UNEXPECTED
OUTCOMES

Unexpected Outcomes

How Emerging Economies Survived the Global Financial Crisis

Carol Wise

Leslie Elliott Armijo

Saori N. Katada

editors

BROOKINGS INSTITUTION PRESS
Washington, D.C.

Library of Congress Cataloging-in-Publication data
Unexpected outcomes : how emerging economies survived the global financial crisis / Carol Wise, Leslie Elliott Armijo, and Saori N. Katada, editors.
    pages   cm.
    Includes bibliographical references and index.
    ISBN 978-0-8157-2476-6 (pbk. : alk. paper)—ISBN 978-0-8157-2477-3 (e-book)   1. Developing countries—Economic conditions—21st century. 2.   Developing countries—Economic policy—21st century. 3.   Finance—Developing countries. 4.   Financial crises—Developing countries. 5.   Global Financial Crisis, 2008–2009.   I. Wise, Carol.
    HC59.7.U468 2015
    330.9172'4090511—dc23   2014036717

9 8 7 6 5 4 3 2 1

Printed on acid-free paper

Typeset in Minion

Composition by R. Lynn Rivenbark
Macon, Georgia

Contents

Foreword   vii
Joshua Aizenman

Acknowledgments   xi

1   The Puzzle   1
Carol Wise, Leslie Elliott Armijo, and Saori N. Katada

2   Chinese Financial Statecraft and the Response to the
Global Financial Crisis   25
Shaun Breslin

3   Korea's Victory over the Global Financial Crisis
of 2008–09   48
Barbara Stallings

4   India's Response to the Global Financial Crisis:
From Quick Rebound to Protracted Slowdown?   74
John Echeverri-Gent

5   Southeast Asia's Post-Crisis Recovery:
So Far, So Good   102
Mark Beeson

6   The Global Financial Crisis and
Latin American Economies   123
Eric Hershberg

7   Macroprudence versus Macroprofligacy:
     Brazil, Argentina, and the Global Financial Crisis   148
     Carol Wise and Maria Antonietta Del Tedesco Lins

8   Mexico's Recovery from the Global Financial Crisis   181
     Gerardo Esquivel

9   Lessons from the Country Case Studies   202
     Leslie Elliott Armijo, Carol Wise, and Saori N. Katada

Contributors   231

Index   233

JOSHUA AIZENMAN

Foreword

Emerging economies suffered a string of severe macroeconomic crises between 1994 and 2001, starting with Mexico (1994) and East Asia (1997) and continuing with Russia (1998), Brazil (1998–99), Argentina (2000–01), and Turkey (2000–01). Those crises coincided with a period of growing external financial integration. In spite of the reforms subsequently undertaken by emerging economies, few would have predicted that they would perform as well as they did during the 2008–09 global financial crisis and the accompanying Great Recession.[1] Not only did developing countries and emerging economies display considerable resilience during the 2008–09 crisis but their economic take-off—including that of the most populous countries, China and India—also resulted in a situation in which more than half of global GDP growth had originated in these countries by 2010 (at purchasing power parity exchange rates). This volume provides an insightful overview and evaluation of their remarkable performance during and after the global financial crisis by methodically studying the diverse experiences of China, Korea, India, the Southeast Asian countries, Argentina, Brazil, and Mexico. It distills those experiences into a comprehensive analysis and presents the lessons learned from the surprising resilience of emerging economies.

The analysis concludes that the market structural reforms of earlier decades provided the fiscal and monetary space that enabled emerging economies to invoke robust countercyclical expansionary macroeconomic policies in response to the global economic crisis. Remarkably, the countercyclical response of several of those economies exhibited an agility and a flexibility that exceeded that of the responses of the OECD countries. The lessons that the emerging economies had learned from the financial crises of the mid-1990s paid off: they aimed at greater exchange rate flexibility buffered by a sizable buildup of international reserves and improved their balance sheet exposure. Those measures increased their resilience, reducing their vulnerability to financial crises and the need to rely on costly and possibly destabilizing bailouts from international financial institutions.

The introduction and the concluding chapters provide an insightful and balanced analysis of the various responses of the emerging markets to the global financial crisis. A key lesson is that strategies aimed at emulating the golden mean—combining neoliberal with heterodox insights—paid off. Prior neoliberal macroeconomic reforms were helpful overall in providing policy space, but they were not a panacea. Defensive strategies, including precautionary hoarding of reserves and reducing balance sheet exposure, helped in times of peril (although countries should beware of the adverse effects and costs of over-insuring themselves). Trade liberalization promotes growth and trade diversification can reduce vulnerability, but neither by itself may succeed in decoupling emerging markets from global turbulence. Countervailing international conditions like high commodity prices helped Latin American and other commodity exporters, though those gains came with costs to large Asian importers (China, India, South Korea, and others). Low interest rates in financial centers helped emerging economies, but they came with greater exposure to destabilizing hot money inflows, with investors chasing yields, and possibly to increasing balance sheet exposure. Applying pragmatic approaches, learning from past mistakes, and investing in policy space and institutions have all been key factors in the resilience of emerging economies. Narrow ideological divides notwithstanding, countries that invested in flexibility and better institutions and buffers gained resilience.

Put in historical context, the global financial crisis has been especially "shocking." Observers dubbed the 1985–2006 period the Great Moderation of the OECD countries. Some credited the Great Moderation to the "good macroeconomic policies" and "mature institutions" of the OECD bloc. The Great Moderation proved to be illusory, and the consequent drop in interest rates, inflation rates, and the price of risk put fiscal issues on the back burner of the United States, the Eurozone, and other OECD countries in the late w1990s and early years of the 2000s. Yet there has been no great moderation for emerging economies—their experience with the massive financial shocks of the 1990s brought painful learning and adaptation of new policies. The global financial crisis vividly showed that volatility is back, ending hope that the Great Moderation of earlier decades reflected enduring gains from better macroeconomic policies. The crisis also illustrated that the financial globalization and financial deregulation of the 1990s and early years of the 2000s overshot the desirable levels. Instead of helping countries cope with global volatility, financial deepening became a growing source of instability, threatening the globalization project. The global crisis also challenged earlier views that held that "crony capitalism" in emerging markets was the source of their exposure to financial instability and crisis, in contrast to the OECD countries, with their more mature institutions and superior macroeconomic policies. Well, not anymore—all countries are facing similar challenges in dealing with and "taming the beast" of financial globalization.

This book should guide us well in the coming years, providing a balanced analysis of the successes and challenges facing emerging economies. While most avoided repeating the old patterns ("When the United States sneezes, emerging economies catch pneumonia"), it would be a mistake for them to rest on their laurels. Past performance does not guarantee future results. Emerging economies benefited from their lower financial exposure to troubled U.S. assets, especially in countries run by prudent central bankers who prohibited sizable exposure to U.S. collateralized mortgage obligations and similar securitized assets. Yet the experience of South Korea illustrates the limits of buffers: South Korea found that its sizable and once highly regarded stock of international reserves failed to isolate its economy from massive deleveraging. The ensuing financial panic was ultimately abated only with the help of the U.S. Federal Reserve's special swap lines.

Korea's experience illustrates the need to supplement reserve hoarding with prudential regulations dealing with the balance-sheet exposure of systemic banking. Indeed, unlike the 1997–98 Korean financial crisis, the global financial crisis did not lead to a large post-crisis increase in the ratio of Korea's reserves to GDP but to prudential regulatory changes.[2] Also, because the United States and other OECD countries no longer act as "demanders of last resort," the post-crisis world has also been less friendly to export-led growth strategies. That, in turn, has induced China to rebalance, giving priority to its need to develop a more mature and vibrant level of domestic demand for Chinese goods and services. Despite their robust performance during the crisis, emerging economies experienced an overall drop in their growth. If the secular stagnation hypothesis rejuvenated by Larry Summers should hold over the next decade or two,[3] the convergence of emerging markets toward OECD indicators will slow down, increasing the risk that these economies will approach stagnation before reaching medium-high income levels and thereby increase their exposure to internal instability. Looking forward, emerging economies should keep experimenting with prudential policies aimed at reducing their balance sheet exposure, reducing their external hard currency borrowing, and shifting to greater reliance on domestic currency borrowing and equity funding.

Joshua Aizenman
Robert R. and Katheryn A. Dockson Chair in Economics and International Relations and professor of International Relations and Economics, University of Southern California, and research associate, National Bureau of Economic Research

December 2014

Notes

1. Development Committee, "How Resilient Have Developing Countries Been during the Global Crisis?" DC2010-0015, prepared by the staff of the World Bank and the International Monetary Fund, September 30, 2010.

2. V. Bruno and H. S. Shin, "Assessing Macroprudential Policies: Case of Korea," *Scandinavian Journal of Economics*, vol. 116, no. 1 (2014), pp. 128–57.

3. Larry Summers, "U.S. Economic Prospects: Secular Stagnation, Hysteresis, and the Zero Lower Bound," *Business Economics*, vol. 49, no. 2 (2014), pp. 65–73.

Acknowledgments

This project was initially launched with a Venture Workshop Grant from the International Studies Association and subsequently supported by the School of International Relations and the Center for International Studies at the University of Southern California. We are especially grateful to Robert English, director of the School of International Relations, and to Patrick James, director of the Center for International Studies at USC, for enthusiastically endorsing the project. We also want to thank the Brookings Institution Press and Eileen Hughes and Janet Walker in particular, for their tireless efforts to transform the original essays into an integrated and professional manuscript. All of the chapters benefited from numerous rounds of editing, formatting, and fact checking by a large team of graduate and undergraduate research assistants at USC. We especially thank Rachel Chan, Connie Chen, Scott Huhn, Gloria Koo, Hannah Kwon, Will Kwon, Michael Perez, Chengxi Shi, and Vijeta Tandon for their excellent research assistance. Very helpful comments were offered by Mariano Bertucci, Fabian Borges-Herrero, Christina Faegri, Stephan Haggard, Gerry Munck, Injoo Sohn, and two anonymous reviewers. The book cover was produced by Susan Woollen and Peggy Archaumbault, whose beautiful work made it difficult to choose from various options. Finally, we thank the book's authors for their patience and tenacity in bringing this project to press.

CAROL WISE, LESLIE ELLIOTT ARMIJO, *and*
SAORI N. KATADA

1 | *The Puzzle*

One of the more surprising features of the 2008–09 global financial crisis was the comparative ease with which emerging economies in Asia and Latin America rebounded. That rebound was a radical departure from the effects of previous crises on these regions, be it the decade-long recession wreaked on Latin America by the 1982 debt shocks[1] or the financial crisis that dramatically slowed Asian economies in the late 1990s.[2] The quick recovery of emerging economies in 2010–12 was, moreover, instrumental in deterring a full-blown global depression. The lingering phenomenon of the "Great Recession" has largely been limited to the wealthier members of the Organization for Economic Cooperation and Development. Most emerging economies, with the notable exception of those in Eastern Europe, weathered the crisis reasonably well.

The resilience of the emerging economies (EEs) in Asia and Latin America in surviving the global financial crisis (GFC) is all the more striking when one considers the substantial differences that exist among the countries both within and across these regions. The EEs that we consider in this volume differ in terms of size, endowment factors, and the domestic institutions that

We are grateful to the Center for International Studies and the School of International Relations at the University of Southern California as well as to the International Studies Association for funding this project. We thank Rachel Chan, Connie Chen, Scott Huhn, Gloria Koo, Hannah Kwon, Will Kwon, Michael Perez, Chengxi Shi, and Vijeta Tandon for their excellent research assistance. Very helpful comments were offered by Mariano Bertucci, Fabian Borges-Herrero, Christina Faegri, Stephan Haggard, Gerry Munck, and Injoo Sohn.

frame economic policymaking. Taking their diversity into account, this introductory chapter summarizes the commonalities and differences among the reforms that they had undertaken before the GFC and the policies that they pursued on the path to recovery in its aftermath. Our focus in this book is on the Pacific Rim, the definition of which we expand to include the important emerging economies of Brazil, Argentina, and India.

This introductory chapter suggests, first, that the ability of these countries as a group to resist the initial financial contagion was due in considerable part to the substantial macroeconomic, financial sector, and trade reforms that EE governments throughout Asia and Latin America had undertaken over the previous two decades. Second, a timely rebound was supported by the implementation of countercyclical policies in major emerging economies.[3] Third, EEs also benefited from some countervailing conditions in the international economy, including high commodity prices since the early 2000s; these conditions were fortuitous, not the result of conscious prior policy choices. Fourth and perhaps most important, old labels used to distinguish neoliberal (market-based)[4] from developmentalist (state-oriented)[5] strategies do not accurately describe the foundations of EE recovery. We argue that policy learning and reforms adopted in response to previous crises prompted EE policymakers to combine both state and market approaches in coping with the GFC.[6] Policy pragmatism trumped ideological rigidity.

In the Wake of Crisis: What Do the Data Tell Us?

Since the 1980s, calls for financial market deregulation in the United States have arisen on both sides of the political aisle. One result was the passage by Congress of the Financial Services Modernization Act of 1999, which repealed the Glass-Steagall Act of 1933, which had prohibited mergers among investment banks, commercial banks, and insurance companies.[7] The bursting of the dotcom bubble in 2000 followed quickly on the heels of that deregulatory legislation, as did the 9/11 attacks on the United States. Those double recessionary shocks prompted the Federal Reserve to maintain low interest rates from 2000 to 2004, which pumped massive liquidity into both the U.S. economy and global markets.[8] At the same time, newly merged mega-institutions like Citicorp and the Goldman Sachs Group began offering a range of innovative, if not always sound, financial instruments that spurred an unprecedented boom in credit card, personal, and mortgage debt.[9] In 2005 alone, around US$1 trillion was issued in interest-only "subprime" mortgages, which were one of the key financial instruments generated in the new low interest rate environment. However, many of those flexible-rate mortgages fell into default after the Federal Reserve began gradually raising interest rates in 2004–05. The global financial crisis of 2008–09 originated in this high-risk, subprime segment of the U.S. housing market, and it was exacerbated by the creation of various mortgage-backed financial instruments and unregulated derivatives that had attracted investors in the United States and Europe.[10]

Once the U.S. housing bubble burst, the defaults affected heavily leveraged hedge funds as early as the summer of 2007. The crisis quickly spread from the United States and Europe to other parts of the world, driven by massive runs on excessively leveraged private assets, the withdrawal of investments, the sudden collapse of export markets in the advanced economies, and a sharp but temporary decline in commodity prices.[11] As a consequence, according to the World Bank, global growth fell by approximately 5 percentage points from its pre-crisis peak to its trough in 2009, nominal world trade (in U.S. dollars) fell by around 30 percent year-on-year in the first quarter of 2009, and trade volumes fell by more than 15 percent. The magnitude of the losses made this the worst global economic crisis since the 1930s, when the Great Depression spread throughout the world.[12] But the results and pattern of global contagion in this crisis differed from those in previous financial crises in recent decades. Despite initial fears, the emerging economies as a group had a relatively easy go of it and recovered rapidly.

One piece of the puzzle is the fact that poorer countries were already growing faster than those with higher per capita income. Economic theory has long predicted that backward economies, which have considerable absorptive capacity and could ostensibly benefit from imported new technologies, investment capital, and relatively abundant supplies of cheap labor, *should* grow faster than mature industrial economies; however, for many decades they did not.[13] Yet by the late 1990s developing country growth rates were up to the extent that some argued that a "great convergence" was finally under way.[14] Subramanian and Kessler report that, on average, developing countries' growth surpassed that of the United States by about 3.25 percent annually from 2000 to 2007.[15] Table 1-1 shows that in the immediate pre-crisis years of 2005–07, the advanced industrial economies had steady average annual GDP growth of 4.0 percent— but the developing economies grew at an average annual rate of 7.7 percent. Nonetheless, the near universal assumption was that growth in developing economies was both fragile and volatile. Common wisdom held that as long as these economies lagged behind in the implementation of deep structural

Table 1-1. *Crisis and Recovery: Aggregate GDP Growth, Various Economies*[a]
Percent

Economy	Pre-crisis (2005–07)	Crisis (2008–09)	Recovery (2010–12)
World	5.6	0.0	3.5
Advanced economies	4.0	–1.3	2.3
G-7	3.7	–1.5	2.3
Developing economies	7.7	1.6	4.9
Developing Asia	9.3	3.8	6.2
Latin America and the Caribbean	5.9	–0.4	3.8

Sources: Data from International Monetary Fund, *World Economic Outlook*, April 2013.

a. Compound annual growth rates, using purchasing power parity GDP, with aggregates weighted by countries' economic size.

reforms and remained highly dependent on financial inflows from overseas markets, financial crises would continue to plague them. Any subsequent disruptions were expected to be just as severe as those witnessed, for example, in Mexico (1994); Indonesia, Malaysia, Thailand, and South Korea (1997–98); Russia (1998); Brazil (1998–99); and Argentina (2001–02).

Instead, it was the advanced industrial economies that suffered a deep contraction during and long after the global financial crisis. Average annual GDP growth for the countries in the Organization for Economic Cooperation and Development fell to –1.3 percent in 2008–09; the equivalent figure for the G-7 major advanced economies was –1.5 percent. The burden of maintaining global growth had shifted decisively to the developing countries, which grew by an average of 1.6 percent annually on the same GDP-weighted basis in 2008–09. Even Latin America and the Caribbean—which includes Mexico, Central America, and the Caribbean Basin countries, all of which were closely tied to the hard-hit U.S. economy—shrank less than half a percentage point in 2008–09. These patterns hold not merely in the aggregate but for most of the major economies among the advanced industrial, Asian developing, and Latin American developing countries. Among the 14 large emerging economies shown in table 1-2, only Venezuela—which has been the least inclined to implement modernizing reforms since the debt crisis of the 1980s—failed to recover on par with the countries shown in table 1-2.[16]

Nonetheless, this collective emerging market resistance to the 2008–09 shock has not yet resulted in the recuperation of pre-crisis growth rates, and growth recently has slowed in a number of emerging economies in our sample, including Argentina, Brazil, China, India, and Korea.[17] Although this selec-

Table 1-2. *Crisis and Recovery: National GDP Growth, Various Countries*[a]
Percent

Country	Pre-crisis (2005–07)	Crisis (2008–09)	Recovery (2010–12)
Canada	3.6	−1.0	2.8
France	3.6	−1.2	1.9
Germany	4.5	−2.1	2.6
Italy	3.3	−2.4	0.6
Japan	3.4	−2.4	1.8
United Kingdom	4.1	−1.6	1.7
G-7 mean	**3.7**	**−1.7**	**2.0**
China	11.0	5.0	7.0
India	8.6	2.9	5.2
Indonesia	6.0	2.7	5.6
Korea	5.5	0.6	3.2
Malaysia	6.0	−0.3	4.5
Philippines	6.0	1.0	4.8
Thailand	5.5	−0.7	3.5
Asian 7 mean[b]	**6.9**	**1.6**	**4.8**
Argentina	7.8	0.9	4.9
Brazil	5.4	0.3	2.5
Chile	5.8	0.0	5.1
Colombia	6.6	1.3	4.9
Mexico	4.9	−2.6	3.9
Peru	7.6	0.9	5.7
Venezuela	6.3	−3.6	0.7
Latin American 7 mean[c]	**6.3**	**−0.4**	**4.0**

Sources: Data from International Monetary Fund, *World Economic Outlook*, April 2013.

a. Compound annual growth rates, using purchasing power parity GDP, with unweighted means.

b. The Asian 7 countries include China, India, Indonesia, Korea, Malaysia, the Philippines, and Thailand.

c. The Latin American 7 countries include Argentina, Brazil, Chile, Colombia, Mexico, Peru, and Venezuela.

tive slowing confirms the need for deeper structural reforms in several countries,[18] it does not negate the unprecedented achievement of developing and emerging economies as a group in rebounding from the global financial crisis. Moreover, although EE post-crisis growth rates have not yet recovered, they remain well above those in the advanced industrial countries when growth is measured both by aggregate rates weighted by economic size (as in table 1-1) and by simple group means (as in table 1-2). Subramanian and

Kessler calculate that in 2010–12 the mean growth rate of developing economies as a group remained about 3 percent above the U.S. growth rate.[19] What explains the resilience of most emerging economies in the face of the most daunting financial crisis to hit the global economy in more than seven decades?

The Missing Crisis: Contending Explanations

Both Latin America and Asia have had their share of tough times in recovering from earlier disruptions. Most fresh are memories of the "lost decade" in Latin America, which was triggered by the 1982 debt crisis, and the massive downturn in the Asian economies in the aftermath of the Asian financial crisis of the late 1990s.[20] In each case, major internal policy debates took place in economic ministries in Latin America, Asia, and beyond over what went wrong and what could be done to restore stability and growth in these crisis-ridden countries and regions. The standing explanations of these crises in the literature differed with respect to the weight given to domestic/institutional and international/systemic variables as causes of the crises. The domestic/institutional explanation, for example, faulted sovereign borrowers for failing to properly channel funds lent by foreign commercial banks into the kinds of macro-stabilization and micro-economic restructuring projects for which they were ostensibly borrowed; the international/systemic explanation stance blamed private international financiers for imposing the costs of their own poor lending decisions almost solely on borrowers.[21]

The subsequent prescriptions for policy reform offered by each camp were, unsurprisingly, quite different. They also reflected the usual divide between neoliberals, who called for economic opening and more market-based solutions to crises, and developmentalists, who called for more targeted public policies and strategic state intervention. In the end, the need for massive International Monetary Fund–backed bailout packages in both regions—Latin America in the 1980s and Asia in the 1990s—meant that market liberalizers, who dominated the international financial institutions (IFIs) and could impose obligatory conditions on borrowers, prevailed. Most countries were induced to adopt austerity measures in order to make balance-of-payments adjustments. It is that time-worn recipe that gradually morphed into what has been termed the "Washington Consensus,"[22] a package of measures based on liberalization, privatization, and deregulation that by the late 1990s had been implemented in varying degrees throughout the developing and post-communist world.

In recent debates over the missing crisis in the emerging market countries both during and after 2008–09, both sides seem to be claiming victory. Market-oriented analysts point to the success of prior neoliberal reforms in preparing emerging economies to defend their financial sectors from the kinds of contagion that spread so quickly across emerging markets when the Mexican peso collapsed in 1994 and the Thai baht crashed in 1997.[23] The fact that the recent contagion emanated from the United States and subsequently from Western Europe makes the continued macroeconomic stability and growth within the emerging market countries all the more impressive. Although the global financial crisis highlighted massive market failures in the OECD bloc, the pro-market chorus has been quick to claim the EE rebound as a victory of its own. Meanwhile, those with a more heterodox bent argue that EE staying power in the 2000s rests just as much on strategic interventions and innovative public policies.[24]

Our approach to sorting out some of these claims is intentionally eclectic, drawing on both quantitative and qualitative evidence from the now vast secondary literature and from our case studies. What such a methodology loses in parsimony it gains by bringing together contending explanations that are seldom considered jointly. A second novel element of our analytical strategy is our intentional focus on the experiences of larger emerging economies. Rather than following the typical econometric practice of considering each country's experience as a single observation and assigning equal weight to each in arriving at eventual research findings, we argue that there are both economic and political reasons to pay particular attention to regional leaders and larger economies. Given that regions such as East Asia and South America have trading patterns that are somewhat intraregionally integrated and that economic ideas and practices also diffuse intraregionally, it makes economic sense to focus on the bigger economies. In addition, our interest in evaluating the causal role of pre-crisis government policy choices leads us to concentrate on those countries whose material, cultural, and political capabilities tend to make them sources of regional policy innovation and diffusion.

We have generated three broad hypotheses drawn from the long-running debates over the virtues of policies that lean more heavily toward the market ("neoliberal") and those of more proactive policies undertaken by the state ("developmentalist"). We also consider an alternative explanation: the presence of countervailing international conditions—for example, the decade-long commodity price boom that took off in 2003 and the phenomenon of historically low interest rates in the G-7 bloc since the 2000–03 global recession, both of which have provided readily available liquidity and capital inflows to many EEs. These external factors are less related to national policy choices and obviously cannot be taken for granted in the future. The contending explanations are summarized in table 1-3, which divides each explanation into components plausibly related to surviving the initial shock ("crisis resistance") and those tied to resumption of the respectable growth rates ("crisis recovery") depicted in tables 1-1 and 1-2.

Our first hypothesis suggests that the critical factor in enabling crisis resistance among the majority of Asian and Latin American EEs was the presence of *prior pro-market (neoliberal) macroeconomic reforms.* That is, if economic distortions created by state intervention had been the main source of prolonged economic hardship in developing countries in the past,[25] then the basic package of macroeconomic reforms implemented in the 1990s by a number of East Asian and Latin American countries under the auspices of the Washington Consensus (WC) had given policymakers in those countries the tools necessary to survive the shocks of 2008–09. A related proposition under this same umbrella hypothesis is that prior monetary and fiscal reforms—including reduction in budget deficits, stabilization of inflation, and key institutional reforms, such as granting greater operational independence to central banks—were necessary to give incumbent governments the macroeconomic "space" that they needed to implement the kinds of countercyclical policies that ultimately saved the day for these countries in 2008–09. During earlier crises, heavily indebted national governments across the Pacific Rim were in no position to finance local variants of the countercyclical policies that the United States implemented so forcefully in 2009.[26]

Hypothesis 2, which posits the importance of *prior financial sector reforms,* comes in two versions, one neoliberal and the other developmentalist. The neoliberal version holds that by the time that the global financial crisis struck in 2007–09, emerging economies on both sides of the Pacific had instituted substantial reforms to deepen and liberalize their financial sectors and that those reforms are what accounted for EEs' resilience when the GFC struck. Reforms typically included lowering barriers to entry into the banking sector (and thus reducing oligopolistic rents long enjoyed by domestic commercial banks), freeing interest rates, improving bank balance sheet transparency, and

Table 1-3. *Hypotheses Regarding the Quick Rebound of Emerging Economies*

Hypothesis	Effects on crisis resistance	Effects on crisis recovery
1. Prior (neoliberal) macroeconomic reforms	Strong economies with sound public finances are better able to resist crises.	Fiscal and monetary "space" enables countercyclical policies.
2. Prior financial reforms (neoliberal and/or developmentalist)	Strong, independent central bank and private banks help to avoid twin crises (neoliberal). Foreign exchange reserves can act as a buffer (developmentalist).	State banks speed recovery (developmentalist). Foreign exchange reserves support policy space.
3. Prior trade reforms (neoliberal and/or developmentalist)	An open trade regime bolsters economic growth (neoliberal). State promotion increases exports (developmentalist). Diversified trade reduces vulnerability.	Effects are the same as those for crisis resistance.
4. Countervailing international conditions	Resistance is due to luck more than to explicit emerging economy policies.	Recovery is due to luck more than to emerging economy policies, countercyclical or otherwise.

Source: Authors' hypotheses.

recapitalizing banks once the problem of nonperforming loans had been adequately addressed.[27] Micro-level reforms in the banking and financial sectors rendered these EEs less susceptible to the "twin crises" of earlier times, which inevitably combined a currency (foreign exchange) shock with a domestic banking crisis.

The developmentalist stance on prior financial reforms holds that along with incremental interest rate liberalization and gradual banking deregulation, the governments of many EEs intentionally retained or created a number of defensive financial policy tools that both limited the effects of the initial crisis and enabled them to rekindle growth more quickly. One developmentalist financial policy was the setting of some controls on potentially volatile inflows of portfolio capital—for example, by lowering taxes on longer-term, more stable inflows, such as foreign direct investment (FDI).[28] Other policies included building up foreign exchange reserves as insurance against speculative attacks on the currency and relying on state-owned banks to channel fiscal stimulus funds, especially with regard to the implementation of countercyclical policies.[29]

Hypothesis 3 suggests that the critical determining factor was *prior trade reforms,* also undertaken in response to the wave of EE financial crises in the 1980s and 1990s. Neither the mainstream neoliberal nor the developmentalist stance on trade posits a direct relationship between prior trade reforms and the ability to fight off international financial contagion, but two positions can be inferred. As with financial reform, there exists both a neoliberal and a developmentalist concept of trade reform. Far-reaching trade liberalization was a major prong of the pro-market Washington Consensus. In the neoclassical model of market-determined comparative advantage, countries cannot influence their trading patterns nor should they try, because doing so simply introduces inefficiencies. However, the WC assumes that a free trading state will develop a stronger, faster-growing economy than a country less integrated into the global economy. Deep trade integration ("hyperglobalization," in the words of Subramanian and Kessler[30]) ostensibly nurtures strong, resilient economies that are better able to withstand crises.[31]

In contrast, the developmentalist approach to trade assumes a global economy rife with market failures, implying the need for governments to intervene in order to nurture targeted sectors, capture external markets, and reduce economic vulnerabilities. Under such conditions, trade integration must be managed.[32] In particular, it is important for the state to regulate trade with the explicit goal of promoting exports that promise to increase a given country's competitive ranking in the global economy. Although both neoliberals and developmentalists generally support the goal of diversifying exports and trading partners as a way to reduce volatility in the demand for a country's products, the two may differ in how involved the government should be in engineering that outcome.

Each of these three hypotheses assumes that the surprisingly mild crisis experienced in 2008–09 by emerging economies around the Pacific Rim (and by Brazil and India) resulted from deliberate policy choices made by their governments as a result of policy learning from the earlier financial crises (and sometimes external pressure, as with conditions imposed by IFIs). A fourth hypothesis suggests that the relatively good performance of emerging economies in 2008–09 and thereafter was not a matter of economic policy learning; rather, EEs simply benefited from fortuitous *countervailing external conditions*. That is, the milder effect of the global financial crisis on emerging economies in Asia and Latin America raises the possibility that their quick recovery was due to such global environmental circumstances as high commodity prices and low international interest rates. In other words, the luck of the draw helped to foster EE recovery once financial contagion originating in the United States and Europe had been effectively resisted.

To a great extent, the high-commodity-prices theory reflects the extraordinary rise of China over the past 30 years and the fact that China has reached a stage in its ambitious export-led growth model that now requires massive inputs of such commodities as copper, petroleum, iron ore, fishmeal, and soybeans—precisely those resources that are abundant in Latin America (see table 1-4).[33] The low interest rates argument is the flip side of the enduring difficulties that the advanced industrial countries have experienced in fully recovering from the Great Recession. In other words, the sluggish growth rates that continue to plague the United States and Western Europe (minus Germany) have led to historically unprecedented government decisions to maintain a loose monetary policy in hopes of reviving business activity, investment, and job creation.[34] Coupled with near-zero interest rates in the United States since 2008, this loose monetary policy has provided a strong impetus for massive outflows of private capital into EEs, which have offered yield-seeking investors substantially higher returns. Of course, to rely on capital inflows stimulated by stagnant global growth, a commodity price boom, and countercyclical policies in the major advanced economies is a very risky and unreliable strategy. In the country case studies that follow, only Argentina flirted with this option in the post-GFC period, with results that were less than appealing.

Plan of the Book

Again, our approach here is eclectic. Although we acknowledge the substantial differences in historical development trajectories and policy choices among the countries chosen here, what unites them is a subtle yet important similarity in their policy responses to the global financial crisis. While their responses themselves defy neat categorization, the overall trend since the GFC and thereafter has been toward adopting pragmatic and flexible policies, not

Table 1-4. *Annual Commodity Price Trends in Real Dollars, 2000–13*

Year	Copper ($/metric ton)	Crude oil ($/barrel)	Soybeans ($/metric ton)	Iron ore ($/dry metric ton)	Fishmeal ($/metric ton)
2000	2,279.38	35.48	266.26	36.19	519.11
2001	2,061.05	31.80	255.73	39.22	635.53
2002	2,060.54	32.94	281.00	38.73	800.60
2003	2,234.60	36.30	331.58	40.13	767.05
2004	3,370.60	44.38	360.48	44.57	762.81
2005	4,194.64	60.88	313.20	74.11	833.43
2006	7,475.17	71.49	298.74	77.10	1,296.99
2007	7,459.13	74.52	402.44	128.88	1,233.63
2008	6,764.19	94.32	508.43	151.69	1,101.86
2009	5,338.61	64.02	452.94	82.91	1,275.37
2010	7,534.78	79.04	449.80	145.86	1,687.50
2011	8,103.66	95.47	496.29	153.99	1,411.24
2012	7,400.30	97.60	549.67	119.43	1,448.33
2013	6,913.32	98.13	507.66	127.63	1,647.37

Source: World Bank Global Economic Monitor (GEM) Commodities (http://databank.world-bank.org/data/views/variableselection/selectvariables.aspx?source=global-economic-monitor-%28 gem%29-commodities).

some of the staunch dogmas that prevailed during earlier times. We begin with the Asian case studies, including separate chapters on China, Korea, and India and a fourth chapter that analyzes the economic performance and policy responses of countries within the Southeast Asian bloc. We then turn to the Latin American cases, beginning with a chapter that provides a view of the region as a whole vis-à-vis the GFC. That is followed by two chapters on the top EEs in the region, one comparing the responses of Argentina and Brazil to the crisis and the other analyzing Mexico's response.

Why begin with China? Because it has become the top emerging market destination for foreign direct investment and has risen to the upper ranks of world trade more quickly than any other developing country in the post–World War II period. Especially since its accession in 2001 to the World Trade Organization (WTO), China has engaged economically—through trade, loans, aid, and investment—in every region of the global economy, in developed and developing countries alike, and it currently accounts for about 25 percent of world reserves. In a matter of just a decade, China has displaced Germany as the top exporter of goods to the rest of the world and in the process "has gone from being one of the most insignificant high-technology exporters to the number-one high-technology manufacturer in the world."[35] In the heat of the 2008–09 crisis, China's fiscal stimulus effort was on par— in absolute terms and as a share of domestic GDP—with the stimulus packages implemented by the United States, Germany, and Japan.

China has thus mattered immensely for the recovery of the global economy since the 2008–09 debacle. In contrast with the shocks of the global financial crisis in the other Asian cases examined here, the shocks to China's economy were transmitted through a drop in demand for exports to Europe and North America rather than through the financial system. As table 1-5 shows, China's total trade (exports and imports) with Europe accounted for 19.7 percent of China's total trade in 2007 but dropped to 17.7 percent by 2012. China's trade with North America, which stood at 15.3 percent of total Chinese trade in 2007, was down to 13.9 percent by 2012. In chapter 2, Shaun Breslin notes that the Chinese Communist Party leadership had already expressed the need to modify the country's long-standing policy of export-led growth in order to foster more efficient domestic investment and spur domestic consumption. Other negative offshoots of the prevailing development strategy—including rampant corruption, dire pollution, and rising income inequality—also brought the government's single-minded focus on export-led growth into question. Although the GFC was both a trade shock for China and a confirmation of the need to shift the focus of the country's development strategy, Breslin emphasizes that the responses of the Chinese leadership were on the financial side, akin to those of other countries analyzed in this volume.

Breslin assesses how the hypotheses presented earlier in this chapter hold up in the Chinese case. Fearing social instability if an economic slowdown were to trigger widespread unemployment, the Chinese authorities moved quickly to implement a vast stimulus package that the International Monetary Fund declared a "quick, determined, and effective" response to the crisis.[36] That, Breslin argues, could not have occurred in the absence of credible macroeconomic reforms prior to the global financial crisis. Moreover, the previous implementation of financial sector and banking reforms enabled the disbursement of the stimulus funds through state-held domestic banks and other financial levers controlled by the government. Ironically, even though China's countercyclical policy responses to the GFC failed to follow neoliberal prescriptions, the strategy worked and even won praise from the IFIs. As other chapters in this volume show, China's rapid recovery was a boost for some of the other EEs in both Asia and South America.

Table 1-5. *Distribution of China's Trade with the World*

Percent

Country/region	2000	2001	2002	2003	2004	2005	2006	2007	2008	2009	2010	2011	2012
Destination of China's exports													
Asia	53.1	53.0	52.6	50.8	49.8	48.1	47.0	46.6	46.4	47.3	46.4	47.4	49.1
Africa	2.0	2.3	2.1	2.3	2.3	2.5	2.8	3.1	3.6	4.0	3.8	3.8	4.2
Europe	18.3	18.5	17.9	20.1	20.6	21.7	22.2	23.6	24.0	22.0	22.5	21.8	19.3
Latin America and the Caribbean	2.9	3.1	2.9	2.7	3.1	3.1	3.7	4.2	5.0	4.8	5.8	6.4	6.6
North America	22.2	21.7	22.8	22.4	22.5	22.9	22.6	20.7	19.2	19.9	19.4	18.4	18.6
Oceania	1.6	1.5	1.6	1.7	1.7	1.7	1.7	1.7	1.8	2.1	2.1	2.2	2.2
Origin of China's imports	2000	2001	2002	2003	2004	2005	2006	2007	2008	2009	2010	2011	2012
Asia	62.8	60.4	65.0	66.1	65.8	66.9	66.4	64.9	62.0	60.0	59.9	57.8	57.3
Africa	2.5	2.0	1.8	2.0	2.8	3.2	3.6	3.8	4.9	4.3	4.8	5.4	6.2
Europe	18.1	19.9	17.6	16.9	15.9	14.6	14.5	14.6	14.8	16.1	15.6	16.5	15.8
Latin America and the Caribbean	2.4	2.8	2.8	3.6	3.9	4.1	4.3	5.3	6.3	6.4	6.6	6.9	7.0
North America	11.6	12.4	10.5	9.3	9.3	8.5	8.5	8.4	8.3	8.9	8.4	8.3	8.6
Oceania	2.6	2.6	2.3	2.1	2.4	2.7	2.7	3.0	3.6	4.2	4.7	5.1	5.1
Percent of total China trade	2000	2001	2002	2003	2004	2005	2006	2007	2008	2009	2010	2011	2012
Asia	57.7	56.5	58.5	58.2	57.6	56.8	55.7	54.6	53.3	53.1	52.7	52.3	53.0
Africa	2.2	2.1	2.0	2.2	2.6	2.8	3.2	3.4	4.2	4.1	4.3	4.6	5.1
Europe	18.2	19.2	17.8	18.6	18.3	18.4	18.8	19.7	20.0	19.3	19.3	19.3	17.7
Latin America and the Caribbean	2.7	2.9	2.9	3.2	3.5	3.5	4.0	4.7	5.6	5.5	6.2	6.6	6.8
North America	17.2	17.2	16.9	16.0	16.0	16.2	16.2	15.3	14.4	14.9	14.2	13.6	13.9
Oceania	2.1	2.0	2.0	1.9	2.0	2.2	2.1	2.3	2.6	3.1	3.3	3.6	3.5

Source: Calculation based on Comprehensive Economic, Industry and Corporate Data (CEIC Data) (www.ceicdata.com).

In South Korea, which Barbara Stallings writes about in chapter 3, the drastic fiscal and monetary contraction (largely imposed by the IFIs) that the country experienced in the throes of the Asian financial crisis (AFC) stands in striking contrast to its much milder experience in 2008–09. The formidable macroeconomic and financial sector reforms undertaken by the government in the decade following the AFC makes this perhaps the strongest example of policy learning in this volume. The Korean case also exhibits a compelling combination of developmentalist strategies from the 1960s through the mid-1990s, followed by deep market-based reforms from the late 1990s onward. Although near-complete financial liberalization had left Korea vulnerable to capital outflows when the global financial crisis struck and the country's GDP plummeted for three economic quarters beginning in late 2008, the government was on solid ground when it came to confronting the crisis. The emergency bank restructuring implemented in the aftermath of the Asian financial crisis was one vital factor, because, as a result of restructuring, the financial sector had strong capital adequacy, a low level of nonperforming loans, and few toxic assets going into the global financial crisis.

Korea's previously tight monetary policy also gave the government the leeway necessary to lower interest rates at the height of the external shock. Like the other countries analyzed here, Korea was sitting on an arsenal of foreign exchange reserves, and policymakers stood ready to deploy them to combat financial contagion. The government infused a fiscal stimulus into the economy that was second only to China's stimulus among the Asian EEs; in addition, like China, Korea relied on its policy banks to implement countercyclical measures to fend off shocks from the GFC. Stallings points to the country's recently rediscovered tradition of macroprudential management, reflected in its surplus position in both the current account and the national budget, as crucial to its ability to quickly rebound from the GFC. On the trade side, Korea was able to rely on China, which became its top trading partner in 2004, and Chinese demand for Korean exports helped to offset the drop in demand from Europe and the United States. Stallings notes that because its liberal economy was so well run and because government officials were willing to act assertively when the need arose, Korea was able to weather the GFC successfully.

India sits at the other end of the continuum from Korea and to a certain extent from China. In the two latter countries, domestic politics was obviously an important consideration when it came to quelling the impact of the GFC. However, in India, they were at center stage. In addition, India's reform timeline was much shorter than that of China or of Korea, as the country did not embark on a serious program of market reform and structural adjustment until the early 1990s. As a result, there was a considerable backlog of reforms to be made, along with serious rifts within the political and policymaking establishment over whether further reforms should take a developmentalist or a neoliberal direction. Furthermore, there was a good deal of acrimony over the pace at which reforms should be enacted. For most of the 2000s, the prevailing government coalition resisted liberalization and deep reform of the banking and financial sector. On the upside, the virtually nonexistent exposure of Indian banks and financial entities to the mortgage-backed securities and other toxic assets that originated on Wall Street in the 2000s meant that financial contagion was readily resisted when the GFC struck. On the downside, the severe credit crunch in Europe and the United States left India's trading companies and other corporate institutions scrambling to secure credit.

On the political front, John Echeverri-Gent details in chapter 4 how the timing of India's national elections coincided with the outbreak of the global financial crisis. In anticipation of the vote, the government had already adopted an expansionary economic policy; as a result, the Reserve Bank of India (RBI) was able to maintain the policy already in place when the GFC hit, and that amounted to a considerable fiscal stimulus. Monetary expansion, however, was not painless: it led to mounting deficits, persistent inflation, a dramatic depreciation of the rupee, and abrupt outflows of portfolio investment. The RBI responded, among other ways, by raising the interest rate ceiling on foreign currency deposits and easing restrictions on external commercial borrowing. The policy responses were far from perfect, but the Indian economy did rebound from the crisis until growth slowed in 2012. India's quick recovery was assisted by a heterodox—and largely fortuitous—policy mix that combined cautious prior liberalizing reforms; credit extended through state banks; prior trade liberalization that had reoriented trade away from the recessionary North Atlantic countries and more toward Asia; election-related debt waivers; and public works employment projects. As with the other countries profiled in this volume, it helped considerably to have some macroeconomic room to maneuver.

The final Asian chapter in the volume covers the experiences of the Southeast Asian countries, which are smaller and less developed that the countries discussed thus far. In chapter 5 Mark Beeson describes the ten countries that belong to the Association of Southeast Asian Nations (ASEAN) as being more politically, economically, and ethnically diverse than their larger Asian neighbors.[37] The three largest ASEAN countries—Indonesia, Malaysia, and Thailand—were also the ones most stricken by the AFC in 1997–98. Like Korea, these countries exhibited some policy learning from their AFC experience. Each had accumulated significant foreign currency reserves and had the wherewithal to avoid a repeat of the twin banking and currency crises that sent all of them into a tailspin in the late 1990s. Still, Beeson emphasizes that most of these countries had very limited scope for adopting creative emergency policies to fend off the GFC.

Instead, the ASEAN bloc was able to ride out the 2008–09 crisis on the tailwinds of the large fiscal stimulus packages deployed by both China and Japan. Its ability to take that approach was facilitated by the increased integration of these countries into cross-border production of manufactured goods and intra-industry trade involving primarily the Chinese market. Table 1-5 shows that China's total trade with Asia held steady from 2008 to 2012. In 2010, the China-ASEAN Free Trade Area (CAFTA) had gone into effect, which reduced average weighted tariffs on covered goods down to less than 1 percent across CAFTA. Much of that trade is embedded in global production chains, and most countries in Southeast Asia still rely heavily on the United States and Europe to import their finished products. But despite the region's high external economic integration and heightened dependence on the Chinese market, China's recovery had positive multiplier effects for this smaller group of nations. Unfortunately, the reverse also holds true: in the event of an AFC-style crash in China, the economies of these Southeast Asian countries would be severely tested.

The Latin American cases are introduced in chapter 6 in an overview of the region by Eric Hershberg that emphasizes how widely these countries vary in terms of their development, ongoing economic strategies, and responses to the global financial crisis. Despite its diversity, Latin America differs from the similarly heterogeneous Asian bloc in at least two main ways. First, it has shown a stronger affinity for WC-style reforms since the early 1990s, with Chile, Mexico, and Peru leading the pack. Many Latin American countries implemented much of the WC agenda by reducing public debt, slashing trade protections, deregulating commercial banks, and promoting deeper stock markets. Yet when the dust had finally settled on the GFC, Latin American policy responses, in general, reflected the flexibility and pragmatism that previously had been more emblematic of the Asian EEs.

A second contrast with Asia is that Latin America has, on average, benefited greatly from the decade-long commodity boom that took off in 2003. Especially for such South American countries as Argentina, Brazil, Chile, and Peru, the sale of the commodities that appear in table 1-4 was a huge boon. With China as their main customer, all four countries have lessened their trade dependence on the U.S. market. But not all of these lottery winners kept their wits about them when the global financial crisis struck. Brazil, Chile, Colombia, and Peru did best; all had undertaken prior macroeconomic reforms and considerable financial sector modernization and had achieved some trade diversification, including by strengthening their commercial ties with China. With high reserves, current account and budgetary surpluses, and the cultivation of strong technocratic expertise, these countries led in crafting effective countercyclical policy packages in 2008–09. Argentina and Venezuela, on the other hand, continued with the same populist, expansionary policies that they had embraced off and on for the past two decades. That approach served to mitigate the shocks from the crisis, but it was hardly cohesive and did little to put either country on the path to sustainable growth.

Hershberg also stresses that the effect of the global financial crisis on Mexico, Central America, and some of the Caribbean countries was much less benign and their recovery was slower. That is partly because these countries are bound more closely to the U.S. market and therefore were on the frontlines of the contagion that spread so quickly in 2008. For the countries in this group, the shocks were transmitted largely through the abrupt contraction in trade and remittances, and Mexico was the hardest hit. Its lack of excess commodities to sell to China and the massive flow of Chinese manufactured imports into the country since the advent of the 2000s has placed tremendous stress on Mexico's current account for the past decade. Remarkably, Mexican policymakers actually raised interest rates and adopted procyclical policies when the GFC erupted—an ironic response, since deep macroeconomic and banking sector reforms in the 1990s meant that Mexico was well-positioned to adopt the full range of countercyclical measures undertaken by its South American counterparts. A severe recession finally led the government to loosen its monetary and fiscal policy, but some of the country's excess economic pain was self-inflicted.

The final two chapters on Latin American EEs elaborate on the cases of Argentina, Brazil, and Mexico. In chapter 7, Carol Wise and Maria Antonieta Del Tedesco Lins undertake a comparative political economy analysis of prior reforms and domestic policy responses to the global financial crisis of Brazil and Argentina. Whereas Brazil has stuck with a more gradual strategy of economic opening and structural reform since 1994, Argentina embraced a more rapid implementation of market reforms along the lines of the Washington Consensus in the early 1990s. Brazil thus moved steadily toward reform of its banking and financial sector and adoption of macroprudential measures such as inflation targeting, fiscal overhaul, and a floating exchange rate. Argentina, on the other hand, resorted to a fixed exchange rate from 1991 to 2001 that distracted from the kinds of fiscal, monetary, and overall macroprudential reforms that served its South American neighbors so well in the throes of the GFC. Wise and Lins emphasize that despite Argentina's 2001–02 financial meltdown, the country's policy learning curve from the 1990s still accounted for the government's ability to survive the GFC; moreover, thanks to the commodity lottery, up until the crisis Argentina had succeeded in balancing its budget, achieving equilibrium in its external accounts, and rallying a large fiscal stimulus when the crisis hit.

But this is where Brazil and Argentina part ways. Despite the global financial crisis, Brazilian policymakers never lost sight of the macroprudential goals that they had set for themselves back in the 1990s.[38] To combat inflation, monetary policy remained tight and measures were imposed to deter speculative capital inflows. Fiscal policy was lenient, and Brazil's national development bank (BNDES) was tasked with infusing liquidity into the real economy through the country's public banks. Brazil, in other words, implemented a pragmatic combination of state and market-based policies to weather the worst of the GFC. Wise and Lins argue that while Argentina still had a chance to get back on the path to macro-stability with steady growth when the crisis erupted, it instead continued a populist-style spending spree that eradicated any semblance of equilibrium. Old-fashioned financial repression has set in, including negative interest rates, double-digit inflation, multiple exchange rates, and controls on capital outflows. The slowing of growth in Brazil since 2012 suggests the need for a further round of structural reforms to address the impediments to productivity and efficiency. The same could be said for Argentina, although political leaders and policymakers there appear to have simply given up on the notion of structural reform for the time being.

The final chapter is Gerardo Esquivel's examination of Mexico. In chapter 8, Esquivel focuses less on pre-crisis reforms than on fortuitous—and largely favorable—external factors that affected Mexico's economy during the first decade of the 2000s, including strong economic growth in the United States, rising oil prices, and high remittances from Mexicans living and working abroad. These positive factors bolstered Mexico's balance of payments and fostered the accumulation of foreign exchange reserves. However, given the dependence of the country's exports on the U.S. market and the sharp contraction in U.S. consumer demand, the global financial crisis hit the Mexican economy disproportionately hard. Esquivel argues that despite the sharp contraction, Mexican policymakers underestimated the magnitude of the crisis and therefore took far too long to act.

Despite praise for Mexico's eventual economic recovery and strong growth in 2010–12, Esquivel cautions that unemployment is still high and per capita output is anemic. Much of the recovery, he notes, was simply a bounce back from the plunge in GDP growth that occurred in 2008–09. Although Mexico was the first of the emerging economies to jump on the neoliberal bandwagon, Esquivel emphasizes that consecutive administrations since the late 1980s relied too much on market tenets and macroeconomic prudence at the expense of crucial structural reforms in the realm of fiscal, regulatory, and antitrust policy. That sheds some light on why Mexico took by far the biggest hit from the GFC and why the country's pre- and post-crisis growth rates have been among the lowest in the LAC-7, the seven largest economies in Latin American and the Caribbean (see table 1-2).[39]

Summing Up

This chapter begins with a set of hypotheses concerning the rapid recovery of the Pacific Rim emerging markets in the wake of the 2008–09 global financial crisis. These hypotheses are probed throughout the country case studies that follow and are thoroughly discussed in the concluding chapter of this volume. Inherent in the discussion in this chapter are three assertions. First, institutional innovations and policy learning from the experience of coping with previous crises assisted emerging market policymakers around the Pacific Rim and in Brazil, Argentina, and India in weathering the GFC and its rocky aftermath. Second, policymakers in emerging economies stepped outside their usual comfort zones to embrace a combination of market-based and state-oriented policies that served them especially well in the face of the crisis and made long-standing policy labels such as "neoliberal" and "developmentalist" less relevant. Finally, the combination of longer-run macroeconomic and institutional reform and the increased confidence to engage in more flexible policy approaches has enabled emerging economies to cope effectively with ongoing global challenges, including high levels of capital liquidity since 2008. Obviously, there are outliers in our country sample, especially on the Latin

America side, and the weight that can be assigned to our causal variables differs considerably across countries and regions.

What stands out in the majority of the cases analyzed in this volume is a steady but marked pattern of improvement in the key macroeconomic indicators (inflation, external debt, and public debt) and an ongoing, albeit variable, pattern of financial sector reform. Despite different reform trajectories in Asia (gradual reform, higher growth since the 1980s) and Latin America ("big bang" reform, lower growth until it hit the commodity lottery in 2003), the economic indicators for these emerging economies are converging across the Pacific Rim. In other words, while there is considerable variation in the choice of economic restructuring programs, the timelines involved, and the actual policies employed, the bulk of countries in our database appear to be approaching the same destination. When we analyzed longer-run patterns of macroeconomic and institutional reform, two groups emerged. Chile, Mexico, and Korea all relied more heavily on a market-based reform strategy, while still tweaking some strategic levers (capital controls, state banks) along the way; Brazil, China, and India came down much more heavily on the side of state-led reform strategies, with market reforms embraced at the margin but implemented nonetheless.

The management of capital inflows has been the most obvious challenge for all of the EEs in our sample but especially for the South American countries in their efforts to cope successfully with ongoing global economic challenges. To date the track record reflects a strong commitment among the EEs to combat currency appreciation and inflationary pressures, with the shadow of earlier financial crises as a constant reminder of how quickly the economy can unravel when policymakers depart from the basics. However, as the European Union continues to sort out its own banking crises and the U.S. Federal Reserve remains committed to a zero–interest rate policy, many of the emerging economies will continue to attract unusually high capital inflows. We therefore expect that the kinds of agility that we have seen thus far—including the resort to some types of taxes and regulations that even some International Monetary Fund staffers have recommended—will become increasingly common in the more market-oriented countries in our sample. With the emergence of these countries—led by China, the motor for global growth and the locus of global liquidity in the post-GFC period—a profound structural shift is under way. With that, some ideological blinders are finally dropping off, with pragmatism trumping dogmatism and flexibility in policy approaches beginning to have greater sway.

Notes

1. Jeffry Frieden, *Debt, Development, and Democracy* (Princeton University Press, 1992); Stephan Haggard, C. H. Lee, and Sylvia Maxfield, *The Politics of Finance in Developing Countries* (Cornell University Press, 1993); Robert Wade, "The Asian Debt-and-Development Crisis of 1997–?: Causes and Consequences," *World Development*, vol. 26, no. 8 (1998), pp. 1535–53; Gregory W. Noble and John Ravenhill, *The Asian Financial Crisis and the Architecture of Global Finance* (Cambridge University Press, 2000).

2. Stephan Haggard, *The Political Economy of the Asian Financial Crisis* (Washington: Institute for International Economics, 2000); Andrew MacIntyre, "Institutions and Investors: The Politics of the Economic Crisis in Southeast Asia," *International Organization*, vol. 55, no. 1 (2001), pp. 81–122.

3. Jeffrey A. Frankel, Carlos A. Vegh, and Guillermo Vuletin, "On Graduation from Fiscal Procyclicality," *Journal of Development Economics*, vol. 100 (2013), pp. 32–47.

4. The "neoliberal" label is most commonly applied to Latin American policies in the post–cold war period of the 1990s. See Susan Stokes, *Mandates and Democracy: Neoliberalism by Surprise in Latin America* (Cambridge University Press, 2001); Carol Wise and Riordan Roett, *Post-Stabilization Politics in Latin America* (Brookings, 2003); and Kurt Weyland, *The Politics of Market Reform in Fragile Democracies* (Princeton University Press, 2004).

5. For more on the developmentalist model, which has been used to explain the various East Asian miracles over the past three decades, see Alice Amsden, *The Rise of the Rest* (Oxford University Press, 2000) and *Asia's Next Giant: South Korea and Late Industrialization* (Oxford University Press, 1989); Meredith Woo-Cumings, *The Developmental State* (Cornell University Press, 1999); and Atul Kohli, *State-Directed Development: Political Power and Industrialization in the Global Periphery* (Cambridge University Press, 2004).

6. Andrew MacIntyre, T. J. Pempel, and John Ravenhill, *Crisis as Catalyst: Asia's Dynamic New Political Economy* (Cornell University Press, 2008).

7. Nuriel Roubini and Stephen Mihm, *Crisis Economics: A Crash Course in the Future of Finance* (London: Penguin Group, 2010), pp. 72–76.

8. Benjamin Bernanke, "The Global Saving Glut and the U.S. Current Account Deficit," March 10, 2005 (www.federalreserve.gov/boarddocs/speeches/2005/2005 03102/).

9. Andrew Ross Sorkin, *Too Big to Fail* (New York: Penguin Books, 2010); Alan Blinder, *After the Music Stopped* (New York: Penguin Books, 2014).

10. Michael Lewis, *The Big Short* (New York: W.W. Norton and Company, 2010).

11. See Roubini and Mihm, *Crisis Economics,* and Philip Arestis and Elias Karakitsos, *The Post "Great Recession" U.S. Economy: Implications for Financial Markets and the Economy* (New York: Palgrave Macmillan, 2010).

12. World Bank, "Globalized, Resilient, Dynamic: The New Face of Latin America and the Caribbean,"October 6, 2010 (http://siteresources.worldbank.org/EXTLAC

OFFICEOFCE/Resources/870892-1197314973189/NewFaceofLAC_AnnualMtgs
Report_Eng.pdf).

13. William Easterly, *The Elusive Quest for Growth* (MIT Press, 2002).

14. Alfredo Saad-Filho, "The 'Rise of the South': Global Convergence at Last?," *New Political Economy,* vol. 10, no. 4 (2014). This author warns that while there are signs of convergence in the empirical data, it is important not to exaggerate these claims.

15. Arvind Subramanian and Martin Kessler, "The Hyperglobalization of Trade and Its Future," Working Paper 13-6 (Washington: Peterson Institute for Economics, July 2013), p. 3. See also Dani Rodrik, "The Past, Present, and Future of Economic Growth," *Towards a Better Global Economy Project* (Switzerland: Global Citizen Foundation, 2013) (www.gcf.ch/?page_id=5758).

16. Omar D. Bello, Juan S. Blyde, and Diego Restuccia, "Venezuela's Growth Experience," *Journal of Latin American Economics,* vol. 48, no. 2 (2011), pp. 199–226.

17. Sebastian Mallaby, "Beware Membership of the Elite Club," *Financial Times,* December 5, 2012.

18. Mauro Guillén and Emilio Ontiveros, *Global Turning Points* (Cambridge University Press, 2012).

19. Subramanian and Kessler, "The Hyperglobalization of Trade and Its Future"; also see Rodrik, "The Past, Present, and Future of Economic Growth."

20. A vast literature exists on these crises. On the Latin American debt crisis see, for example, Frieden, *Debt, Development, and Democracy,* and Arturo C. Porzecanski, *Latin America: The Missing Financial Crisis,* Studies and Perspectives Series 6 (Washington: Economic Commission on Latin America and the Caribbean, 2009); on the Asian financial crisis see Haggard, *The Political Economy of the Asian Financial Crisis,* and MacIntyre, "Institutions and Investors."

21. William Darity and Bobbie L. Horn, *The Loan Pushers: The Role of Commercial Banks in the International Debt Crisis* (Cambridge, Mass.: Ballinger Publishing, 1988); Steven Radelet and Jeffrey Sachs, "The East Asian Financial Crisis: Diagnosis, Remedies, Prospects," *Brookings Papers on Economic Activity,* no. 1 (1998), pp. 1–90.

22. John Williamson, "What Washington Means by Policy Reform," in *Latin American Adjustment: How Much Has Happened?,* edited by John Williamson (Washington: Institute for International Economics, 1990), pp. 5–20; Dani Rodrik, "Goodbye Washington Consensus, Hello Washington Confusion," *Journal of Economic Literature,* vol. 44, no. 4 (December 2006), pp. 973–87; John Williamson, "A Short History of the Washington Consensus," in *The Washington Consensus Reconsidered: Towards a New Global Governance,* edited by Narcis Serra and Joseph E. Stiglitz (Oxford University Press, 2008).

23. Porzecanski, *Latin America*; Mauricio Cardenas, "Curbing Success in Latin America," April 14, 2011 (www.brookings.edu/opinions/2011/0414_curbing_success_cardenas_yeyati.aspx).

24. Dani Rodrik, *One Economics, Many Recipes: Globalization, Institutions, and Economic Growth* (Princeton University Press, 2007); Mario Cimoli, Giovanni Dosi, and Joseph E. Stiglitz, *Industrial Policy and Development* (Oxford University Press,

2007); Multidisciplinary Institute for Development and Strategies, "Brazil's Alternative to Austerity: Increased Employment and Reduced Inequality" (Washington: New America Foundation, June 14, 2013) (http://newamerica.net/publications/policy/brazils_alternative_to_austerity).

25. Anne O. Krueger, "Government Failures in Development," in *Modern Political Economy and Latin America*, edited by Jeffry Frieden, Manuel Pastor, and Michael Tomz (Boulder, Colo.: Westview Press, 2000).

26. Ben Bernanke, *The Federal Reserve and the Financial Crisis* (Princeton University Press, 2013).

27. The best overview of this process, with case studies on both East Asia and Latin America, is Barbara Stallings with Rogerio Studart, *Finance for Development: Latin America in Comparative Perspective* (Brookings, 2006).

28. Leslie Elliott Armijo, "Mixed Blessing: Expectations about Foreign Capital and Democracy in Emerging Markets," and "Mixed Blessing: Conclusions," in *Financial Globalization and Democracy in Emerging Markets,* edited by Leslie Elliott Armijo (New York: Palgrave/St. Martin's, 1999).

29. See Leslie Elliott Armijo and Saori N. Katada, "Theorizing the Financial Statecraft of Emerging Powers," *New Political Economy* (www.tandfonline.com/doi/full/10.1080/13563467.2013.866082#.VBm4VxaH8sQ).

30. Subramanian and Kessler, "The Hyperglobalization of Trade and Its Future."

31. Martin Wolf, *Why Globalization Works* (Yale University Press, 2004).

32. Joseph Stiglitz and Andrew Charlton, *Fair Trade for All* (Oxford University Press, 2005), pp. 107–55.

33. Carol Wise and Yong Zhang, "China and Latin America's Emerging Markets: Debates, Dynamism, Dependence," paper presented at the International Studies Association Meetings, Buenos Aires, July 23–26, 2014.

34. Bernanke, *The Federal Reserve and the Financial Crisis.*

35. Kevin Gallagher and Roberto Porzecanski, *The Dragon in the Room: China and the Future of Latin American Industrialization* (Stanford University Press, 2010).

36. "People's Republic of China: 2010 Article IV Consultation," International Monetary Fund Country Report 10/238 (July 2010), p. 4.

37. The ten members of ASEAN are Brunei, Cambodia, Indonesia, Laos, Malaysia, Mayanmar, the Philippines, Singapore, Thailand, and Vietnam.

38. Albert Fishlow, *Starting Over: Brazil since 1985* (Brookings, 2011).

39. The LAC-7 includes Argentina, Brazil, Chile, Colombia, Mexico, Peru, and Venezuela.

SHAUN BRESLIN

2

Chinese Financial Statecraft and the Response to the Global Financial Crisis

In a comparative project such as this, which looks at emerging economy responses to the 2008–09 global financial crisis and the varieties of capitalist development that influenced them, the Chinese case seems to be a shining example of effective crisis management by a proactive developmentalist state. The government's swift action to stimulate other sources of growth once exports declined dramatically in November 2008 was facilitated by prior macroeconomic reforms—which, crucially, were not neoliberal ones. A number of reforms to help strengthen the Chinese financial system had already been implemented; although they were undertaken largely to correct perceived domestic weaknesses, they were also influenced by what happened during the Asian financial crisis. The intention was not to replace developmentalism with a neoliberal alternative but to improve the developmentalist state and make it more resilient. Those reforms had left China in a strong national fiscal position, with large and growing currency reserves. Banking sector reforms also played their part by ridding the banks of nonperforming loans and bad debts.

Most important, however, was that once the decision to act was made, strategic financial statecraft came to the fore. As early as November 2008, well before the full impact of the crisis on Chinese exports became clear, the government announced a massive stimulus package to promote consumption in order to spark an investment-led recovery. The immediate crisis was averted,

This chapter acknowledges the support of the FP7 large-scale integrated research project GR:EEN (Global Re-ordering: Evolution through European Networks).

and despite the fact that exports continued to perform badly through much of 2009, the much-vaunted target of achieving 8 percent growth for the year was reached with ease and even surpassed. With capitalism in crisis in much of the West, such a strong performance led to debate over whether a "China model" of strong state developmentalism might replace neoliberalism as a guide to development elsewhere.[1] More concretely, China's recovery sucked in imports from other developing states, thereby contributing to the counter-vailing environmental conditions that aided recovery in some of the other economies that are dealt with in this volume.

But once we shift from short-term to broader, longer-term analyses, a number of issues come into sharper focus and threaten to take some of the shine off China's initial successes in withstanding the crisis. The contribution of the government's response to speculative bubbles and the disposition of the debt that funded growth in 2009 and 2010 are two high-profile examples of outcomes that may have long-term detrimental consequences. It is also unclear how the response to the crisis will help the Chinese leadership achieve its stated desire to decrease dependence on exports and investment and promote domestic consumption as the basis of growth.[2]

The response to the crisis highlighted two key elements of Chinese state developmentalism. First, while China's economy might be a market economy, it is not a neoliberal free market one, despite the retreat from socialism and the introduction of market mechanisms over the years. Despite the fact that the nonstate sector is much more productive than the state sector, that it accounts for the majority of GDP (and an even bigger share of growth), and that it has been overwhelmingly the most important source of new jobs, the state sector remains important. The state retains the ability to shape the way in which the market operates, partly because of residual state ownership in key industrial sectors—perhaps most notably energy, which directly impacts other economic activity. However, the argument here is that the state's control over finance remains an essential determinant of how the Chinese economy works. Therein lies the key to China's success in surviving the global financial crisis (GFC).

Second, there is more to the Chinese state than the central government. Although the central leadership first identified the challenges and then announced the stimulus package in response, it committed itself to directly funding less than half of the stimulus. Bank lending became the major source of the subsequent credit boom—and through their often intimate relations with local banks, local governments became (indirectly) the major recipients of the credit. Investigating the way in which local governments are funded might not seem the most exciting task, but is essential to understanding both how the Chinese response was implemented and how, as a consequence, financial problems may emerge in the long run.

Considering these two elements together, we can begin to understand how the Chinese response evolved over time. What started out as a central government response became a local government project fueled by bank loans that proved difficult to coordinate and control.

What for China had started as a crisis in the real economy (in manufacturing trade) soon had clear effects on the financial sector too. As a result, the central government's strategic statecraft shifted from an initially proactive position to a more reactive one as local policymakers moved to prevent those effects from developing into a full-blown financial crisis.

The Chinese Developmentalist State

Although the idea of a China model of development built around strong state control of the economy has gained considerable interest in recent years, Huang Yasheng reminds us that for much of the post-Mao period, the emphasis has been on the introduction of the market rather than its suppression. For Huang, it was the move to the market—in particular the explosion of township and village enterprises (TVEs)—rather than the residual strength of the state that provided the foundation for China's economic miracle.[3] Although pragmatic experimentation might be the hallmark of the Chinese development experience and might offer a key lesson to others,[4] that pragmatism has entailed accepting rather than overturning key elements of the neoliberal agenda in some areas. As the World Bank's Philip Karp argues, "on questions of trade, FDI and regulation, China's actual reform experience is pretty much in line with the policy prescriptions attributed to the Washington Consensus."[5]

For private and foreign companies that wish to invest in China to produce exports, the trade regime is indeed rather liberal. But notwithstanding the regulatory changes that followed China's entry into the World Trade Organization (WTO) in 2001, trying to compete with Chinese firms in the Chinese domestic market reveals another side to the Chinese economy. Protecting key companies from competition includes the use of practices that seem to violate the government's formal commitments to reform as well as practices that occupy the "murky ground" between being outright illegal (according to WTO law) and violating the spirit of WTO law.[6] And of course, China's exchange rate policy has led to calls—from, for example, Argentina, Brazil, and the United States—to label China a "currency manipulator."[7] Some even consider China's exchange rate policy to be at least one of the causes of the global imbalances that created the potential for a global economic crisis.[8]

The market that has been constructed in China is thus one wherein the state retains significant levers of control—a market shaped by state ownership and state interests. For example, direct state control of pricing has declined, and the price of almost all retail goods and agricultural products is set by supply and demand. But crucially, the prices that the state still sets (such as energy prices and some wages) impact virtually every area of economic activity and result in "factor price distortions" across the economy.[9] Moreover, if the need arises, the government can and does step in to reimpose price controls, provide price and consumer subsidies, release strategic state reserves, and move goods and commodities to where they are needed. Perhaps most significant of all, while land has been commoditized and gained a market price, it has not been privatized and remains largely under the ownership and control of local governments.[10] It has become an important source of local government income in what appears to be an unsustainable link between banks, local governments, and land prices.

A similar pattern emerges with ownership. In the second half of the 1990s, the state sector shrank through privatization, mergers, and other kinds of ownership reform.[11] As employment in state and collectively owned urban enterprises fell by roughly half,[12] the nonstate sector rose to become the major driver of growth and almost the only source of new jobs by the end of the millennium.[13] The remaining state-owned enterprises (SOEs) were expected to reform to adapt to the realities of life in a market system and in the global economy.[14]

However, while they are supposed to be commercial entities, Chinese SOEs occupy a very privileged place in the market. According to a Chinese think tank report, the profitability of the state sector rests almost entirely on the relationship between SOEs and the state. In many sectors SOEs are monopoly actors, have easy access to bank loans at around a third of the official market interest rate, pay a fraction of the market rate for land, pay less than half of the tax that private companies pay, receive cheap energy and fiscal subsidies and other direct injections of capital if and when the need arises, and remit only a tiny fraction of their profits back to the state.[15] The state sector is also larger than it might appear at first sight. Many of the firms that are listed on Chinese stock markets and that appear to be private entities are actually owned by holding companies and conglomerates that ultimately can be traced back to SOEs.[16]

But in many respects, size is not as important as the sectors where SOEs still dominate. Ownership reform has left the central state in control of "strategically important sectors" (战略重要部分 [*zhanlue zhongyao bufen*]) that are "the vital arteries of the national economy and essential to national security" (energy, communications, distribution, and so on) and in a dominant position in "pillar" sectors (machinery, automobiles, information technology, construction, steel, base metals, chemicals, land surveying, and R&D).[17] Moreover, while the central government controls only 117 enterprises (at the time of writing), focusing just on the national level ignores the 100,000 SOEs or more that are owned by and responsible to local governments. While some of them are very large industrial groups that have a global reach, even the smaller local SOEs play key roles in shaping the contours of local economic activity.

Finally, China's banks have a key role as levers of financial statecraft. As China moved from a state-planned economy to one more influenced by markets and capitalism, direct financial transfers from the state were partly replaced by bank-based credit as a source of financing (although direct capitalization still takes place at times). When that first occurred in the mid-1980s, local governments treated the banks in effect as a continuation of the old planning system and as a means of supporting local SOEs. Often loans were extended with little or no chance of ever being repaid, resulting in a massive accumulation of bad debts. In an attempt to solve the problem, the 1995 Commercial Bank Law mandated that banks were to use commercial criteria when assessing requests for loans and were not to be swayed by political pressure. But the law also refers to their role in supporting "national industrial policies,"[18] and available evidence suggests that political leverage and pressure remain key determinants of who gets what through the financial system. That does not mean that only state enterprises get funded but that it is much easier for a business to secure financing at good rates if it is part of the state. If it is not part of the state, then it has to try to get close to it by developing personal relations with party or state officials or by building strong corporate relations with the state sector. The fact is that "state officials have the ultimate capacity either to make an enterprise a business star or make it go bankrupt."[19]

Reforming the Developmentalist State

As discussed in more detail later, the ability of China's leaders to respond effectively to the global financial crisis with a set of measures that resulted in short-term objectives (at least) being met owes much to the continued sources of power and financial statecraft of the central government. Through its direct relationship with SOEs, its indirect influence via the banking system, and its willingness and ability to shape supply and demand, the state was able to off-set the impact on growth of the decline in imports in 2008 and 2009.

A number of reforms over the previous decade had established a macro-economic situation that made it relatively easy to respond, a crucial factor in China's ability to weather the crisis. But while some of those reforms might have introduced more room for market forces and nonstate actors to influence economic activity, they should certainly not be confused with the type of market-oriented reforms proposed by advocates of neoliberalism.

For much of the 1990s, there was real concern that economic reform might lead to a disastrous financial crash. In addition to loss-making SOEs and non-performing bank loans, the way in which taxes were levied and distributed left the central government short of funds to support its objectives. With local governments seemingly more concerned with their own narrow interests than with national plans, the fragmentation of the Chinese economy looked more likely than the emergence of a clear and coherent strategy for long-term sus-tainable development.[20] Yet by the time that the impact of the GFC began to be felt in China, the economy was in a much stronger position not only to sur-vive but also to respond than might have been the case a few years earlier.[21] Four key issues warrant attention here. First, the exposure of the key banks to debt and nonperforming loans was greatly reduced through recapitalization—transferring bad debts out of the banks and into asset management compa-nies—and initial public offerings of major banks launched in Hong Kong. The cost was enormous. In 2006, Chi Lo calculated that all told, "China has spent US$260 billion on cleaning up its banking system. The amount is about twice as much as Korea spent on restructuring its banks after the 1997–98 Asian crises."[22]

It is important to note that the fundamental source of the problem was not dealt with and that political pressure still seems to be a major factor when it comes to decisionmaking within many banks. Indeed, there is a strong case for saying that fundamentally, China's banks are as "fragile" as they ever were.[23] And cleaning up the debts certainly did not entail replacing a developmentalist banking paradigm with a neoliberal one. But at least when the crisis began to hit China, individual banks were in a stronger position than they had been in the mid-1990s.

Second, fiscal reforms first implemented in 1994 began to shift fiscal authority back to the central government. Although local governments responded by finding new ways to raise money by levying fees, that avenue also was gradually closed off.[24] With the abolition of the much-hated agricultural tax in 2006, local governments as a whole became increasingly dependent on the transfer of funds from the central government to cover their fiscal responsibilities.[25] One of the negative consequences has been the inability of a number of local governments to carry the burden of increasingly costly health, education, and welfare services. In contrast, because of the increase in its share of national finances combined with strong economic growth, the central government had a very low level of debt, in part because of the reform of the state-owned sector, which moved from being a drain on state finances to being a source of profits in 2004.[26] Thus, China was running a budgetary surplus by 2007 and in the first half of 2008, just before the impact of the GFC began to be felt. Quite simply, as the influential Chinese economist Yu Yongding put it: "In contrast to many developing countries, which do not have adequate fiscal and financial resources, for China, it is not only affordable, but sustainable to carry out a very expansionary fiscal policy."[27]

Third, the lack of national debt was mirrored at the household level. To be sure, the increase in domestic consumption in 2009 owed a huge amount to government actions. But the government's short-term success in boosting consumption was aided by beneficial preexisting conditions.[28] Fourth, the long-term benefits of holding large foreign currency reserves are questionable and holding such reserves makes the process of managing domestic economic growth (and inflation) rather problematic. Throughout the 2000s, the People's Bank of China spent considerable time, effort, and money trying to sterilize inflows to prevent pressure on the exchange rate and the monetary supply and to keep inflation from derailing growth targets. The buildup of China's foreign currency reserves, which rose from US$165 billion in 2000 to US$2 trillion in April 2009, is especially striking. Between 2006 and 2009 alone, the country's foreign currency reserves doubled. In addition to providing an emergency bulwark against global shocks, those reserves have enabled China to diversify its economic relationships through loans and investments to other developing states. That, too, helped to create countervailing environmental conditions that helped other emerging economies (EEs) to rebound from the GFC.[29]

In sum, reforms in different areas might have put China in a relatively strong position on the eve of the crisis, but they were a far cry from Washington Consensus–style neoliberal/good governance reforms. It is the relative lack of financial liberalization in China (despite at times considerable external pressure) that has allowed its leadership to manage exchange rate fluctuations and build up strategic reserves. In the case of the banks and bad debts, reform was brought about by moving liabilities between different state agencies rather than by introducing the kinds of neoliberal macroprudential measures discussed in chapter 7 of this volume. Once the impact of the crisis began to be truly felt, it was primarily a developmentalist strategy that enabled China's policymakers to reinvigorate growth.

Responding to the Crisis: Back to the Future?

As discussed, China was in an advantageous position to cope with the impact of the GFC and preserve economic growth. The fundamentals (though not neoliberal fundamentals) were in place to allow it to fund a new wave of growth without generating unsustainable levels of debt. But to some extent the crisis can be seen as a case of especially bad timing—at least by those who have been pointing for some time to the need for China to change direction and put in place a new growth and development paradigm.

For a number of years, consensus had been growing in China on the pressing need to change the direction of economic policy. At the 2007 National People's Congress, Premier Wen Jiabao's comments that the national economy was "unstable, unbalanced, uncoordinated, and unsustainable" gained significant international attention.[30] But in reality, China's leaders had been pointing to a systemic problem for a number of years. Rather than signaling a new policy course, Wen's comments perhaps more aptly reflected his frustration at his inability to oversee a fundamental change from the existing growth model to a new "scientific concept of development" (科学发展观 [kexue fazhan guan]) that had first been announced in 2003.[31]

The existing growth model, so the argument goes, was just that—a "growth" model. Raising GNP had become the major benchmark against which success was measured, and little attention was paid to the longer-term implications of how growth had been attained. Furthermore, not only had this growth model failed to generate desired developmental results, it had in some ways made things worse—particularly in terms of environmental destruction and social inequality. What China needed instead was a sustainable long-term development strategy. "Sustainable" here does not refer just to environmental sustainability, although the urgent need to at least slow the rate of environmental destruction in China has long been accepted by Chinese policymakers. It also refers to the sustainability of the way in which economic growth is generated. Three issues are especially relevant to this discussion.

The first is the extent to which the relationship between the Chinese political system and economy, outlined above, had created the conditions for corruption to flourish—particularly when combined with political control and influence over the police and the judiciary (more particularly, at the local level). Even when there was no outright corrupt activity, the leadership acknowledged wide-scale dissatisfaction, not necessarily with inequality per se but with inequality of opportunity. Those who were getting rich seemed to do so through either their political connections or inherited power and wealth.

The second issue brings us back to the question of local versus national economic objectives. Despite the relative success of its attempts to restore central fiscal and economic power from the mid-1990s on, the central leadership was still concerned about the failings of macroeconomic policy to "persuade" local governments to rein in local spending and conform to central government plans and objectives. Fixed-asset investment was exceeding GDP growth, and many sectors were suffering from overcapacity as a result of competition between producers from different parts of the country. Perhaps ironically, the recentralization of fiscal power had not only failed to solve the problem but in some ways had also made things worse. With insufficient funds to meet their development commitments at a time when they were being pressed to expand access to health, education, and welfare services, local governments' "reliance on value-added tax . . . and business tax means they tend to encourage investments that maximize their fiscal incomes regardless of the overall market situation."[32] In addition to the generic problems of local control, the growth of property and land (rent) prices had become particularly sharp in and after 2003, leading to the possibility that burstable bubbles were emerging in many parts of the country.

The third issue brings us back to the issue of trade policy reform, discussed in the introduction to this volume, and the balance between domestic consumption, investment, and exports as drivers of Chinese growth. The extent to which Chinese growth has become dependent on exports has been much debated, with very little consensus. Those who argue that export dependence has been overstated point to the importance of imported goods and components in the manufacturing of Chinese exports. The key, they argue, is to focus instead only on the value added during the manufacturing of exports, stripping out the value of the imported components.[33] When that is done, rather than accounting for 40 percent of GDP before the crisis, exports account for around 10 percent.[34]

While it is entirely reasonable to try to factor in the net, rather than gross, impact of exports, it is easy to overlook the fact that "policies designed to promote exports also encouraged rapid investment growth."[35] Factoring spillovers back in is far from an exact science, although Akyüz calculates that what might be called "export-related growth" accounts for at least half of Chinese GNP.[36]

Thus, calculating the exact respective contributions of investments and exports to China's growth (either pre- or post-crisis) is far from a straight-forward process. But what is clear is that China's central and local leaders have employed export-promotion strategies that have played a significant (if not easily quantifiable) role in generating both GNP and investment-related growth. It is also clear that private household consumption contributed less to growth in the first decade of the new millennium than it did in the 1990s, accounting for not much more than a third of GNP on the eve of the crisis. Whatever the statistics, China's leaders appeared very concerned that China had become too dependent on exports and that its dependence made it (perhaps more specifically, made employment in certain export sectors in China) vulnerable to changing market conditions elsewhere.

In the short term, then, Chinese policy in 2007 and early 2008 sought to slow growth to a more sustainable and controllable level. In the long term, the aim was to move toward a growth pattern that depended much more on private consumption than on state investment and exports. It was clear that doing so would be far from an easy task. Indeed, although Wen Jiabao announced a planned growth rate of 7 percent for 2007, the target was exceeded by almost half as much—notwithstanding a concerted monetary tightening strategy throughout the year.

Even without the global crisis, changing the nature and direction of the Chinese economy would have been far from easy. Margins in many low-tech, low-value-added export industries were very thin, meaning that they were quite sensitive to policy changes that affected their price competition in foreign markets. With the renminbi (RMB) being allowed to appreciate (by some 20 percent from 2005 to 2008) and many tax rebates removed, exporters began to complain and lay off workers in early 2008. As a result, those policies were partially reversed to help exporters maintain their margins and employment levels.[37]

The response to the crisis entailed a number of initiatives that should contribute to rebalancing: the promotion of green projects, infrastructure projects that might facilitate domestic economic expansion, and policies designed to increase domestic consumption. There also has been a renewed embrace of relations with other developing states that might reduce trade dependence on Western developed economies in the long term. But while there was a rebalancing away from exports, in the short term at least it was increased investment that took up most of the slack. In facilitating this investment boom, the central government allowed the very same sort of unstable, unbalanced, uncoordinated, and unsustainable expansion of bank loans that had been seen as the problem, not the solution, just a few years earlier. Why then did the leadership decide in the autumn of 2008 to reverse policy and run the risk of reigniting financial fires that they had previously spent so much time and money trying to put out?

China's Developmentalist Statecraft Response

The reason for the leadership's policy reversal seems to lie in an "obsession with stability"[38] that was based on a rather negative assessment of the party's ruling capacity[39] and an acute awareness of the rise in social instability. Add to those concerns the perception (correct or not) of China's dependence on the global economy, and a case for a quick response is relatively easy to make. The speed at which exports collapsed also is significant—a year-on-year increase of 21.9 percent in October 2008 was followed by a year-on-year reduction of 2.2 percent only a month later.

Soon there were reports of factories closing and millions of migrant workers returning home from factories on the coast. Exact figures are difficult to ascertain—partly because official unemployment figures focus on the permanent urban population and partly because when only job losses are considered, workers who are subsequently reemployed can be overlooked. A figure of 20 million became the standard reported total, although Fang Cai and Kam Wing Chan's more detailed investigation pointed to 23 million job losses and a 1 percent increase in the overall unemployment rate in China by the summer of 2009.[40] There also were reports of increasing social tensions, including a number of riots, as a result of factory closings and managers disappearing without paying wages.[41]

The legitimacy of Communist Party rule does not rest just on performance; meeting targets (or even better, exceeding them) also has become one self-imposed measure of the party's leadership ability. Having established recovery from the GFC and attainment of 8 percent annual growth as a major policy goal for 2009, the party had to ensure that the target was reached. Short-term political pragmatism, not longer-term economic rationality, became the priority of the day.

The Chinese Stimulus Package

One of the supposed strengths of authoritarian leadership is the speed with which it can respond to crises. Without the need, as in democratic polities, to build a popular consensus for action or to forge coalitions in order to win parliamentary votes, monetary tightening decisions can be made and implemented quickly because the state controls key economic levers. The Chinese response to the global crisis seems to be a classic example of what the IMF referred to as "quick, determined, and effective" action.[42] Chinese monetary easing started in September 2008, and a two-year RMB4 trillion stimulus package was announced in November, with a first tranche of RMB100 billion released in November and December. Nicholas Lardy notes in comparison that it was not until February 2009 that the American Recovery and Reinvestment Act became law.[43]

Working out what the stimulus package actually entailed was not an easy task, as perhaps best illustrated by Barry Naughton.[44] Where the money was meant to go was relatively clear. Data released by the National Reform Development Council showed that a quarter of the total amount was devoted to recovery from the massive earthquake that had hit Sichuan Province in May 2008. Plans had been under way since the quake to help redevelop the affected areas, a fact that might partially explain the speed of the Chinese response to the global financial crisis. The greatest focus was on transportation and power infrastructure development, which was initially slated to receive 45 percent of the total (that figure was dropped to 37.5 percent when the plan was revised in March 2009). If earthquake recovery funds are deducted from the total stimulus amount, infrastructure development accounts for half of the remaining amount. The other areas (after the revision and as a percent of the whole RMB4 trillion) were low-income housing (9.75 percent), projects to boost rural areas and technological innovation projects (9 percent each), green projects (5.25), and spending on health, education, and welfare (3.75).[45]

The problems emerge in identifying where the money to fund these projects was to come from. Although the central government committed its own funds (RMB1.8 trillion) and issued RMB200 billion in bonds to help fund local government projects, the banking sector became the key source of increased liquidity across the country. By the end of 2009, new bank loans in China had reached RMB9.6 trillion, more than twice the figure for the previous year, and a further RMB7.96 trillion in new loans was disbursed in 2010. About RMB1.4 trillion went to new mortgages, with Lardy calculating that by the end of the year, a third of all outstanding household mortgages had been approved in that year alone.[46] Around a quarter of all bank loans went to households in 2009 and more than a third in 2010. When combined with tax cuts and subsidies to encourage the sale of cars and durable consumer goods, domestic consumption accounted for around a third of overall net economic growth in 2009. While net exports were a drain on growth in 2009, the reintroduction of rebates for exporters worth at least RMB670 billion[47] and a minor diversification of trade relations seemed to have had some impact: the rate of decline slowed in the second half of the year and exports grew in December 2009, albeit from a rather low level in December 2008. In other words, the negative impact of exports on growth was probably not as bad as it might otherwise have been.

The Local Developmentalist State

In the end, around two-thirds of overall net growth in 2009 was due to increases in investment. And that brings us back to the nature of Chinese capitalism and the relationship between local governments and economic activity. Although local governments are not formally allowed to borrow money through the banking system, they circumvented the restrictions by establishing local investment platform companies (LIPCs) (地方融资平台公司 [*difang rongzi pingtai gongsi*]), which then applied for loans and issued bonds. When we think of local governments in China, we perhaps first think of provincial governments (including the four municipalities and the five autonomous regions that share the same first-level rank). But while the provincial level is a very important component of the distribution of power in China, much of the day-to-day business of "guiding" economic activity—including funding projects through LIPCs—takes place at lower levels.

How many LIPCs exist is unclear. While the National Audit Office (NAO) surveyed 6,576 of them in 2011,[48] a People's Bank of China regional development report referred to a total of 10,000 at all levels of local government.[49] Collectively, the LIPCs surveyed by the audit office spent 62 percent of their money on infrastructure projects and 11 percent on land purchases. Not surprisingly, working out statistics for the LIPCs as a whole is fraught with difficulty and entails mixing information from different sources and taking a leap of faith at times. With that very big caveat, it appears that around half of new loans issued in 2009 went toward local government infrastructure projects via LIPCs.[50] Even if the math is a bit hazy, it is clear that the combined investments of LIPCs was the single biggest reason that Chinese growth continued despite the severity of the global financial crisis.

While the government's strategy was successful in its own right—the target was set and surpassed—the way in which growth was attained brings us back to the question of the sustainability of China's predominant mode of growth promotion and to the three key sustainability issues identified above. First, the expansion of credit created the opportunity for those who approved bank financing for projects to target their preferred beneficiaries. That might entail spending money on refurbishing government buildings or buying new fleets of cars, but it also could involve outright corruption. In May 2010, the Ministry of Supervision announced that penalties had been imposed on more than 5,000 officials by the Chinese Communist Party. Of those, over 3,000 had also been referred to the judicial system.[51] In particular, it seems that the state's residual ownership of land put officials in an especially strong position to benefit—legally or otherwise—from the expansion of credit. The selling of farmers' land rights without consultation and adequate compensation has been the cause of a number of protests against local governments, including the Wukan "Uprising" in December 2011[52] and riots in Zuotan in June 2012.

This brings us to the second issue: the financial relationship between central and local governments. Provincial governments receive just under half of their income through transfers from the central government—44 percent in 2010. The rest is made up of two sources: fiscal income that they share with the central government and income that they directly control themselves. It is the latter that has been growing overwhelmingly fast because local governments have increasingly come to rely on selling land use rights (国有土地使用权出让收 [*guoyou tudi shiyongquan churang shou*]) as a means of raising income. That source of income increased by over 40 percent in 2009[53] and by 100 percent in 2010.[54] Following a more modest year-on-year increase of 14 percent in 2011, the sale of land use rights accounted for 87 percent of all locally controlled income (RMB3.32 trillion).[55] That is not net income because local governments collectively use about 71 percent of the money on compensation for land expropriation, housing demolition, and resident relocation. But it still means that local governments earned just under RMB1 trillion from selling land rights in 2011 alone.

Moreover, loans made through local investment platforms typically are underwritten (implicitly if not explicitly) by expectations of rising prices in the future, creating an even stronger link between local government finances, debt and land prices, ownership, and usage. Rising house and land prices, which contribute to inflation and land appropriations, have been the cause of social discontent. But if land prices did not rise, then local governments would lose an important source of income and LIPCs might find it harder to pay off their debts.[56]

The extent of those debts is significant—but, once again, not easy to pin down. The official NAO report put LIPC debt in 2010 at just under RMB5 trillion; with local governments holding slightly more debt in other forms, the combined total rises to RMB10.71 trillion. There is a huge regional variation in debt levels, with levels tending to be higher and the ability to repay debts lower in the central and western regions.[57] A second audit in 2013 found that local government debt had reached RMB17.9 trillion, with RMB10.6 trillion in direct liabilities and the rest in contingent debt that could fall on local governments through their guarantees.[58] Although it registered a significant increase in debt in three years, the second audit was at the lower end of expectations. The Chinese Academy of Social Sciences previously had reported that total local government debt was RMB19.94 trillion at the end of 2011,[59] while a Nomura survey suggested that LIPC debt *alone* had reached RMB19 trillion in 2012.[60]

Whatever the true figures, it seems likely that some local governments are going to find themselves under severe financial strain. While that does not necessarily augur financial crisis on a national scale, it does point to the ongoing struggle to strike a financial relationship between central and local governments that not only serves the interests of both but also averts social disorder and potential further fracturing of the relationship between the party-state and the people. The current system, which has seen such an emphasis on debt financing and local control of land, seems economically unsustainable and potentially dangerous in political terms.

The state of local finances also points to other conclusions that are important to the analysis in this chapter. First, focusing on what is said and done in Beijing gives us just part of the picture of the nature of state-economy relations and the financial levers available to influence economic activity. To be sure, regulation and innovation by the central government are crucial, but so too are actions at the local level, where the daily relationship between the state, the financial system, and economic actors is often quite intimate. More-over, the local level encompasses not only the provinces but also the thousands of lower-level administrative units. It is noteworthy that more than two-thirds of overall local government debt is held at the city and county level. A change in central government policy laid the foundation for the response to the GFC, and central agencies like the Ministry of Railways were key actors in efforts to develop infrastructure projects (and they generated considerable debt in the process). But taken together, the actions of local governments in using credit to pursue local projects were also a key source of the 8 percent plus growth in 2009 and 2010.

Second, for those who already thought that the Chinese growth model was unsustainable, the collapse in exports in 2008 seemed to prove the point.[61] But the extent to which the response to the crisis has led to a fundamental rebal-ancing seems debatable. Given the collapse in exports for much of 2009 and the amount of money that was pumped into the economy, it would have been astonishing if exports had not played a less important role in generating growth than before. Continuing problems in a number of China's major mar-kets have also made the prospect of a long-term export-driven recovery rather unlikely. But the argument for rebalancing is not as clear cut as might appear at first sight. As *The Economist* argued in 2012: "Unfortunately, China has rebalanced externally without rebalancing internally. Its current-account sur-plus has narrowed largely because of an increase in domestic investment, not consumption."[62]

Indeed, investment in real estate alone might have accounted for as much as 20 percent of GDP in 2011.[63] There are also questions over the long-term contribution that real estate investment will make to the economy. The need for and the extent and safety of the extension of China's railway network has been widely debated. For example, Edward Chancellor has argued that much investment has been "frittered away on trophy infrastructure projects, such as the country's expensive high-speed rail network, with low prospective returns."[64] In extreme cases, "some local governments are literally digging holes and then filling them in to ratchet up the GDP."[65]

In its immediate response to the global financial crisis, the central govern-ment, after having spent years trying to deal with "unstable, unbalanced, unco-ordinated" economic growth, went back to policies that could increase instability, that appear to be unbalanced, and that were clearly uncoordinated. For Lardy, while this response has created problems in terms of bad debts and inflationary pressures, it was a price worth paying to avoid the alternative, "an even sharper drop in economic growth."[66] Nevertheless, if a paradigm shift was necessary but difficult to make before the crisis, the consequences of the response to the GFC might have made the shift even more difficult, by creating more problems that must be overcome first and by further entrenching the position of those in the central and local governments who benefited from the provision of credit in 2009.

Conclusion

The Chinese stimulus project worked. It did what it was meant to do: to allow China to recover from the impact of the decline in exports in 2008 and 2009. Whether it will be considered a long-term success depends on how the dysfunctional consequences of the response to the crisis are managed over the coming years. Since 2010, Chinese economic policy has shifted from a focus on monetary tightening to expansion and a possible mini-stimulus. This shift largely reflects a "normal" cyclical policy response as the challenge of dealing with slow and even reduced real estate and housing prices up to the summer of 2012 gave way to the challenge of dealing with slowing overall growth. But there are also suggestions that it reflects a lack of consensus and perhaps even a lack of will and ability among China's top leaders to move ahead with fundamental reforms. The first and major recommendation of a report called *China 2030* was that China should

> implement structural reforms to strengthen the foundations for a market-based economy by redefining the role of government, reforming and restructuring state enterprises and banks, developing the private sector, promoting competition, and deepening reforms in the land, labor, and financial markets.[67]

Given that the World Bank produced this report, the emphasis is not surprising. That it was produced in collaboration with the Development Research Center at China's State Council suggests that it also closely represents the views of at least some top political stakeholders in Beijing. Yet such changes would undermine the power and ability of powerful vested interests to generate profits where the state and economy interact. One result is the danger of falling into what has been termed a "transition trap."[68] One of the conclusions of this chapter is that even when there is resolve at the top, the central government does not have total control. Again, much of what happens in China—including investment and spending—is at the very least influenced by local governments.

Two changes would seem to be essential, for political and social stability as well as economic growth. First, the way in which local finances are organized seems to be dysfunctional and unsustainable. Pursuing expansionary investment strategies worked well as a response to the crisis, but it does not always result in a coherent, coordinated, and sustainable *national* strategy. The local government emphasis on selling land use rights to raise revenues seems, in the long term, to be a recipe for asset bubbles, corruption, and popular protests. Second, although access to health and welfare services has increased, in large parts of the country there remains a profound lack of confidence that people will get what they need when they need it. Perhaps as many as 500 million people live at risk of falling back into absolute poverty if they or a family member falls ill in old age. While the state still plays a key role in the Chinese economy, it no longer provides the welfare guarantees and security that it once did. Until that security is restored, millions of people, particularly in the countryside, are likely to retain their propensity to save.

With respect to the hypotheses discussed in the introduction to this volume, the importance of countervailing economic conditions seems to be more a *consequence* of China's recovery (for others), rather than a *cause* of it (in China). Chinese trade policy (including currency policy) and macroeconomic reforms—specifically banking-related reforms—meant that China was in a relatively strong position in 2008–09 to respond to the collapse in exports and its impact on economic growth. While those reforms did entail a degree of liberalization, collectively they fall much more clearly in the developmentalist camp and in some quarters have come to be seen as an alternative to neoliberal strategies. That meant that when financial statecraft was needed, the state had the tools that it needed to *launch* a quick response—although, as shown, not necessarily to *control* the response.

Whether China's leaders can effectively control the long-term consequences of their response to the global financial crisis remains to be seen. Local government and banking debt is not widely perceived to be a systemic threat because the central government is expected to step in and provide bailouts where needed; indeed, the expectation of implicit state guarantees is a key reason why that debt built up in the first place. Nevertheless, while the GFC might not have generated a Chinese financial crisis as such, it has led to renewed focus on how the Chinese financial system functions and on its longer-term viability if left unreformed. We might hypothesize, however, that wherever China goes from here, the recent experiences of more neoliberal financial reformers do not provide an alluring model that Chinese elites will strive to emulate.

Notes

1. Shaun Breslin, "The 'China Model' and the Global Crisis: From Friedrich List to a Chinese Mode of Governance?," *International Affairs,* vol. 87, no. 6 (November 2011), pp. 1323–43.

2. Yu Yongding, "A Different Road Forward," *China Daily,* December 23, 2010, p. 8.

3. Huang Yasheng, "Rethinking the Beijing Consensus," *Asia Policy* 11 (January 2011), pp. 1–26.

4. An argument made in detail in Sebastian Heilmann, "Maximum Tinkering under Uncertainty: Unorthodox Lessons from China," *Modern China,* vol. 35, no. 4 (May 2009), pp. 450–62.

5. Philip Karp, "China's Development Experience: Key Lessons for other Developing Countries," in *The Global Financial Crisis: International Impacts and Responses,* edited by the Beijing Forum Organizing Committee (Beijing: Beijing Forum, 2009), p. 204.

6. Aaditya Mattoo and Arvind Subramanian, "China and the World Trading System," World Bank Policy Research Working Paper 5897 (December 2011), p. 14.

7. See Fred Bergsten, "A Proposed Strategy to Correct the Chinese Exchange Rate," testimony before the Hearing on the Treasury Department's Report on International Economic and Exchange Rate Policies, Committee on Banking, Housing, and Urban Affairs, U.S. Senate, September 16, 2010 (www.iie.com/publications/testimony/bergsten20100916.pdf)."

8. Martin Wolf, *Fixing Global Finance: How to Curb Financial Crises in the 21st Century* (Yale University Press, 2008).

9. Zhang Shuguang and Cheng Lian, "The Achilles' Heels of Growth: Factor Price Distortions and Wealth Transfer in China," SSRN Working Paper (Beijing: Chinese Academy of Social Sciences, 2011) (http://papers.ssrn.com/sol3/papers.cfm?abstract_id=1960360).

10. When land rights are transferred, incumbents are compensated for their losses, but the local government that owns the land gets the higher market-driven price from the new user. So the market sets the price that the local government gets, but not the compensation given to the incumbents. See Zhang Shuguang and Cheng Lian, "The Achilles' Heels of Growth"; and Hsing You-tien, *The Great Urban Transformation: Politics of Land and Property in China* (Oxford University Press, 2010).

11. Jean Oi, "Patterns of Corporate Restructuring in China: Political Constraints on Privatization,"*China Journal,* vol. 53 (January 2005), pp. 115–36.

12. John Giles, John Park, and Cai Fang, "How Has Economic Restructuring Affected China's Urban Workers?," *China Quarterly,* vol. 185 (March 2006), pp. 61–95.

13. Fan Gang, 论体制转轨的动态过程 (Lun Tizhi Zhuangui de Dongtai Guocheng [On the Dynamic Process of Institutional Transition]), *Jingji Yanjiu* [Economic Review] (January 2000), pp. 11–21.

14. From 2003 the State-Owned Assets Supervision and Administration Commission took over the shareholding responsibility of SOEs.

15. 国有企业的性质、表现与改革 (Guoyou Qingye de Xingxhi, Baoxian yu Gaige [The Nature, Performance, and Reform of the State-Owned Enterprises])," Unirule Institute of Economics, April 12, 2011 (www.unirule.org.cn/xiazai/2011/20110412.pdf).

16. See Barry Naughton, "Top-Down Control: SASAC and the Persistence of State Ownership in China" (2006) (www.nottingham.ac.uk/gep/documents/conferences/2006/june2006conf/naughton-june2006.pdf); and Barry Naughton, "China: Economic Transformation before and after 1989" (2009) (www.democracy.uci.edu/files/democracy/docs/conferences/naughton.pdf).

17. See "China Defines Key National Economic Sectors," *China Daily,* December 18, 2006; and Mikael Mattlin, "Chinese Strategic State-Owned Enterprises and Ownership Control," *Asia Paper,* vol. 4, no. 6 (Brussels: Brussels Institute of Contemporary China Studies, 2009) (www.vub.ac.be/biccs/site/assets/files/apapers/Asia%20Paper%204 (6).pdf).

18. Andrew Szamosszegi and Cole Kyle, "An Analysis of State-Owned Enterprises and State Capitalism in China" (Washington: U.S.-China Economic and Security Review Commission, 2011), p. 51.

19. Keming Yang, "The Dependency of Private Entrepreneurs on the Chinese State," *Strategic Change,* vol. 1 (May 2012), p. 111.

20. Kellee Tsai, "Off Balance: The Unintended Consequences of Fiscal Federalism in China," *Journal of Chinese Political Science,* vol. 9, no. 1 (September 2004), pp. 7–26.

21. Of course, for those who see the origins of the crisis in global imbalances and look for root causes in the source of the surpluses as much as in the sources of deficit, this was no mere accident of timing.

22. Unpublished paper, cited with author's permission.

23. Carl Walter and Fraser Howie, *Red Capitalism: The Fragile Financial Foundation of China's Extraordinary Rise,* 2d ed. (Singapore: Wiley, 2012).

24. Ray Yep, "Can 'Tax-for-Fee' Reform Reduce Rural Tension in China? The Process, Progress, and Limitations," *China Quarterly,* vol. 77 (March 2004), pp. 42–70.

25. However, the extent of their dependence varies greatly from place to place.

26. Barry Naughton, "Understanding the Chinese Stimulus Package," *China Leadership Monitor,* vol. 28 (May 2009).

27. Yu Yongding, "The Impact of the Global Financial Crisis on the Global Economy and China's Policy Responses," Third World Network Working Paper 25 (2010), p. 11.

28. David Janoff Bulman, "China and the Financial Crisis: Stimulating and Understanding Household Consumption," *Stanford Journal of East Asian Affairs,* vol. 10, no. 2 (Summer 2010), p. 22.

29. Daniel Chow, "China's Response to the Global Financial Crisis: Implications for U.S.-China Economic Relations," *Global Business Law Review,* vol. 1, no.1 (2010), p. 49.

30. "Premier: China Confident in Maintaining Economic Growth," *Xinhua,* March 16, 2007 (http://news.xinhuanet.com/english/2007-03/16/content_5856569.htm).

31. After the 2012 annual NPC session, Wen more clearly expressed his frustration, accompanied by regret, at not dealing effectively with China's problems.

32. *Overcapacity in China* (Beijing: Roland Berger Strategy Consultants for the European Union Chamber of Commerce in China, 2010).

33. He Dong and Zhang Wenliang, "How Dependent Is the Chinese Economy on Exports and in What Sense Has Its Growth Been Export Led?," *Journal of Asian Economics,* vol. 21, no. 1 (February 2010), pp. 87–104; Paul Bowles, "Rebalancing China's Growth: Some Unsettled Questions," *Canadian Journal of Development Studies,* vol. 33, no.1 (April 2012), pp. 1–13.

34. Jonathan Anderson, "Is China Export-Led?," UBS Investment Research Asian Focus, September 26, 2007 (www.allroadsleadtochina.com/reports/prc_270907.pdf).

35. Ed Dew and others, "China's Changing Growth Pattern," *Bank of England Quarterly Bulletin,* vol. 51, no.1 (February 2011), p. 51.

36. See Yilmaz Akyüz, "Export Dependence and Sustainability of Growth in China," *World Economy and China,* vol. 19, no. 1 (2011), pp. 1–23.

37. Barry Naughton, "A New Team Faces Unprecedented Economic Challenges," *China Leadership Monitor,* vol. 26 (2008).

38. Shi Jiangtao, "Closed Doors to Reform," *South China Morning Post,* January 30, 2012.

39. 中共中央关于加强党的执政能力建设的决定 (Zhonggong Zhongyang Guanyu Jiaqiang Dangde Zhizheng Nengli Jianshe de Jueding [The Party Central Committee Decision on Strengthening Governing Capacity Construction]) (September 2004) (www.china.com.cn/chinese/2004/Sep/668376.htm).

40. Fang Cai and Kam Wing Chan, "The Global Economic Crisis and Unemployment in China," *Eurasian Geography and Economics,* vol. 50, no. 1 (2009), pp. 1513–31.

41. Kam Wing Chan, "The Global Financial Crisis and Migrant Workers in China: 'There Is No Future as a Labourer; Returning to the Village Has No Meaning,'" *International Journal of Urban and Regional Research,* vol. 34, no. 3 (September 2010), pp. 659–77.

42. "People's Republic of China: 2010 Article IV Consultation," International Monetary Fund Country Report 10/238 (July 2010), p. 4.

43. Nicholas Lardy, *Sustaining China's Economic Growth* (Washington: Peterson Institute for International Economics, 2012), p. 5.

44. Naughton, "Understanding the Chinese Stimulus Package."

45. Ibid., p. 7; Yu Yongding, "The Impact of the Global Financial Crisis," p. 13; and Stefan Myers, "China's Fiscal Stimulus and Implications for the Future," in *China and the Great Recession of 2007–2009,* edited by J. Connolly and M. Grubb (Washington: Jackson School of International Relations, 2010), p. 77.

46. Lardy, *Sustaining China's Economic Growth,* p. 10.

47. Yu Yongding, "The Impact of the Global Financial Crisis," p. 17.

48. 全国地方政府性债务审计结果 (Quanguo difang zhengfu xing shenji jieguo [The Result of the Audit of the Nature of Local Government Debt]), PRC National Audit Office Audit Report Announcement 2011/35 (2011) (www.audit.gov.cn/n1992 130/n1992150/n1992500/2752208.html).

49. 2010 年中国区域金融运行报告 (2010 nian zhongguo quyu jinrong yunxing baogao [Report on 2010 Regional Finance Development]) (Beijing: People's Bank of China, 2011), p. 6.

50. Wang Xinyuan, "Local Government Debt Balloons," *Global Times*, April 7, 2010.

51. "Land, Construction Management 'High-Risk' Posts for Official Corruption: Watchdog," Xinhua, May 20, 2010.

52. The protests actually began in September but turned into an uprising against the local leadership in December.

53. Barry Naughton, "The Turning Point in Housing," *China Leadership Monitor*, vol. 33 (2010), p. 32.

54. Ministry of Finance, 关于2010年中央和地方预算执行情况 与2011 年中央和地方预算 草案的报告 (Guanyu 2010 zhongyang he difang yusuan zhixing qingkuang yu 2011 nian zhongyang he difang yusuan can'an de baogao [Report on the Implementation of the 2010 Central and Local Budget and the Draft Budget for 2011]), Report to the National People's Congress, March 17, 2011 (www.mof.gov.cn/zhengwuxinxi/caizhengxinwen/201103/t20110317_505087.html).

55. Ministry of Finance, 关于2011年中央和地方预算执行情况 与2012 年中央和地方预算 草案的报告 (Guanyu 2011 zhongyang he difang yusuan zhixing qingkuang yu 2012 nian zhongyang he difang yusuan can'an de baogao [Report on the Implementation of the 2011 Central and Local Budget and the Draft Budget for 2012]), Report to the National People's Congress, March 17, 2012 (www. esocial sciences.org/Download/repecDownload.aspx?fname=A2012315133115_20.doc&f category=Articles&AId=4856&fref=repec).

56. Kai Yuen Tsui, "China's Infrastructure Investment Boom and Local Debt Crisis," *Eurasian Geography and Economics*, vol. 52, no. 5 (November 2011), pp. 686–711.

57. 全国地方政府性债务审计结果 (Quanguo difang zhengfu xing shenji jieguo [The Result of the Audit of the Nature of Local Government Debt]).

58. 全国政府性债务审计结果 (Quanguo zhengfu xing zhaiwu shenji jieguo [National Government Debt Liability Audit Report]), National Audit Office, December 30, 2013. (www.audit.gov.cn/n1992130/n1992150/n1992500/n3432077.files/n343 2112.pdf).

59. Chinese Academy of Social Sciences, 中国国家资产负债表2013 (Zhongguo guojia zichanfuzhaibiao 2013 [China National Balance Sheet 2013]) (Beijing: 2013).

60. Zhiwei Zhang, Changchun Hua, and Wendy Chen, "China's Heavy LGFV Debt Burden," Nomura Asia Special Report, September 24, 2013.

61. Yao Yang, "The End of the Beijing Consensus? Can China's Model of Authoritarian Growth Survive?," *Foreign Affairs*, February 2, 2010 (www.foreignaffairs.com/articles/65947/the-end-of-the-beijing-consensus); and Ding Xueliang,

警惕中国模式的"慢性病 (jingti zhongguo moshi de 'manxingbing [Look Out for the Chronic Illness of the China Model]), *Nanfang Zhoumou*, December 9, 2010, p. 31.

62. "China's Economy: Fears of a Hard Landing," *The Economist*, March 17, 2012.

63. The officially announced figure was 13 percent. See Patrick Chovanec, "BBC: China's 2011 GDP Numbers," January 17, 2012 (http://chovanec.wordpress.com/2012/01/17/bbc-chinas-2011-gdp-numbers/).

64. Edward Chancellor, "Corruption Threatens China's Future," *Financial Times*, March 22, 2012.

65. Yu Yongding, "A Different Road Forward," *China Daily*, December 23, 2010, p. 8.

66. Nicholas Lardy, "The Sustainability of China's Recovery from the Global Recession," Policy Brief Pb10-7 (Washington: Peterson Institute for International Economics, 2010), p. 3 (www.piie.com/publications/pb/pb10-07.pdf).

67. World Bank, *China 2030: Building a Modern, Harmonious, and Creative High-Income Society* (Washington: World Bank, 2012).

68. This is from Sun Liping, "Research Report Series on Social Progress," January 9, 2012, produced by Tsinghua University. The report and newspaper reports citing it were subsequently removed from the Internet. For details, see David Bandurski, "Critical Report Pulled from China's Web," *China Media Project*, January 12, 2012 (http://cmp.hku.hk/2012/01/12/17967/).

BARBARA STALLINGS

3

Korea's Victory over the Global Financial Crisis of 2008-09

Korea's response to the global financial crisis of 2008–09 was exemplary. Although the economy was negatively impacted, especially by massive capital outflows and the collapse of exports, government policy was able to offset the shocks. GDP growth was negative for only three quarters, measured year on year (from the fourth quarter of 2008 through the second quarter of 2009), and never turned negative on an annual basis. In 2010, the economy expanded by more than 6 percent. Moreover, the stimulus did not seriously undermine the country's fiscal balance or the level of government debt.

How can this positive scenario be explained, especially given the devastating impact on Korea of the Asian financial crisis (AFC) a decade earlier? The most important element of an explanation is precisely that crisis and what Korea learned as a result of it. The government had undertaken a number of important reforms in the years following the AFC, especially in the financial sector; therefore, Korea did not have a *financial* crisis in 2008–09, although it suffered serious *economic* problems. That is a crucial distinction, since finan-

This chapter was funded by a grant from the WCU (World Class University) program through the National Research Foundation of Korea, funded by the Ministry of Education, Science, and Technology of the Republic of Korea (Grant R32-20077). I appreciate the comments from participants in the roundtable "Unexpected Outcomes across the Pacific Rim" at the 2011 International Studies Association Annual Convention in Montreal and the workshop "Pacific Rim Emerging Economies in the Post Global Financial Crisis," University of Southern California, July 27–28, 2012.

cial crises are the hardest to overcome. In addition, the government continued to manage macroeconomic policy in a very cautious way; therefore, the macroeconomic conditions that existed in 2008–09 allowed for implementation of a large stimulus package without much damage to the government's balance sheet. Finally, earlier trade reforms, together with continuing trade promotion and the signing of several free trade agreements, provided for both an economic stimulus and a large reserve cushion.

Korea provides positive evidence for all four of the hypotheses considered in this volume. I argue that the most important hypothesis in Korea's case concerns financial reform. Financial reforms were of two types. On one hand, liberalization and privatization of the financial sector accompanied the cleanup of bad loans in the private banks. On the other hand, Korea still had three policy banks in 2008–09, and they participated in the stimulus package in a minor way. In addition, some limits on the capital account were reintroduced after the global financial crisis (GFC) to slow capital inflows and exchange rate appreciation. The hypothesis about macroeconomic policy management is also relevant, although Korea has rarely had large deficits on either its fiscal or current account balances. Exchange rate policy became more flexible after the Asian financial crisis. Prior trade reforms dating back to the 1960s were the third major component of the Korean response, as they led to a large trade surplus in the aftermath of the AFC. Finally, the external—or, more precisely, the regional—context was important in relation to trade. China became Korea's main trade partner in 2004, and the Chinese stimulus package helped to offset the fall in Korea's other export markets. Korea did not, however, benefit from positive terms of trade, as did some countries featured in this volume, because its exports are almost all industrial goods and its imports are raw materials.

Korea and the 2008–09 Crisis: A Look at the Data

Korea was similar to but also different from other countries considered in this volume. On one hand, Korea is becoming increasingly different from other emerging economies (EEs). The World Bank classifies it as a high-income country; it has very sophisticated, competitive industrial exports; and its education level is above that of many "developed" countries. It also has the slowing growth rate of a maturing economy, as seen in figure 3-1, where the trend line indicates that average annual growth has slowed from about 9 percent in 1970 to about 4 percent today. Indeed, *The Economist* recently discussed the

Figure 3-1. *GDP Growth, Korea, 1970–2012*

Percent

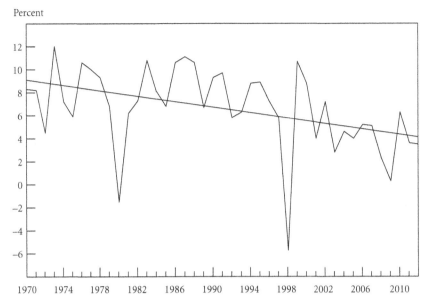

Source: World Bank, World Development Indicators, various years (http://data.worldbank.org/
data-catalog/world-development-indicators).

problems that Korea now faces because it can no longer rely on a catch-up model as its main strategy for resource allocation.[1] On the other hand, Korea's experience with the recent crisis—a sharp decline followed by a strong rebound—was similar to that of some other Asian countries (although not China or India) and most of Latin America. The rest of this chapter explores whether the response to the crisis in Korea also was similar to responses elsewhere and whether the effects of those responses are sustainable.

Table 3-1 shows the pattern of the crisis in Korea through two measures of quarterly data on GDP. By both measures, a sudden contraction occurred in the fourth quarter of 2008. With respect to the previous quarter in the same year (see the second data column in the table), the decline was 4.6 percent, but it lasted only one quarter. Compared with the same quarter the previous year (see the first data column), the recession persisted for three quarters, through the second quarter of 2009, with negative growth of 3.2, 4.0, and 2.0 percent, respectively.

Two main causal mechanisms were at work, both coming from the international economy. First was a contraction in international credit: with the

Table 3-1. *Quarterly GDP Growth, Korea, 2007–12*
Percent

Quarter	Year-on-year	Quarter-on-quarter	Quarter	Year-on-year	Quarter-on-quarter
Q1/2007	4.4	1.4	Q4/2009	6.3	0.2
Q2/2007	5.3	1.4	Q1/2010	8.6	2.2
Q3/2007	4.9	1.2	Q2/2010	7.4	1.4
Q4/2007	5.8	1.6	Q3/2010	4.4	0.7
Q1/2008	5.3	1.0	Q4/2010	5.0	0.6
Q2/2008	4.2	0.4	Q1/2011	4.0	1.3
Q3/2008	3.2	0.2	Q2/2011	3.5	0.8
Q4/2008	−3.2	−4.6	Q3/2011	3.7	0.8
Q1/2009	−4.0	0.1	Q4/2011	3.4	0.3
Q2/2009	−2.0	2.5	Q1/2012	2.9	0.9
Q3/2009	1.2	3.4	Q2/2012	2.3	0.3

Source: Calculated from Organization for Economic Cooperation and Development, Quarterly National Accounts (http://stats.oecd.org/index.aspx?queryid=350#).

collapse of Lehman Brothers in September 2008, Korean banks faced a sharp reduction in credit lines and rollover rates on short-term bank debt from international lenders. The deterioration of the capital account of the balance of payments actually exceeded that during the Asian financial crisis.[2] The situation was especially problematic since Korean banks—unlike most of their Asian counterparts—relied on wholesale funding to supplement deposits. Consequently, both the exchange rate and local equity markets fell by about 30 percent in the months following the Lehman collapse.

A second blow to the Korean economy came with the collapse of many of its export markets, especially in the United States and Europe. The low point came in January 2009, when exports were down by about 35 percent year on year. For an economy that is highly reliant on exports to support growth, that was another serious problem. Not surprisingly, it spilled over into domestic demand as both investment and consumption fell sharply.

Despite the seriousness of the crisis for the Korean economy, it assumed a V-shaped pattern, evidenced by Korea's strong recovery in 2010, when GDP growth reached 6.3 percent. By 2011–12, however, the recovery spurt was over and slower growth had resumed, at 3.6 percent (2011) and 2.0 percent (2012). International Monetary Fund (IMF) projections for coming years show GDP expanding at around 4 percent annually.[3]

In the case of Korea, then, the main puzzle is how the economy was able to return to a respectable positive growth rate so rapidly, despite the depth of the financial and commercial challenges from international markets. At the same time, there remains the question of the sustainability of the recovery and the growth potential of the economy. I argue that Korea's longer-term post-crisis growth is unlikely to be as high as that found in the rest of developing Asia or even as high as the Latin American average.

Historical Background

To understand the issues related to the crisis of 2008–09 in Korea and the nature of the response, it is necessary to briefly review two prior periods of Korean history: the years of rapid growth from the late 1960s to the mid-1990s and the Asian financial crisis of 1997–98.

As widely discussed in the literature, Korea was one of the "economic miracle" countries in East Asia, which grew very rapidly for several decades during the post–World War II period.[4] At the end of the Korean War, South Korea was one of the poorest nations on earth, with an annual per capita GDP of less than US$100. Initially the recipient of large amounts of foreign aid, mainly from the United States, the country experienced rapid economic improvement under a strong state that exerted significant control within a relatively closed economy, except in terms of export promotion. Under a series of authoritarian governments, particularly that of Park Chung-Hee (1961–79), Korea became an export powerhouse and that in turn stimulated rapid economic growth in the economy as a whole.[5]

Partly as a result of its economic success, Korea came under pressure to liberalize its economy, and it began to do so in the 1980s. The plan was to carry out the liberalization gradually in order to avoid the kinds of vulnerabilities that other countries had encountered. However, with the initiation of a democratic government in the early 1990s, Korea began negotiations to join the advanced economies as a member of the Organization of Economic Cooperation and Development (OECD), which led to an acceleration of both internal and external reforms. As is generally acknowledged, the sequencing of the financial liberalization process was poorly planned, and significant short-term debt was built up through borrowing by both financial firms and the large business conglomerates (*chaebol*).[6] Those trends set the stage for contagion to spread from Southeast Asia and engulf Korea once the Asian financial crisis began to unfold.

Once the AFC hit the region in mid-1997, the holders of Korea's large short-term debt refused to roll it over, and Korea exhausted its foreign exchange reserves in trying to help the banks and prop up the exchange rate. Floating the won resulted in a large devaluation that brought about dramatic twin crises: severe financial stress in the banking sector and a currency free fall.[7] With its foreign exchange reserves virtually depleted, the government saw no choice but to approach the IMF for assistance. In December 1997, the fund approved a US$21 billion loan, part of an overall package of US$55 billion to be jointly provided by the World Bank, the Asian Development Bank, and the G-7 governments. In absolute terms, it was the largest rescue package ever assembled, but as a share of the Korean economy it was much smaller than the US$50 billion package authorized for Mexico three years earlier by the IMF, the U.S. government, and assorted other lenders. Moreover, the disbursement was to be spread out over more than two years, contingent on the government's progress in implementing structural reforms and tightening fiscal and monetary policy.[8] Foreign creditors viewed these steps as inadequate, the crisis worsened, and the Korean government turned to the United States for help. The U.S. government persuaded the IMF to frontload its resources and used its influence with international banks to roll over Korea's short-term loans, thereby restoring a semblance of investor confidence in Korea; attention could then turn to longer-term measures.

Korea's economic meltdown was the main surprise of the AFC. Foreigners asked how such a strong, dynamic economy could succumb to financial contagion that had begun in neighboring countries with much weaker economic fundamentals. But the crisis was an even bigger shock to the Koreans themselves. As such, it transformed the entire context of decisionmaking. As one former high official put it, "We had been very arrogant and refused to listen to outsiders' advice before the crisis. All of that changed in 1997."[9] In addition to a new perception of the economy's vulnerability, the Korean government needed money, and it came with conditions.

Analysts differ on the importance of foreign actors in general, on which foreign actors took the lead, and on the extent to which foreign views diverged from the views of Korean officials. One group of mainly foreign analysts argued that the IMF and the U.S. government essentially coerced the Korean government into accepting a package of reforms that disregarded Korean preferences.[10]

A more nuanced view was expressed by some Korean analysts, who emphasized the importance of timing with respect to the election of President Kim

Dae-Jung in December 1997 and his willingness to back the IMF reform package. Since Kim was an outsider with strong links to the labor movement, he was able to obtain its support. The *chaebol* were unable to object, even to corporate restructuring, because of the dire nature of the crisis and the fact that their public image had been badly damaged by the role that their own indebtedness had played in bringing on the crisis.[11] A variant of this view argues that Kim Dae-Jung had his own strategy, which involved bringing in foreigners to offset the power of the *chaebol*.[12]

A third view stressed the importance of democratization in Korea and its impact on the relative power of domestic actors. Specifically, democratization limited the power of bureaucrats in the economic ministries, increased the fragmentation in the legislature, created conflict between the president and the legislature, and increased the power of big business. All of those trends left the government weaker than it had been under military rule.[13]

Changes since 1997

As a result of the 1997 crisis, a number of changes were made to Korea's economic policy. I categorize them in line with the four hypotheses presented in chapter 1 of this volume concerning prior macroeconomic reforms, prior financial reforms, prior trade reforms, and countervailing external conditions.[14]

Macroeconomic Policy

Like most other East Asian economies, Korea has traditionally followed fairly prudent macroeconomic policies. With the exception of a few years in the early 1980s when Korea embarked on its heavy-industry initiative and encountered a debt crisis similar in some ways to that of Latin America, both its fiscal and current account have usually been in rough balance.[15] This can be seen in table 3-2, which presents those balances for the period since 1994, along with government debt as a share of GDP and the volume of reserves in absolute terms and in terms of the number of months of imports that the reserves cover.[16] The table shows also that there was a deficit in the current account in the years leading up to the Asian financial crisis; since then, however, the accounts have been continually in surplus because the government became even more cautious than before. That caution is also reflected in the figures for the fiscal balance, government debt, and reserves. All of them indicate that the country had learned bitter lessons in 1997–98 and was determined to prevent a similar debacle in the future.

Table 3-2. *Macroeconomic Indicators, Korea, 1994–2011*

Year	Current account[a]	Budget deficit[a]	Government debt[a]	International reserves[b] U.S. dollars, billions	Months of imports
1994	−0.8	0.4	10.6	26	2.6
1995	−1.5	0.3	9.4	33	2.5
1996	−4.1	0.2	8.6	34	2.3
1997	−1.6	−1.4	10.7	20	1.4
1998	12.3	−3.5	15.4	52	5.1
1999	5.5	−2.3	17.6	74	5.8
2000	2.8	1.0	18.0	96	5.7
2001	1.7	1.1	18.7	103	6.9
2002	1.3	3.1	18.6	121	7.6
2003	2.4	1.0	21.6	155	8.4
2004	4.5	0.6	24.6	199	8.6
2005	2.2	0.4	28.7	210	7.7
2006	1.5	0.4	31.1	239	7.4
2007	2.1	3.2	30.7	262	6.9
2008	0.3	1.3	30.1	201	4.5
2009	3.9	−1.7	33.8	270	7.9
2010	2.8	1.4	33.4	272	6.6
2011	2.4	1.9	34.1	304	5.8

Sources: Calculated from World Bank, World Development Indicators (http://data.worldbank. org/data-catalog/world-development-indicators); International Monetary Fund, "Republic of Korea: Article IV Consultation," various years (www.imf.org/external/country/KOR/index.htm).
   a. As a percent of GDP.
   b. Total reserves minus gold (end of period).

The main new policy direction in the macroeconomic sphere since 1997–98 concerned the exchange rate. Traditionally Korea had used the exchange rate as part of its trade policy. By pegging it to the dollar and thus keeping it undervalued, Korea both stimulated exports and restrained imports. After the AFC, the Bank of Korea and the Ministry of Finance introduced a flexible exchange rate policy as part of an inflation-targeting approach to monetary policy. That policy clearly fit with the more liberalized policy package in the financial sector, and it succeeded in reducing inflation modestly to low single digits.[17]

Financial Sector Reform

The financial reforms undertaken by the Korean government can be divided into two sets.[18] The first set falls under what is called "neoliberal" reforms in the introduction to the volume. The second, less important, set could be labeled "developmentalist." Six changes fall under the neoliberal rubric. First, the banking sector itself was rehabilitated. Government funds amounting to 30 percent of GDP were injected into the banks to deal with nonperforming loans (NPLs). Five commercial banks were closed, seven were required to submit restructuring plans, and the vast majority of merchant banks were disbanded. A number of banks were temporarily returned to government ownership. Second, the legal and regulatory apparatus was strengthened. The Financial Supervisory Commission (FSC) was established and put in charge of several existing supervisory organs.[19] The Korean Asset Management Corporation (KAMCO) was restructured under FSC guidance, and a fund was created within KAMCO to purchase nonperforming loans.[20] Third, the FSC strengthened prudential regulatory policy through a forward-looking approach to asset classification, limits on short-term foreign borrowing by banks and on bank lending to large borrowers, and increased disclosure requirements. Regulations on mortgage lending also were established so that banks could not get into the kinds of problems that later emerged in the United States and some European countries.

Fourth, to reduce moral hazard, a new deposit insurance scheme was introduced that explicitly limited insurance to 50 million won (around US$40,000 at the current exchange rate) for each depositor at each depository institution. Fifth, the capital account was further liberalized. Restrictions on mergers and acquisitions by foreigners were abolished; foreign investment in the Korean Stock Exchange was fully liberalized; and foreign investment in firms not listed on the stock exchange was permitted. Other measures included liberalization of foreign investment in Korean bonds, money market instruments, and real estate. Sixth, changes were made in corporate governance of the financial sector. Most important, foreigners were allowed to own commercial banks and become bank executives. At the same time, rights of minority stockholders were strengthened.

Table 3-3 shows how the reforms strengthened banking performance indicators. Nonperforming loans peaked at 11 percent of total loans in 1999 but declined rapidly in the next five years to around 1 percent.[21] At the same time, the capital-asset ratio increased; even during the crisis period, it met the Bank for International Settlements requirement of 8 percent, but it increased to more than 12 percent by the mid-2000s. Provisions (money set aside for expected losses on NPLs) rose from 84 percent of the total value of NPLs in 2003 (earliest available data) to more than 200 percent in 2007.

Table 3-3. *Banking Strength Indicators, Korea, 1997–2011*
Percent

Year	NPLs[a]	Provisions[b]	Capital[c]
1997	5.8		
1998	7.6		8.2
1999	11.3		10.8
2000	8.9		10.5
2001	3.3		10.8
2002	2.4		10.5
2003	2.6	84.0	11.1
2004	1.9	104.5	12.1
2005	1.2	131.4	13.0
2006	0.8	175.2	12.8
2007	0.7	205.2	12.3
2008	1.1	146.3	12.3
2009	1.2	125.2	14.4
2010	1.9		14.6
2011	1.3		14.0

Source: Calculated from International Monetary Fund, "Global Financial Stability Report," various years (www.imf.org/external/pubs/ft/gfsr/).
a. Nonperforming loans as share of total loans.
b. Provisions as a share of nonperforming loans.
c. Bank regulatory capital as a share of risk-weighted assets.

Another type of financial performance indicator is the banking sector's contribution to economic growth. Korean banks provide a large volume of credit to the economy in general and the private sector in particular, and loans outstanding were equal to more than 100 percent of GDP by 2007, up somewhat from their share before the crisis. Although in many emerging economies large amounts of credit go to the public sector, in Korea more than 98 percent of credit was going to private borrowers. Also, unlike the loan-to-deposit ratio in most other East Asian countries, Korea's ratio was above 100 percent, a result of competition for market share among Korean banks. To fund the loans that exceeded deposits taken in, banks borrowed on the international market. That was considered the main vulnerability of the Korean financial sector. Capital markets also grew substantially in the period after the AFC. Stock market capitalization as a share of GDP rose from an average of 35 percent in 1992–96 to 78 percent in 2003–07 (and to 107 percent in 2007, calculated separately). Domestic bonds issued by the nonfinancial corporate sector amounted to 22 percent of GDP in 2007, about the same share as before the crisis.[22]

Under developmentalist financial reforms, capital flows and state banks are the most relevant policies. Korea's capital account was completely liberalized following the Asian financial crisis. A decade later, that meant that the economy was vulnerable to large capital outflows by foreign investors, which triggered an exchange rate devaluation and a falling stock market. However, after the economy returned to growth—while the U.S. and European economies remained mired in the Great Recession—the opposite problem arose. The open capital account allowed large inflows into the country, along with the corresponding appreciation of the exchange rate and a rise in stock market prices. As has been discussed extensively in the Latin American context, waves of capital flows into a fairly small economy make it hard to manage macroeconomic policy. Consequently, Korean authorities adopted a set of policy adjustments that were meant primarily to deal with the capital inflow problem at the time that they were introduced but that—if maintained— could also have a positive impact on future outflows as well. As summarized by the IMF, four kinds of measure were introduced:

—regulations to reduce foreign currency mismatches, limit wholesale funding by banks, and limit foreign borrowing by the corporate sector (introduced in November 2009 and June 2010)

—a stability levy on non-core foreign exchange liabilities of banks to a maximum of 100 basis points (introduced in April 2010)

—a withholding tax on nonresident purchases of treasury and monetary stabilization bonds (introduced in January 2011)

—measures to reduce banks' foreign exchange derivative ceilings (introduced in May 2011).[23]

The IMF itself is of the opinion that the foreign exchange regulations on the banks have been more successful than the attempt to limit bond inflows.

Opening bank ownership to foreign participation also was part of the financial reforms. Indeed, the Korean financial system has become the most "Westernized" among the East Asian countries. As of December 2003, 44 percent of bank assets were held by foreigners, including a mix of foreign commercial banks, investment banks, equity funds, and insurance companies; however, no large international banks fully owned any major Korean banks, as they did in other emerging economies.[24] Over the next several years, that pattern began to change. Citibank and Standard Chartered each purchased a medium-size Korean bank, and HSBC considered doing so, but the global financial crisis intervened and the purchase was suspended.

The main way that foreign actors entered Korea's banking sector was through the reprivatization of banks that had been nationalized as part of the bank cleanup process discussed previously. Some of the banks were sold to local holding companies, but others were sold—sometimes controversially—to foreign companies. By 2007, on the eve of the global financial crisis, the main government holdings were in Woori Bank, a commercial bank that had been formed by combining troubled small banks, and the three traditional policy banks, the Korea Development Bank (KDB), the Industrial Bank of Korea (IBK), and the Korea Export-Import Bank (KEXIM). The stated aim was and is to privatize all of these entities except for KEXIM, but that has not been done, for a variety of reasons. Since the banks were still in state hands, they became part of the government response to the 2008–09 crisis.

The policy banks have different functions. KDB specializes in long-term finance for investment purposes. The biggest share of its loans goes to the industrial sector, followed by gas, electricity, and water utilities and telecommunications companies. It also took the lead in corporate restructuring after the Asian financial crisis. IBK focuses on small and medium-size firms (SMEs), providing them with direct finance as well as guarantees and some venture capital–type services.[25] It has smaller divisions that focus on individual and corporate lending. KEXIM, like its counterparts worldwide, provides finance for exports, especially shipbuilding and construction in the Korean case. It now has a division that is in charge of concessional loans, which are part of Korea's rapidly expanding foreign aid program.

The state banks helped during the global financial crisis in two main ways. First, government capital injections enabled the state-owned banks to roll over existing loans. Second, they provided new loans to small and medium-size enterprises. A recent study on Korean banks during the global financial crisis finds that they played a positive role because they—in contrast to the private banks—could operate in a countercyclical manner. The study also finds that government support for financial stability meant that wholesale lending to the Korean banking sector continued during the crisis, although at somewhat higher costs.[26]

Trade Reforms

Korea has been and remains a highly trade-dependent economy. Exports plus imports on the eve of the crisis in 2007 amounted to 82 percent of GDP, far above the ratio for most developing countries and the world as a whole.[27]

Indeed, Korea's export capacity is generally believed to have propelled the country's rise from impoverished nation to economic powerhouse. Trade reform took place very early in Korea, dating back to the 1960s, when the United States began to withdraw its foreign aid. Although Korea, like many other developing countries, went through an import-substitution industrialization phase, it was much shorter than that in many of its EE counterparts, especially those in Latin America.[28]

Korea maintained fairly high tariffs on imports, but exports were promoted by various government policies. Mah identifies the following export promotion measures: tax incentives, financial incentives, low tariff rates for intermediate goods, free trade zones, and trade support organizations.[29] He reports that one estimate of the effective subsidy for Korean exports during the "aggressive [export promotion] period" from the mid-1960s to the early 1980s was as high as 31 percent of gross export receipts.[30] Following WTO regulations—and its own liberalization policies—in recent years Korea eliminated direct subsidies in favor of international marketing support as well as export insurance and duty drawbacks, all of which are allowed under WTO rules. The recent signing of a number of free trade agreements—with the United States, the European Union, and several Asian neighbors—should also boost exports. These policies, together with Korea's competitiveness, have allowed the country to maintain a dynamic export sector.

While trade deficits characterized the economy until the mid-1980s, they turned into surpluses for the rest of that decade. In the years leading up to the AFC, however, the deficits returned, ballooning to more than US$20 billion in 1996 (3.6 percent of GDP). After the AFC, the deficit was quickly eliminated, and the trade account has since shown a surplus, except for the year 2008. A result of the surplus was the accumulation of a large war chest of reserves, which was intended to eliminate the possibility of another crisis such as that in 1997–98.

One important way in which Korea differs from its counterparts in Asia and Latin America is in the composition of its trade, particularly exports. At the beginning of the period of export-oriented growth, labor-intensive products dominated. But by the 1970s and 1980s, the drive to promote heavy and chemical industries had pushed steel, autos, and shipbuilding to the forefront of the country's exports. From the 1990s on, large investments in research and development produced a significant increase in the technological content of Korea's exports, among which electronics, telecommunications, biotech products, and capital equipment have been most important. Because Korea is a natural resource–poor country, most of its imports are raw materials.

Figure 3-2. *Terms of Trade Index, Korea, 1980–2010*[a]

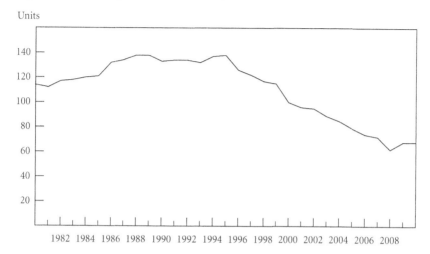

Units

Source: World Bank, World Development Indicators, various years (http://data.worldbank.org/data-catalog/world-development-indicators).
a. Terms of trade index = unit price of exports divided by unit price of imports.

International Context

Because Korea exports mainly industrial products and imports raw materials, the favorable terms of trade that benefited Latin American commodity exporters and some of the developing Asian countries did not help Korea at all. Many of those countries had been able to take advantage of booming export prices for copper, oil, soybeans, and other raw materials, hence their positive terms of trade; for Korea, the situation was quite different. As seen in figure 3-2, Korea's terms of trade had been deteriorating since the mid-1990s. A small recovery occurred during 2008–10, but that did little to make up for adverse trends over the two previous decades. Low international interest rates also were a boost for other EEs, but because Korea's foreign debt was not high, they were of little benefit.

The international context did benefit Korea in regard to the change in Korea's trade partners. In the early post–World War II period, Korea's principal trade partner was the United States, followed closely by Japan. The United States was the most important export market for Korea, while Japan provided the largest share of Korea's imports. Even as late as 1990, the United States and Japan together accounted for half of Korea's total trade, but by 2000, their joint share had fallen to 36 percent. Meanwhile, developing Asian neighbors were increasing their share of Korea's trade, with China being the most important among them. In 2004, China overtook the United States as Korea's main export market, although the United States and Japan continued to surpass China as a provider of Korea's imports.[31] As shown in table 3-4, that pattern still continues. The dynamism of the Chinese economy and other emerging markets was the main way that Korea benefited from the international context during the crisis and continues to be the main way that Korea benefits today.[32]

The 2008–09 Global Financial Crisis and the Korean Response

The Korean response to the global financial crisis was swift, large, and based mainly on traditional fiscal and monetary policy. It was made possible by the changes that Korea had undertaken in the aftermath of the Asian financial crisis a decade earlier. The financial sector was in good shape, with strong capital adequacy and a low level of nonperforming loans. Because the banking sector was operating in a conservative manner, banks did not have large quantities of "exotic" mortgage-backed financial instruments on their books.[33] The fiscal balance was positive, government debt was low, and the main interest rate, controlled by the government, was high; therefore, a stimulus package could be put together that would not have serious negative implications for deficits and debt. The situation looked more manageable than it did in 1997, although clearly there were factors that made Korea vulnerable: the high loan-to-deposit ratio, which required wholesale funding; a high level of household debt; and a high short-term debt ratio.

As noted previously, Kim Dae-Jung, who became president just as the Asian financial crisis struck, played a key role in the response to that crisis. Lee Myung-Bak, who assumed the presidency in February 2008, was not a pivotal actor in the response to the global financial crisis in the same way that Kim Dae-Jung had been in 1997–98. A former Hyundai executive and mayor of Seoul, Lee was supported by a conservative coalition and elected on a platform that promised to restore Korea's traditionally high rate of growth. In April 2008, Lee's party and coalition partners won a landslide victory in elections for the National Assembly, which helped to pave the way for the stimulus measures, which were introduced under the motto "Decisiveness, Sufficiency, Preemption."[34] In Korea, then, it was the conservatives who were promoting a

Table 3-4. *Trading Partners, Korea, 2000, 2007, and 2011*

Percent

Partner	2000			2007			2011		
	Exports	*Imports*	*Total*	*Exports*	*Imports*	*Total*	*Exports*	*Imports*	*Total*
United States	22.0	18.3	20.2	12.4	10.5	11.4	10.0	8.5	9.3
Japan	11.9	19.8	15.8	7.1	15.8	11.4	7.1	13.0	10.0
Other industrial	17.4	16.2	16.8	21.3	16.2	18.8	19.0	21.0	19.9
China	10.8	8.0	9.4	22.1	17.7	19.9	23.9	16.5	20.3
Hong Kong	6.2	0.8	3.6	5.0	0.6	2.9	5.5	0.4	3.1
Other Asia	18.3	15.2	16.8	11.9	13.6	12.7	13.3	10.3	11.8
Other developing	13.3	21.7	17.4	20.2	25.6	22.9	20.0	30.2	24.9

Source: Calculated from International Monetary Fund, *Direction of Trade Statistics Yearbook*, various years (http://elibrary-data.imf.org/FindDataReports.aspx?d=33061&e=170921).

stimulus, in line with Lee's promises of high growth, and the liberal opposition supported the plan.

The fiscal stimulus package was large by international standards, amounting to around 6 percent of GDP during the period 2008–10.[35] It was larger in relative terms than the U.S. stimulus but probably smaller than China's, and it was put in place very rapidly. Shortly after the Lehman collapse in the United States in September 2008, the Korean government announced a supplementary budget for 2008, which was expanded by the National Assembly in April 2009. The two budgets together amounted to 4.5 percent of GDP in expenditures and tax cuts. Spending was front-loaded to the first half of the year in order to have maximum impact. In 2010, the stimulus was expanded further but weighted more heavily toward tax cuts.

Table 3-5 shows the composition of the stimulus, based on the OECD's projected sum of 6 percent of GDP. Spending, which amounted to 3.2 percent of GDP, was divided into government investment (1.2 percent of GDP), transfers to business (1.0 percent), transfers to households (0.7 percent), and transfers to states and municipalities (0.3 percent). Tax cuts, which amounted to 2.8 percent of GDP, went mainly to individuals (1.4 percent) but also to businesses (1.1 percent) and consumption (0.2 percent).

The other main element of the stimulus package involved monetary policy. The government's policy interest rate had been raised to 5 percent in 2007, which provided ample space to lower it as necessary. Between September 2008 and January 2009, the rate was indeed lowered several times; at the latter date, it reached 2 percent, where it remained until a small increase occurred in July 2010.

The government's traditionally prudent macroeconomic stance was reflected in two different ways in the stimulus process. First, the country's budget surplus and low debt level made it relatively easy to carry out countercyclical policies in 2009. Likewise, tight monetary policy facilitated the use of the interest rate as a complement to the fiscal measures. Second, the stimulus signaled that the government was eager to return to "normal" as soon as possible. In practice, that meant beginning to withdraw the fiscal stimulus in 2010, although monetary policy continued to support growth. The budget went into deficit for 2009 (1.7 percent of GDP) but returned to surplus in 2010. Budget numbers include social security funds; if they are excluded, the deficit for 2009 is larger (4.1 percent of GDP). The deficit fell to 1.1 percent of GDP in both 2010 and 2011, and a small deficit still continues.

There were other important measures besides fiscal and monetary policy that involved the financial sector.[36] Since all of the major commercial banks

Table 3-5. *Fiscal Stimulus, Korea, 2008–10*

Spending measures	Percent of GDP	Tax cuts	Percent of GDP
Total	3.2	Total	2.8
Public investment	1.2	For individuals	1.4
Transport	0.4	Low-income groups	0.6
Energy	0.2	Housing-related	0.4
Other	0.6	Personal income tax	0.3
Transfers to households	0.7	For businesses	1.1
Pensions	0.3	R&D	0.1
Unemployment benefits	0.2	Investment	0.3
Other	0.1	Corporate tax cut	0.7
Transfers to businesses	1.0	Consumption	0.2
SMEs	0.4	General consumption tax	0.1
Public financial institutions	0.3	Car-related tax	0.1
Job-creating companies	0.2	Other	0.2
Construction and transport	0.1		
Transfers to subnational levels	0.3		
Other	0.1		

Source: Organization for Economic Cooperation and Development, "Economic Survey of Korea 2010" (Paris: 2010), p. 51 (www.oecd.org/economy/surveys/economicsurveyofkorea2010.htm).

were well capitalized and had low NPL ratios, the main issue was liquidity, a result of their reliance on wholesale funding from abroad to cover the excess of loans over deposits. With the withdrawal of international finance, a dollar shortage emerged. The Bank of Korea provided foreign currency loans and announced in October 2008 that it would guarantee up to US$100 billion in bank short-term liabilities.

To help fund those arrangements and to increase international confidence, the Bank of Korea entered into three swap agreements: a US$30 billion swap with the U.S. Federal Reserve (October 2008); a US$20 billion swap with the Bank of Japan (December 2008); and an RMB180 billion (approximately US$26.5 billion) swap with the People's Bank of China (December 2008). The U.S. and Japanese arrangements expired in 2010, while the swap with China was rolled into a new regional swap arrangement.

Measures also were taken to deal with domestic liquidity problems. To alleviate a domestic credit crunch, the Bank of Korea provided liquidity amounting to 2.7 percent of GDP by increasing and broadening the range of assets eligible for open market operations; paying interest on bank reserve deposits; and contributing to the Bond Market Stabilization Fund and the Bank Recapitalization Fund. The two funds, together with a fund to buy bad assets from the banks, were part of a program to further strengthen banks, although they were already capitalized well beyond standards set by the Bank for International Settlements.

In addition, measures were taken to respond to liquidity problems in the real economy. Because SMEs were of special concern, several of the measures to assist banks required them to continue funding SMEs (by the Korean definition, an SME is a firm with fewer than 500 employees). Direct measures also were introduced, including credit guarantees worth 5.6 percent of GDP, an increase of 34 percent over previous SME support programs. In addition, central bank "guidance" encouraged commercial banks and the government-controlled Industrial Bank of Korea to roll over maturing SME debt. All of these measures began to be unwound in 2010.

Finally, distressed households were offered assistance. A fund financed by contributions from private financial institutions bought bad loans and helped borrowers to lower the interest rate on their existing debt. A credit counseling service helped individuals with debt workouts. Banks, under instructions from the Financial Supervisory Service, extended maturities and lowered interest rates. Moral hazard fears were partially dealt with by attaching some conditions to offers of assistance.

As a result of these policies and the partial recovery of the international economy, growth resumed in Korea. By year-on-year measures, growth resumed strongly in the fourth quarter of 2009 (see table 3-1). With respect to the previous quarter of the same year, growth resumed even earlier in 2009. This performance reflects hard-learned lessons from the 1997–98 crisis with respect to not only the speed and size of the various steps taken to support the economy but also the strength of the real and financial sectors when the crisis struck.

Sustainability

Most studies of responses to the global financial crisis have focused on the short term. Nonetheless, it is also important to ask whether the "quick rebounds" documented in this volume can be sustained over the medium run. As discussed previously, Korea experienced a V-shaped recovery (6.3 percent GDP growth in 2010, following 0.3 percent growth in 2009), but by

2011–12 the growth rate had fallen to less than 4 percent. Most economists agree that a 4 percent rate represents Korea's potential growth for the remainder of this decade (see figure 3-1). To finish this analysis, I want to briefly review three points about the sustainability of economic growth in Korea. First, additional steps have been taken since 2008 to strengthen some aspects of the economy. Second, political trends need to be taken into account when analyzing the future of the economy. Third, some long-term structural issues must be considered.

The main steps taken to reduce Korea's vulnerability in a future crisis have involved lengthening the country's debt profile, instituting macroprudential measures to curb bank reliance on external funding, lowering household debt, setting up swap arrangements with regional central banks, increasing foreign exchange reserves, and reintroducing some capital controls. These steps have had the effect of mitigating the vulnerabilities that existed in 2008; they also may have contributed to lowering of the growth rate.[37]

Moving somewhat in the opposite direction are political trends in Korea. All three candidates to replace President Lee Myung-Bak in the December 2012 election proposed policies to return to historically high growth rates. The new president, Park Geun-Hye, the daughter of former president Park Chung-Hee, has stressed growth and jobs as her priority, but GDP growth continues below 4 percent. While Korean growth rates would be seen as highly successful in many developed economies today, the domestic dissatisfaction in Korea reflects the contradiction between Korea's desire to join the "developed countries" and its desire not to suffer the slower growth that typically characterizes them.[38] In addition, there is political pressure for greater equality and more and better social services, which arguably could conflict with prudent macroeconomic policies.

Finally, structural changes are occurring or may occur that interact with the first two points. One is the issue of the aging population, which means fewer workers to contribute to growth. It is projected that by 2050, Korea will have the second-oldest population among the OECD countries. At the same time, rebalancing the economy toward a service-based rather than manufacturing-based economy and increasing domestic demand to avoid such a high dependence on exports are also likely to slow growth somewhat.[39] Both of these trends are exacerbated by the hope and fear that North and South Korea will be reunited. Such a process would be exceedingly expensive, as in Germany in the 1990s, and there is pressure for both government and individual households to save for that possibility.[40]

Keeping these points in mind, I believe that the sustainability of the Korean recovery will be heavily influenced by the interaction of the following three goals of the Korean government: to ensure security from a possible future economic crisis, to achieve higher growth, and to reunify the two Koreas. Any discussion of how they relate must take place within the structural constraints of an aging population and Korea's place in the international political economy.

Conclusions

I conclude by returning to the hypotheses presented in the introduction to this volume. Although they are divided into the traditional "neoliberal" or "developmentalist" categories, the introduction notes that the more successful economies may use a combination of both neoliberal and developmentalist strategies. Likewise, the hypotheses contribute to both "resistance" to the crisis and "recovery" from it. The Korean case supports such a mixed approach.

As discussed earlier, Korea's experience in the last few years provides support for all of the hypotheses. My own argument is that earlier financial sector reforms (hypothesis 2) were essential to Korea's success in addressing the global financial crisis in 2008–09. The reason is simple. Because the major Korean banks were in a strong position when the GFC struck, there was virtually no financial crisis in Korea. No banks had to be rescued; on the contrary, they could help support the real economy. According to the Reinhart and Rogoff analysis, which has become the consensus view in the last few years, financial crises are especially damaging and long lasting.[41] Yet sufficient time had passed for Korea to fully recover from the 1997–98 crisis, and the second time around policymakers and domestic institutions were well prepared to fend off the contagion.

The macroeconomic hypothesis (hypothesis 1) also is important for understanding the Korean response to the recent crisis. The surpluses in both the current account and government budget in the years leading up to the 2008–09 crisis were essential in facilitating the large stimulus, which got the economy back on track quickly. But I consider this hypothesis less important in the Korean case because Korea has a long-standing tradition of prudent macromanagement.

Both of the above hypotheses could be labeled neoliberal. Trade reforms (addressed in hypothesis 3) are a combination of neoliberalism and developmentalism. Clearly in the early years (1960–90), Korea had a very developmentalist trade policy: promoting exports through a variety of government subsidies and an undervalued exchange rate and restraining imports through high tariffs. Those policies changed in the 1990s, especially after the Asian financial crisis. In line with WTO rules, Korea now limits itself to the few WTO-approved policies for export promotion and has liberalized its exchange rate. It also has signed several important free trade agreements. Thus its trade dynamism continues, providing a large cushion of foreign exchange reserves. These factors were important both in preventing an overwhelming crisis and in stimulating a swift recovery.

The developmentalist version of the hypothesis regarding financial sector reforms was less relevant in Korea. Because the process of privatizing several policy banks had proved difficult, those banks remained in the public sector after financial liberalization, but they played only a small role in the crisis response. Likewise, some capital controls were reintroduced, but after the crisis had been contained. Indeed, they were implemented because the success of the response meant that capital flows into Korea were considered dangerously large and potentially volatile.

Finally, the external context (hypothesis 4) was important, particularly in the form of a change in trade partners. Trade between Korea and China and other EEs, which had surpassed trade between Korea and its traditional industrial country partners, provided ballast for its recovering economy in 2008–09 and beyond. Of course, the current slowdown in those economies may be a source of future problems.

In summary, then, the Korean experience suggests that a well-run, liberalized economy can successfully confront an international crisis. Government controls are not necessary, although they may be useful at the margin. The location of a country within the international economic geography of trade and investment flows also plays a significant role in accounting for outcomes.

Notes

1. "South Korea's Economy: What Do You Do When You Reach the Top?," *The Economist*, November 12, 2011.

2. International Monetary Fund, "Republic of Korea: 2009 Article IV Consultation—Staff Report," Country Report 09/262 (Washington: 2009).

3. The reason for Korea's slowing growth is now a point of debate. Is it simply the maturing of the economy, which traditionally leads to slower growth? Or were the "neoliberal" reforms of the 1990s and 2000s responsible because they ended the state-directed policies of past decades? On the first explanation, see International Monetary

Fund, "Republic of Korea: 2012 Article IV Consultation–Staff Report," Country Report 12/275 (Washington: 2012). On the second explanation, see Jang-Sup Shin and Ha Joon Chang, *Restructuring Korea, Inc.* (New York: Routledge, 2003); and Keun Lee and others, "Visible Success and Invisible Failure in Post-Crisis Reform in the Republic of Korea: Interplay of Global Standards, Agents, and Local Specificity," Policy Research Working Paper 3651 (Washington: World Bank, 2005).

4. World Bank, *The East Asian Miracle: Economic Growth and Public Policy* (Oxford University Press, 2003).

5. Stephan Haggard, *Pathways from the Periphery: The Politics of Growth in the Newly Industrialized Countries* (Cornell University Press, 1990); Alice Amsden, *Asia's Next Giant: South Korea and Late Industrialization* (Oxford University Press, 1992); Eun Mee Kim, *Big Business, Strong State: Collusion and Conflict in South Korean Development, 1960–1990* (SUNY Press, 1997); Atul Kohli, *State-Directed Development: Political Power and Industrialization in the Global Periphery* (Cambridge University Press, 2004).

6. See Thomas Kalinowski and Hyekyung Cho, "The Political Economy of Financial Liberalization in South Korea," *Asian Survey,* vol. 49 (2009), pp. 221–42. These authors argue that the sequencing was a deliberate policy to protect the *chaebol* from competition by foreign firms.

7. Yoon Je Cho, "Financial Repression, Liberalization, Crisis, and Restructuring: Lessons of Korea's Financial Sector Policies," Research Paper 47 (Toyoko: Asian Development Bank Institute, 2002); David T. Coe and Se-Jik Kim, *Korean Crisis and Recovery* (Seoul: International Monetary Fund and Korean Institute for International Economic Policy, 2002); Choong Young Ahn and Cha Baekin, "Financial Sector Restructuring in South Korea: Accomplishments and Unfinished Agenda," *Asian Economic Papers,* vol. 3 (2004), pp. 1–21.

8. International Monetary Fund, "Republic of Korea: IMF Standby Arrangement" (Washington: 1997).

9. Author's interview of a former Korean economic official, Seoul, June 24, 2010.

10. Paul Blustein, *The Chastening: Inside the Crisis That Rocked the Global Financial System and Humbled the IMF* (New York: Public Affairs, 2001); Joseph Stiglitz, *Globalization and Its Discontents* (New York: W.W. Norton, 2002); Leonardo Martinez-Diaz, *Globalizing in Hard Times: The Politics of Banking-Sector Opening in the Emerging World* (Cornell University Press, 2009).

11. Wonhyuk Lim and Joon-Ho Hahm, "Financial Globalization and Korea's Post-Crisis Reform: A Political Economy Perspective," Working Paper 2004-01 (Seoul: Korea Development Institute, 2004); Lee and others, "Visible Success and Invisible Failure in Post-Crisis Reform in the Republic of Korea."

12. Kalinowski and Cho, "The Political Economy of Financial Liberalization in South Korea."

13. Heeran Lim, "Democratization and the Transformation Process in East Asian Developmental States: Financial Reform in Korea and Taiwan," *Asian Perspectives,* vol. 33, no. 1 (2009), pp. 75–110.

14. For a complementary view of the post-1997 changes in Korea, which focuses more on the corporate reforms, see Byung-Kook Kim, Eun Mee Kim, and Jean C. Oi, *Adapt, Fragment, and Transform: Corporate Restructuring and System Reform in South Korea* (Brookings, 2012).

15. Korea had a debt-to-GDP ratio similar to that of Latin American debtor countries, but it had a much lower debt service-to-exports ratio because of its strong export sector. Consequently, Korea's debt crisis did not approach the magnitude of that in Latin America. See Barbara Stallings, "The Role of Foreign Capital in Economic Development," in *Manufacturing Miracles: Path of Industrialization in Latin America and East Asia*, edited by Gary Gereffi and Donald L. Wyman (Princeton University Press, 1990).

16. Another measure, which came to prominence after the Asian financial crisis, is the ratio of reserves to short-term external debt. Korea had a ratio of 240 percent in 2005, which fell rapidly in the years leading up to the current crisis as short-term debt increased. In 2008, the ratio was only 105 percent. Since then, it has risen again, and in 2012 reserves were double the amount of short-term debt. See Organization for Economic Cooperation and Development, *OECD Economic Surveys: Korea 2012* (Paris: 2012), "Overview," p. 5, figure 3.

17. Barry Eichengreen, "Monetary and Exchange Rate Policy in Korea: Assessments and Policy Issues," paper prepared for Bank of Korea Symposium, August 25, 2004; Soyoung Kim and Yung Chul Park, "Inflation Targeting in Korea: A Model of Success?," BIS Papers 31 (Basel: Bank for International Settlements, 2006).

18. The Korean reforms are described in many publications. See, for example, Lim and Hahm, "Financial Globalization and Korea's Post-Crisis Reform"; Lee and others, "Visible Success and Invisible Failure in Post-Crisis Reform in the Republic of Korea"; Martinez-Diaz, *Globalizing in Hard Times*; Lim, "Democratization and the Transformation Process in East Asian Developmental States"; Kim and Park, "Inflation Targeting in Korea: A Model of Success?"

19. The FSC is now called the Financial Services Commission.

20. KAMCO bought more than US$63 billion of loans (face value) for a cost of around US$24 billion between the end of 1997 and the end of 2001.

21. Unofficial estimates were much higher. World Bank economists estimated that NPLs, at their peak, represented 30 to 40 percent of total loans. See Gerard Caprio and Daniela Klingebiel, "Episodes of Systemic and Borderline Banking Crises," in *Managing the Real and Fiscal Effects of Banking Crises*, edited by Daniela Klingebiel and Luc Laeven (Washington: World Bank, 2002), pp. 31–49.

22. Data on bank loans and stock market capitalization are from World Bank, World Development Indicators (http://data.worldbank.org/data-catalog/world-development-indicators); bond data are from Bank for International Settlements, "Debt Securities Statistics" (www.bis.org/statistics/secstats.htm).

23. International Monetary Fund, "Republic of Korea: 2011 Article IV Consultation: Staff Report," Country Report 11/246 (Washington: 2011).

24. Unpublished data provided by the Bank of Korea.

25. It should be noted that an SME in Korea is defined as a firm with fewer than 500 employees. This is very different from an SME in Latin America, which could have fewer than five employees.

26. Larissa Leony and Rafael Romeu, "A Model of Bank Lending in the Global Financial Crisis and the Case of Korea," *Journal of Asian Economics*, vol. 22 (2011), pp. 322–34.

27. The ratio for the world was 57 percent; for low- and middle-income countries, 62 percent; for East Asia and Pacific developing countries, 83 percent; and for Latin America and the Caribbean, 46 percent. World Bank, World Development Indicators (http://data.worldbank.org/data-catalog/world-development-indicators).

28. Gary Gereffi, "Paths of Industrialization: An Overview," in *Manufacturing Miracles*, edited by Gereffi and Wyman.

29. Jai S. Mah, "Export Promotion Policies, Export Composition, and Economic Development of Korea," *Law and Development Review*, vol. 4 (2011), pp. 3–27.

30. Ibid., p. 11.

31. Byung-Jun Song, "Korean Economic Trend and Economic Partnership between Korea and China," paper prepared for the conference China and the World Economy and Global Economy, University of Washington, Seattle, March 16–18, 2012; Joon-Kyung Kim and Chung H. Lee, "Between Two Whales: Korea's Choice in the Post-Crisis Era," in *Economic Meltdown and Geopolitical Stability*, edited by Ashley J. Tellis, Andrew Marble, and Travis Tanner (Seattle, Wash.: National Bureau of Asian Research, 2009).

32. In the Asian region, Korea plays a key role in the new division of labor, whereby together with Japan it exports capital goods and industrial inputs to China and other low-wage economies where final goods are assembled. Some of those final goods are then sent to Korea and Japan themselves, but most are sold in the United States and Europe.

33. In an interview with a director of the Financial Service Commission (Seoul, June 24, 2010), I was told that this final point was a matter of luck in the timing of the crisis. The FSC was in the process of making its rules more flexible so that Korean banks would be able to participate more extensively in the derivative markets.

34. Deok Ryong Yoon, "The Korean Economic Adjustment to the World Financial Crisis," *Asian Economic Papers*, vol. 10 (2010), pp. 106–27.

35. The figure of 6 percent comes from the Organization for Economic Cooperation and Development, *OECD Economic Surveys: Korea 2010* (Paris: 2010). Two papers by government officials place the total amount at 6.9 percent of GDP. See Deok Ryong Yoon, "The Korean Economic Adjustment to the World Financial Crisis"; and Jun-Kyu Lee, "Korea's Economic Stability and Resilience in Time of Crisis," *Korea's Economy 2010*, vol. 26 (Washington: Korea Economic Institute and Korea Institute for International Economic Policy, 2010). Earlier estimates were lower; the IMF reported that it would be 3.6 percent in 2009 with an additional 1.2 percent in 2010. See International Monetary Fund, "Republic of Korea: 2009 Article IV Consultation—Staff Report," p. 13.

36. International Monetary Fund, "Republic of Korea: 2009 Article IV Consultation—Staff Report"; International Monetary Fund, "Republic of Korea: 2010 Article IV Consultation—Staff Report," Country Report 10/270 (Washington: 2010); International Monetary Fund, "Republic of Korea: 2011 Article IV Consultation—Staff Report"; Organization for Economic Cooperation and Development, *OECD Economic Surveys: Korea 2010.*

37. International Monetary Fund, "Republic of Korea: 2012 Article IV Consultation—Staff Report."

38. Robert Fouser, "An Oddly Dull Election Season," *Korea Times*, October 22, 2012.

39. Organization for Economic Cooperation and Development, *OECD Economic Surveys: Korea 2010.*

40. Joon Seok Hong, "The Economic Costs of Korean Unification" (Stanford University, Stanford Program on International and Cross-Cultural Education, 2011).

41. Carmen Reinhart and Kenneth Rogoff, *This Time Is Different: Eight Centuries of Financial Folly* (Princeton University Press, 2009).

JOHN ECHEVERRI-GENT

4

India's Response to the Global Financial Crisis: From Quick Rebound to Protracted Slowdown?

At first glance, India's response to the global financial crisis (GFC) appears to be one of the most successful of the responses analyzed in this volume. According to data reported by the International Monetary Fund, India's growth rate, at an annual average of 8.6 percent from 2005 to 2007, was second only to that of China among the large emerging economies (EEs). (See table 1-2, chapter 1.) During the crisis, India's growth rate dropped to 2.9 percent, higher than the rate in all countries but China. India's average growth rate during recovery, 5.2 percent, was the fourth-highest rate among all countries. When that average is broken down by fiscal year, as reported by the government of India, India's performance is even more favorable (see table 4-1). Its growth rate rebounded to 8.6 percent in 2009–10 and to 8.9 percent in 2010–11 before dropping to 6.7 percent in 2011–12, 4.5 percent in 2012–13, and 4.7 percent in 2013–14. The last two years were the first time in more than 25 years that India had less than 5 percent growth in consecutive years. The decline raises questions about the sustainability of India's accelerated growth. Will India return to its high growth of the years preceding the GFC, or will it join the ranks of countries that failed to sustain a rapid growth spurt?

At the level of analysis suggested by Wise, Armijo, and Katada in the introductory chapter, India's quick rebound can be explained by a distinctive mix

The author would like to thank Bill Grimes, Herman Schwartz, Carol Wise, Maria Antonieta Lins, and the participants in the workshop "Pacific Rim Emerging Economies in the Post-Global Financial Crisis," University of Southern California, July 27–28, 2012.

Table 4-1. *India's Key Macroeconomic Indicators, 2002–03 to 2013–14*
Percent

Year	Annual GDP growth at factor cost	Central government gross fiscal deficit to GDP	CPI inflation	Current account balance to GDP
2002–03	3.9	5.9	1.4	1.3
2003–04	8.0	4.3	3.9	2.3
2004–05	7.1	3.9	3.8	−0.3
2005–06	9.5	4.0	4.4	−1.2
2006–07	9.6	3.3	6.7	−1.0
2007–08	9.3	2.5	6.2	−1.3
2008–09	6.7	6.0	9.1	−2.3
2009–10	8.6	6.5	12.4	−2.8
2010–11	8.9	4.8	10.4	−2.8
2011–12	6.7	5.7	8.4	−4.2
2012–13	4.5	4.8	10.4	−4.7
2013–14	4.7	4.6	9.7	−1.7

Sources: Government of India, Ministry of Finance, *Economic Survey of India: 2013–2014* (http://indiabudget.nic.in/survey.asp); and Reserve Bank of India, *Handbook of Statistics on Indian Economy, 2013–14* (http://www.rbi.org.in/scripts/AnnualPublications.aspx?head=Handbook %20of%20Statistics%20on%20Indian%20Economy).

of neoliberal and developmentalist policy reforms. Prior macroeconomic reforms enabled the government to provide a substantial fiscal and monetary stimulus in response to the crisis, and both neoliberal and developmentalist trade reforms contributed to India's resilience. External contagion was limited, as there had been little liberalization of the banking sector and capital account controls remained relatively strong. Some contend that a program to sterilize foreign exchange inflows and regulatory interventions to preempt potential volatility in financial markets also contributed to India's rapid rebound, while others criticize the same programs. Central to the controversy is whether economic reformers should concentrate on liberalization for economic efficiency or whether financial institutions, like central banks, should give priority to ensuring financial stability.

Focusing only on the policy mix that contributed to the quick rebound in developing countries neglects the political process, which is central to the formulation of effective policies and which can quickly undermine an effective policy regime. Many experts on India's political economy depict a policy-making process driven by technocratic policymakers at the apex of the state who are insulated from politics at the grass roots.[1] This depiction reflects the reality of the emergence of an institutional sphere located in the Ministry of Finance and the Reserve Bank of India that is insulated from popular politics, if not always from the influence of big business. Within this sphere policymakers formulate economic reforms in a way that minimizes the need for parliamentary approval.

While capturing a noteworthy change in India's political economy, I argue that the distinction between technocratic policymaking and mass politics obscures other important political dynamics that also shape economic policymaking. India's technocrats do not usually speak with one voice, and their efforts to advance their personal views create a political dynamic that shapes the reform process. Overseeing the technocratic sphere are ministers whose political concerns lead them to play a crucial role in the process, either by supporting new reforms or sidetracking them. Finally, the distinction between technocratic and mass politics obscures the manner in which mass politics shapes technocratic politics and vice versa. The impact is clearest in India's fiscal politics, where subsidies to powerful political constituencies and populist election ploys contribute to fiscal and current account deficits that must somehow be managed by the technocrats—but also where responsible fiscal policy reforms may give technocrats the space necessary to implement new policies that respond to the challenges presented by the country's dynamic economic process.

It is difficult to explain India's rebound and subsequent slump by focusing exclusively on policies and institutions, many of which were in place during both periods. While developments in the global economy explain part of the change, exploring the political dimension is crucial to understanding the divergence. I begin by examining the mix of policies that facilitated India's quick recovery from the crisis and then explore aspects of the political process that contributed to its subsequent slump. Ultimately, I argue that analysis of the political process is central to predicting whether India will resume or fail to maintain its impressive post-GFC performance.

Explaining India's Quick Rebound

The policy mix that India followed before and after the global financial crisis goes a long way toward explaining India's quick rebound. Macroeconomic reforms prior to the global financial crisis played a critical role in enabling fiscal and monetary responses that stimulated India's economy when the crisis struck. However, financial sector reforms have been uneven. Banking sector reform, for example, was quite limited. Indeed, some contend that it was the lack of banking reform—that is, the continuing predominance of public sector banks and the limited presence of foreign banks—that insulated India from the crisis. To some degree, trade reforms alleviated the impact of the crisis by reorienting more Indian exports toward Asia. It can be argued that prudent regulatory intervention in the financial sector also minimized the disruption caused by the crisis. Finally, countervailing international conditions proved to be a mixed blessing.

The Role of Prior Macroeconomic Reforms

Prior reform of India's fiscal, monetary, and foreign exchange regimes played an important role in facilitating India's quick rebound. At the same time, failure to develop corporate debt markets added stress to India's financial system by encouraging Indian firms to raise funds abroad. When the global financial crisis froze the credit markets of advanced industrial countries, Indian corporations hightailed it back to India to access credit in order to pay off their foreign obligations. Their hasty retreat imposed stress on elements of the Indian financial system.

India made substantial progress in managing its fiscal deficits in the years prior to the global financial crisis. In August 2003, it passed the Fiscal Responsibility and Budget Management (FRBM) Act. In addition to prohibiting India's central bank, the Reserve Bank of India (RBI), from participating in the primary market for government securities as of April 2006, the FRBM stipulated that the central government's fiscal deficit was to be reduced by 0.5 percent of GDP for each subsequent year until it was brought below 3 percent of GDP in 2007–08. Rapid economic growth, coupled with the introduction of new technology in the form of the electronic tax information network, helped to increase revenue from personal and corporate income taxes from 3.8 percent of GDP in 2003–04 to 6.5 percent in 2007–08.[2] The FRBM's goals were achieved: from 2002–03 to 2007–08, the Indian central government's gross fiscal deficit as a share of GDP shrank from 5.9 percent to 2.5 percent (see table 4-1). The FRBM also encouraged state governments to reduce their fiscal deficits, and the consolidated fiscal deficit of the federal and state governments fell sharply, from about 9.9 percent in 2001–02 to 4.1 percent in 2007–08.[3]

India's success in reducing the fiscal deficit provided needed space for the fiscal stimulus, which facilitated its rapid recovery from the global financial crisis. Some of the stimulus fortuitously came from populist measures taken during the run-up to the 2009 elections. In the wake of the Lehman Brothers collapse, the government issued three supplementary demands for grants that added 3 percent of GDP to overall expenditures.[4] As a consequence, the fiscal deficit increased from 2.7 percent of GDP in 2007–08 to 6 percent for fiscal year 2008–09. The 2009–10 central government budget continued the fiscal stimulus by increasing expenditures on infrastructure, education, health, and rural employment. The government was able to bring the fiscal deficit down to 4.8 percent in 2010–11, but India's fiscal position remained precarious, and as economic growth slowed, the deficit increased to 5.7 percent of GDP in 2011–12 before it was reduced to 4.5 percent in 2013–14.

At the beginning of the 1990s, India lacked the policy instruments needed to implement modern monetary policy. Interest rates were administered by the Reserve Bank of India, and the money supply, according to Arvind Panagariya, "became entirely subservient to the fiscal needs of the government." During the 1980s, the RBI's "extension of credit to the government accounted for as much as 85 percent of the variation in reserve money." At the time of India's 1991 economic crisis, financial repression was such that the RBI obliged Indian banks to provide it with 15 percent of their commercial deposits, interest free, through the mandatory cash reserve ratio (CRR). It also required banks to hold 38.5 percent of their net demand and time deposits in approved public sector securities as required by the statutory liquidity ratio (SLR). Consequently, 53.5 percent of all bank deposits were held either by the central bank at no interest or in securities with below-market rate yields.[5]

The government began to reform India's monetary policy in the 1990s by introducing auctions of government securities and deregulating interest rates on public and private debt. Beginning in 1994, the government gradually curtailed automatic monetization of the fiscal deficit until 1997, when it finally severed the link between fiscal and monetary policy by ending automatic monetization. Throughout the 1990s, the RBI reduced the CRR and SLR, with the former bottoming out at 5 percent in 2004 and the latter reaching its pre-crisis low of 25 percent in 1997. As the RBI reduced the importance of targeting reserve money as a monetary policy instrument, it created a system of liquidity management through open market operations. In 2000, the RBI inaugurated the liquidity adjustment facility (LAF), using auctions to set repo and reverse repo rates to establish a corridor for overnight money market rates. [6] Under the LAF, the repo rate has become the RBI's key policy rate, used to modulate short-term liquidity and signal its monetary policy stance.

The failure of the government to develop India's market for corporate debt highlights the importance of liberal financial sector reforms. Restrictions on foreign purchase of Indian corporate debt contributed to that failure. The high cost of raising debt in India drove a growing number of companies to raise debt abroad, especially from 2004 to 2008, when the interest rate spread was substantial. The share of India's listed firms that had raised 10 percent or more of their debt capital abroad increased from 5 percent at the end of 2001–02 to 14 percent in 2008–09.[7] Outstanding international corporate debt securities rose from US$4 billion at the end of 2000 to US$40 billion at the end of September 2008.[8] In essence, a large share of India's corporate debt market moved offshore.[9]

The growing exposure of Indian firms to foreign debt created a channel through which the GFC affected India. At the onset of the crisis, India remained considerably less integrated into global financial markets than most other emerging markets. De jure measures of capital account openness show that India had a very high level of controls. Nonetheless, private capital flows to India have increased considerably since the 1990s. Average annual capital flows as a share of GDP rose from just 0.1 percent of GDP in 1992 to 2.3 percent by late 2007, just before the eruption of the GFC.[10] Despite the increase, India's cumulative engagement with global financial markets, as measured by the sum of its gross stock of external assets and liabilities as a ratio of GDP, remained lower than that of comparable emerging markets. In 2007, India's ratio was just 85 percent while the comparable averages for the seven Asian and seven Latin American emerging economies reported in table 1-2 of chapter 1 were 131 percent and 115 percent, respectively.[11]

The global financial crisis had a substantial impact despite India's relative insulation from international capital markets. In January 2008, foreign investors began to withdraw their funds from India, which had received unprecedented net inflows of portfolio investment beginning in 2003. After having attracted average annual net inflows of INR441 billion over the previous five years, India experienced a net outflow of INR433 billion in 2008–09. Equity prices swooned: by March 2009, the BSE Sensex had dropped 61 percent from its peak on January 8, 2008. Since portfolio equity inflows contributed to the financing of India's current account deficit (CAD) in the years prior to the crisis, the outflows led to a 30 percent decline in the dollar value of India's currency from January 2008 to March 2009.[12]

The impact on Indian credit markets was even more traumatic. Because of India's capital controls and the relatively high costs of borrowing, many Indian firms shifted their treasury operations abroad to access less expensive foreign money markets. When international money markets collapsed after the Lehman Brothers bankruptcy, Indian firms and banks were unable to roll over their trade credits and external commercial borrowings. In desperate need of dollar liquidity, they began to borrow from the Indian money market and convert their rupees into dollars. The rush back to India increased borrowing and raised interest rates. On Friday, September 12, 2008, the call money rate in India was 6.15 percent and borrowing amounted to a total of INR 144 billion. The collapse of Lehman Brothers was announced over the weekend. By Wednesday, September 17, 2008, the call money rate increased to 13.07 percent and borrowing rose to INR594 billion. Normally the money market interest rate stays within the range set by the RBI. Throughout the rest of September and until late October 2008, money market interest rates consistently remained above the corridor's 9 percent ceiling, often reaching values above 15 percent. The actions of Indian firms and banks led to an unprecedented increase in net capital outflows. As table 4-2 documents, capital outflows through banks ("banking capital") and through other corporations ("foreign direct investment from India") totaled $10.8 billion in the fourth quarter of 2008 while the net outflow in the previous quarter was only $1.1 billion. Consequently, India's total net capital flows plummeted from an inflow of $7.9 billion in the third quarter of 2008 to an outflow of $3.7 billion in the fourth quarter.[13]

In short, the freezing of credit markets abroad created a liquidity crisis in India. In their search for funds, Indian corporations redeemed their investments in money market schemes run by mutual funds. The redemption pressures created by Indian corporations and other private investors along with the liquidity crunch abroad made it difficult for India's nonbanking finance companies (NBFCs) to raise capital, and the rapid growth of NBFC investments and loans in previous years dropped sharply.[14] Declining liquidity and risk appetite deflated equity and real estate prices and put pressure on India's financial institutions. In the midst of the GFC, not only did the market for global depository receipts and American depository receipts freeze but domestic risk capital also became scarce. Medium-size and small firms suffered the greatest loss of access to credit. The scarcity of finance contributed to the decline in the index of industrial production from an average growth rate of 8.5 percent in 2007 to 0.5 percent in the last quarter of 2008.[15]

In the aftermath of the Lehman Brothers crash, the RBI switched to an expansionary monetary regime from October 2008 to April 2009. Overall,

Table 4-2. *The Structure of India's Capital Flows by Quarter, September 2007 to December 2008*

U.S. dollars, millions

Type of capital flow	September 2007	December 2007	March 2008	June 2008	September 2008	December 2008
Loans	9,305	10,942	12,527	4,228	3,561	1,733
Banking capital	6,643	207	5,826	2,696	2,131	−4,956
Total foreign investment	13,027	16,892	4,760	4,778	4,254	−5,000
FDI to India	4,709	7,873	14,197	11,891	8,782	6,684
FDI from India	−2,581	−5,832	−5,701	−2,902	−3,218	−5,864
Net portfolio investment	10,917	14,751	−3,764	−4,178	−1,301	−5,787
Others	4,180	2,976	2,916	−579	−2,904	4,540
Total net capital inflows	33,155	31,017	26,029	11,123	7,852	−3,683

Source: Ila Patnaik and Ajay Shah, "Why India Choked When Lehman Broke," National Institute of Public Finance and Policy Working Paper 2010-63 (New Delhi: January 2010), p. 17 (www.eaber. org/sites/default/files/documents/NIPFP_Patnaik_2010_02.pdf).

the effective policy rate dropped from 9 percent in September 2008 to 3.25 percent in April 2009. In addition, the CRR was cut from 9 percent in September 2008 to 5 percent in April 2009 and the SLR was reduced from 25 percent to 24 percent on November 8, 2008. Those measures together were estimated to inject liquidity equal to 3.6 percent of GDP from September 2008 to September 2009.[16]

Reform of India's foreign exchange policy also contributed to its successful response to the global financial crisis. From the mid-1970s until 1993 India pegged the value of the rupee to an undisclosed basket of foreign currencies. In 1992, the government created a dual exchange rate under which exporters were allowed to sell 60 percent of their foreign exchange earnings in the free market after selling 40 percent to the government at below-market prices. On March 19, 1993, the government established a single, market-based exchange rate, although the RBI continued to intervene in foreign exchange markets to maintain a relatively stable exchange rate. In 1994, the government made the current account convertible. In the following years, the RBI gradually reduced its intervention in the foreign exchange market. After India replaced the 1974 Foreign Exchange Regulation Act with the more liberal 1997 Foreign Exchange Management Act, the average daily foreign exchange turnover grew from US$5 billion in 1997–98 to US$48 billion in 2007–08.[17] The RBI moved slowly toward a policy of allowing the market to determine the rupee's value. Currency futures were introduced in 2008, and currency options were allowed in 2010.

The foreign exchange market functioned relatively well during the crisis. The large withdrawals of investments by foreign institutional investors in January 2008 put pressure on the rupee. After Lehman's bankruptcy, the value of the rupee depreciated sharply. The RBI announced that it would sell foreign exchange, but the rupee continued its sharp decline through October. On November 7, the RBI introduced a rupee-dollar swap facility. The RBI also attempted to ease foreign exchange liquidity through three other measures: it increased the interest rate ceiling on foreign currency deposits to encourage foreign exchange inflows from nonresident Indians; it liberalized restrictions on external commercial borrowing; and it allowed nonbank financial companies and housing finance companies to access foreign credit. Those measures reduced rupee volatility, and with the return of portfolio investment, the rupee gradually appreciated during fiscal year 2009–10.

Limited Banking Sector Reforms

India's balance-of-payments crisis of 1991 and financial sector crisis of 1992 sparked important reforms in the banking sector in the following years. Despite the reforms, liberalization of India's financial sector lagged far behind that of most other EEs. The continued dominance of India's public sector banks, the limited presence of foreign banks, and the conservative regulatory approach of the RBI toward financial innovation all make it difficult to argue that liberalizing reforms were crucial to the resilience of India's banking sector. On the contrary, many argue that it was India's cautious approach to liberalization that was essential to the banking sector's stability.[18]

In the wake of India's financial crises of 1991 and 1992, policymakers initiated reforms to allow more private sector competition in the banking sector, where public banks owned 90 percent of all assets. On January 1, 1993, the RBI announced guidelines for the entry of new banks into the private sector. In addition, restrictions on foreign banks were liberalized. The government encouraged public sector development banks to raise capital and become privately owned, universal banks. Although this limited opening to the private sector resulted in the establishment of new private sector banks, public sector banks still controlled 73.9 percent of aggregate deposits and 72.5 percent of gross credit at the end of June 2014.[19] In 2009, a study of banking sectors in

21 major emerging markets showed that India had the lowest private sector share of all countries but China.[20] India's foreign banks owned only 5 percent of all banking assets, giving India a rank of 79 among a sample of 91 developing countries.[21]

In many countries, the need for banking recapitalization is filled through privatization. After India's financial crisis of the early 1990s, banks were recapitalized in ways that minimized private ownership.[22] By 2002, the government of India had provided INR224 billion for the recapitalization of public sector banks.[23] Public sector banks sold shares in the market, but private ownership of capital was limited to 49 percent. Varma contends that the government established "an anticompetitive regulatory regime" to help Indian banks recapitalize through their retained earnings.[24]

Beginning in the 1990s, the RBI undertook prudential regulation that improved the balance sheets of Indian banks. In April 1992 the RBI ordered India's banks to achieve a minimum 4 percent capital to risk-weighted assets ratio (CRAR) by March 1993 and a CRAR of 8 percent by March 1996. In 2007–08, all scheduled commercial banks had met a 9 percent CRAR norm. Those measures helped the banks to achieve a relatively strong position. In 2010, the RBI noted that the CRAR "stood higher than many of the advanced and emerging market economies indicating that Indian banks were in comparatively better positions in terms of their capitalization across countries."[25] Moreover, the share of nonperforming loans held by Indian banks was lower than the share in most EEs.[26]

In the years prior to the global financial crisis, the RBI came under pressure to follow the example of advanced countries like the United States by allowing the growth of the market for mortgage-backed securities. However, when large inflows of foreign capital created a real estate bubble from 2005 to 2008, the RBI took prudential measures to limit the potential damage. Beginning in July 2005, it gradually increased risk weights on commercial real estate loans, reaching a peak of 150 percent in May 2006. The RBI also raised provisioning requirements and minimized the risk posed by the development of mortgage-backed securities by requiring originating banks to maintain capital against the value of mortgages in the same amount that would have been required if the mortgages had not been securitized. When financial stress peaked, the RBI reduced the extra risk weights and provisioning that it had imposed over the previous three years as a countercyclical measure. The RBI's financial stress index steadily declined from November 2008 to December 2009, reflecting the banking sector's return to normalcy.[27]

The Trade Channel: Export Diversification Increases Resilience

The global financial crisis also affected the Indian economy through the trade channel. India has become a more open economy since 1990, when total trade was only 16 percent of GDP, and by 2012 the trade-to-GDP ratio had grown to 55 percent.[28] As the share of trade in India's GDP rose, the contribution of Indian exports to growth increased. From the 1950s through the 1980s, Indian exports accounted for an annual average of 0.2 percent of India's 4.1 percent growth rate. In the first decade of the new millennium, exports contributed 2.4 percent of India's 7.2 percent annual growth.[29]

The decline in trade credits and consumption abroad that accompanied the global financial crisis produced a drop in Indian exports of 14.3 percent from October 2008 through March 2009, for an overall growth rate of 13.7 percent in 2008–09. The overall export growth rate for 2009–10 was –3.5 percent. In 2010–11 and 2011–12, India's export growth rate rebounded to 40.5 percent and 21.8 percent, respectively, before dropping to –1.8 percent in 2012–13 and to an estimated 4.1 percent in 2013–14.[30]

The impact of the crisis on India's exports was moderated by three factors. First, India's exports of chemical goods and engineering products, particularly transport equipment, remained buoyant in 2008–09, accounting for the total overall expansion of Indian exports during that year.[31] Second, India's service sector exports continued to grow, powered by software services, which rose by 46 percent in 2008–09.[32] Third, the impact of the GFC on Indian exports was offset by an increase in its exports to other developing countries. In the period from 1987 to 1990, the advanced industrial countries absorbed 57.5 percent of Indian exports, but by 2007–08 their share had fallen to 39.5 percent. During the same period, trade with Eastern European countries dropped from 17.5 percent to just 1.1 percent. Under India's "Look East" trade policy, Asia's share of India's exports grew from 13 percent to 28 percent. Trade with other developing countries also increased: the share of the Organization of the Petroleum Exporting Countries in Indian exports grew from 6.2 percent to 21.1 percent; Africa's share rose from 2 percent to 6.3 percent; and Latin America's share increased from 0.5 percent to 3.1 percent.[33]

The RBI's Strategic Intervention in the Foreign Exchange Market

Maintaining monetary stability is a central objective of the RBI, and until very recently India's central bank has sought to maintain the stability of the exchange rate. In the decade prior to the global financial crisis, the RBI implemented policies to facilitate the accumulation of foreign reserves while limiting the appreciation of the rupee and its inflationary impact on the domestic economy. Furthermore, when the global financial crisis led to severe shortages of liquidity in Indian markets, the RBI strategically used the funds available from its sterilization program to inject liquidity into Indian financial markets.

Beginning in the late 1990s, when increasing remittances and foreign investment inflows placed upward pressure on the rupee, the RBI began to purchase foreign exchange to limit the rupee's rise. It then sterilized its rapidly growing foreign exchange reserves to limit inflation.[34] From 2000–01 to 2007–08, India's foreign reserves grew sevenfold, from US$42 billion to US$310 billion.[35] With the rapid increase in foreign reserves, the RBI ran out of securities to use for sterilization. In April 2004, the government announced the Market Stabilization Scheme (MSS), under which the RBI issued special new securities to continue sterilizing capital inflows. The program continued through 2009. The annual average value of MSS bonds issued by the government peaked at 3.42 percent of GDP in 2007–08, when capital inflows to India amounted to US$108 billion dollars, or 9.2 percent of GDP.[36]

In the aftermath of the Lehman crash, the RBI used the MSS to inject liquidity into the economy. It stopped the issue of MSS securities after September 2008, and in November 2008 it began to buy back MSS securities. Although critics of the MSS claimed that it was costly and that the accumulation of foreign exchange should be used to finance infrastructure investment, the RBI claimed that the MSS not only limited rupee appreciation but also provided a source of needed liquidity that did not expand the central bank's balance sheet and that could be calibrated to avoid creating stress in the market.

International Integration Accelerates Growth but Increases Volatility

Integration with the global economy has played an important role in accelerating India's economic growth; however, it has also increased the volatility of the Indian economy. The rapid expansion of global trade was an important factor in India's accelerated growth from 2003 to 2008 and in its quick rebound in 2010 and 2011. From 2003 to 2008, world trade grew at an annual rate of 7.4 percent. After dropping by 10.6 percent in 2009, it resumed growth at a 12.8 percent rate in 2010. Just as the resumption of rapid growth of world trade contributed to India's quick rebound, the decline in world trade—to 6.2 percent growth in 2011 and to 3 percent in 2013—was an important factor in India's slowdown.[37]

Low interest rates in advanced industrial countries following the global financial crisis also benefited India and many other emerging markets by pushing investors to the higher yields available in the EEs. India had suffered the flight from risk that occurred with the global financial crisis. In fiscal year 2008–09, net portfolio investment dropped from an inflow of $27.4 billion in 2007–08 to an outflow of $14 billion. However, once the shock subsided, inflows surged to record levels, totaling $32.4 billion in 2009–10 and $30.3 billion in 2010–11 before declining to $17.2 billion in 2011–12. Foreign direct investment helped to smooth the volatile portfolio investment flows. As a result, after dropping from $43.3 billion in 2007–08 to just $8.3 billion in 2008–09, India's total net foreign investment rebounded to an average of $44.6 billion annually from 2009–10 to 2012–13.[38]

While net foreign investment inflows made a crucial contribution to India's economy,[39] they did not cover the large increases in the merchandise trade deficit (see table 4-3). India's trade deficit quadrupled, from $46 billion in 2005–06 to $190 billion in 2012–13, increasing from 6 percent of GDP to more than 11 percent.[40] One reason for India's burgeoning trade deficit was the slowing growth of exports. In the five years before the global financial crisis (2003–04 to 2007–08), India's exports grew by an annual average of 25.4 percent, but from 2008–09 to 2013–14, exports increased by only 13 percent annually. Much of the decline is explained by the reduction in global demand, especially during the years of the GFC and the euro crisis (2012–13), when Indian exports declined even further. However, there are also deeper problems underpinning India's merchandise trade deficit. Over the 11 years from 2003–04 to 2013–14, the 21.1 percent average annual growth of Indian imports exceeded the 18.7 percent average annual increase in Indian exports (computed from table 4-3). One cause of the imbalance is that India has entered into a number of free trade agreements (FTAs) and comprehensive economic partnership agreements (CEPAs) with countries that are more economically competitive. From 2005 to 2012, India's imports from its FTA/CEPA partners grew at an annual average rate of 26.6 percent, while its exports to these partners grew at a rate of only 12.5 percent.[41] Another reason for the deficits is India's growing dependence on fuel imports during an era of high commodity prices. Fuel as a share of total imports increased from 33.5 percent in 2001–02 to 40.4 percent in 2013–04.[42] A third contributing factor was the surge in gold imports. From 2007–08 to 2011–12, gold imports increased from 6.6 percent of all imports to 11.5 percent.[43]

Table 4-3. *Indian Merchandise Trade, 2003–04 to 2013–14*

Year	Exports[a]	Imports[a]	Trade balance[a]	Exports[b]	Imports[b]
2003–04	63.8	78.1	−14.3	21.1	27.3
2004–05	83.5	111.6	−28.0	30.8	42.7
2005–06	103.1	149.2	−46.1	23.4	33.8
2006–07	126.4	185.7	−59.3	22.6	24.5
2007–08	163.1	251.7	−88.5	29.0	35.5
2008–09	185.3	303.7	−118.4	13.6	20.7
2009–10	178.8	288.4	−109.6	−3.5	−5.0
2010–11	251.1	369.8	−118.6	40.5	28.2
2011–12	306.0	489.3	−183.4	21.8	32.3
2012–13	300.4	490.7	−190.3	−1.8	0.3
2013–14	312.6	450.1	−137.5	4.1	−8.3

Source: Government of India, Ministry of Finance, *Economic Survey of India: 2013–14*, Statistical Appendix, table 71b, p. 70 (http://indiabudget.nic.in/es2013-14/estat1.pdf).
a. U.S. dollars, billions.
b. Percent growth.

After years of inadequate policies to reverse these troubling trends, Indian policymakers launched a series of new initiatives to reduce the capital account deficit beginning in the fall of 2012. The government introduced measures to curb imports by imposing quantitative restrictions on nonessential imports like gold and by increasing duties on gold and silver imports. At the same time, it attempted to augment capital inflows by liberalizing restrictions on foreign direct investment, external commercial borrowing, and foreign investment in the Indian debt market. The government also freed interest rates on nonresident external accounts and created a special swap for banks' foreign currency deposits and overseas borrowings. These measures helped to reduce India's CAD to 1.7 percent of GDP in 2013–14.

The success of these policies, however, leaves no room for complacency. Restrictions have succeeded in reducing gold imports, but unless the government curbs the underlying factors that compel Indians to prefer gold to financial investments, they could simply drive gold purchases to the black market.[44] Without improvement in the competitiveness of Indian exports, further economic opening may lead to growing trade deficits. Because of conservative management of its external financial accounts, India remains in a relatively comfortable position with regard to its overall debt.[45] But opening Indian financial markets to more volatile capital flows is likely to pose hazards over the long term. Minimizing the risks will require better political leadership and concrete policies that truly promote the country's long-term economic health.

India's Political Process: A Crucible for Policy Reforms and Emerging Challenges

India's political process fundamentally shaped its response to the global financial crisis. A range of top scholars analytically distinguish two realms in India's political economy. Varshney divides it into "elite" and "mass" realms distinguished by three factors:
　　—the number of people affected by a policy
　　—the extent to which those affected are organized
　　—whether the policy impact is direct and felt immediately or indirect and felt over a long horizon.[46]

The elite domain occurs in the "upper realms of the public sphere: in the interactions between business and government and in the dealings between New Delhi and foreign governments and international financial institutions."[47] Varshney, Kohli, and Kapur emphasize the insulated, technocratic nature of this realm, with Kohli underscoring the preponderance of business influence.[48] Varshney contends that mass politics constrains liberalizing reforms because such reforms are socially disruptive—especially in a relatively poor country without an extensive social welfare system—and therefore spur the electorate to vote against their sponsors, while Kohli sees mass politics as increasingly decentralized to the subnational level, where political parties pursue a range of strategies to gain popular support despite their narrow pro-business coalition at the national level.[49]

These analytical frames offer insight into the strengths and weaknesses of India's response to the global financial crisis. Technocrats in the elite realm decided policies by introducing new monetary policy instruments, promoting the reorientation of trade toward Asia, and freeing exchange rates, interest rates, and capital controls. Since the private sector has played an increasingly important role in the economy, business has gained privileged access to India's policymakers. At the same time, mass politics has imposed formidable constraints on economic liberalization. Nonetheless, dichotomizing India's political economy obscures important political dynamics that underpin policy change. Technocratic policymakers often advocate disparate solutions to policy challenges, and contestation between elite policymakers creates a dynamic that shapes the reform process. Government ministers supervise policymaking, and their actions are shaped by broader political considerations. Finally, fiscal politics is a domain in which mass politics shapes technocratic politics and technocratic decisions affect mass politics.

Contestation among Technocrats: Relentless Liberalizers versus Calibrating Conservatives

The limited impact of the global financial crisis underscored a long-standing controversy among India's financial sector technocrats. The Ministry of Finance—especially the Department of Economic Affairs and the Planning Commission (at least since Montek Ahluwalia became deputy chair of the commission in 2004)—has consistently pressed for liberalizing reforms in India's finance sector. The "relentless liberalizers" played an important role in developing a plan for turning Mumbai into an international financial center, and they pointed out that further financial liberalization, especially opening to international financial markets, was essential to achieving that objective.[50] When the Planning Commission convened a committee on financial sector reform, it chose economist Raghuram Rajan from the University of Chicago Business School to head it, and it joined other liberalizers in enthusiastically endorsing the Rajan committee's recommendations for financial liberalization.[51]

"Calibrating conservatives" did not oppose financial liberalization but instead advocated a cautious, incremental approach that gave priority to financial stability over liberalization.[52] They were less disposed to float the rupee and more inclined to call for RBI intervention to ensure exchange rate stability. They defended India's public sector banks and were wary of foreign investment in India's financial sector. The best known calibrating conservative was Y. V. Reddy, whose tenure as governor of the RBI from 2003 to 2008 was lauded in 2009 by Nobel laureate Joseph Stiglitz, who declared that "if America had a central bank chief like Y. V. Reddy, the U.S. economy would not have been such a mess."[53] In 2009, Reddy's book *India and the Global Financial Crisis*—a collection of his speeches—became a best-seller.[54]

Reddy's view is that central bank policy should be sensitive to its impact on the common Indian and the disruptive effects that volatility in the financial sector can have on daily life.[55] This attitude is widely shared by the top leadership of the RBI. Reddy's successor as RBI governor, Duvvuri Subbarao, expressed similar sentiments. After business leaders denounced his tight money policy at the beginning of 2013, Subbarao declared,

The RBI has been criticized for hurting growth, and we are all sensitive to that. But one should understand that the person blaming [us] for growth is very articulate and has got proper platforms for speaking up. . . . However, the person pinched by inflation does not have a platform, and I think both the RBI and the government should take care of that part of the population.[56]

The RBI also came into conflict with liberalizers by taking a cautious approach to foreign investment in the banking sector. When the government approved plans for the ICICI Bank, India's largest private sector bank, to establish an intermediate holding company in which foreign investors could own a substantial stake, the RBI insisted on establishing a study group to consider the move. After long deliberations, the study group concluded that it would have difficulties supervising the innovative structure and that therefore the arrangement was not desirable. In the process, it frustrated the ICICI and potential foreign investors and their supporters in the government.[57]

In the wake of the global financial crisis, calibrating conservatives touted the performance of India's public sector banks. Despite liberalizers' extolling of the virtues of privatizing the banking sector, 74 percent of all commercial banking assets still remained in the public sector as of 2010.[58] The financial crisis in the United States can be seen as highlighting the perils posed by private ownership of financial institutions, since a key factor in the crisis was the mispricing of risk by private financial institutions. In contrast, studies show that India's 27 public sector banks, despite their diversity, performed well in providing returns to shareholders.[59]

Liberalizers have learned somewhat different lessons from India's experience in the global financial crisis. They argue that the RBI's efforts to maintain capital controls were increasingly circumvented after 2000.[60] First was the disruption of Indian money markets by Indian multinational firms returning to India to raise funds to pay off their short-term foreign debt and the ineffectiveness of capital controls. Second, liberalizers also view sterilization efforts through the MSS as being costly and ineffective in preventing inflation. Third, liberalizers point to the inability of capital controls to halt the growing pattern of de facto international capital integration, which has created irresistible pressures that tend to override the RBI's commitment to stable exchange rates. As a result, India's exchange rate showed increasing flexibility beginning in 2004.[61]

Whether the views of the relentless liberals or calibrating conservatives are right does not matter for the purposes of my analysis. What matters is that their efforts to implement policies based on their disparate perspectives have created a dynamic that continues to shape India's economic policies. Whether or not that dynamic enabled India to avoid the most severe repercussions of the global financial crisis, it made the process of financial liberalization more gradual and cautious than if liberalizing technocrats had held undisputed reign.

Politicians and Technocrats: Pranab Mukherjee's Term as Finance Minister

India's technocrats are appointed by politicians. Their autonomy and insulation from mass politics depend on the disposition of the cabinet minister who supervises them. Within the government of India, the Ministry of Finance—particularly its Department of Economic Affairs (DEA)—is the agency most insulated from political pressure. Those working in the ministry have been a vital source of ideas and support for economic reform, yet their contributions were undermined and arguably reversed under the tenure of Pranab Mukherjee as minister of finance. Although it would be a gross exaggeration to lay all the blame for India's recent economic slowdown on Mukherjee, his tenure demonstrates the fragility of India's reform process and the fact that its sustainability depends on the underlying political process. Mukherjee's politicization of the appointment of a chairperson of a major mutual fund, his failure to advance foreign direct investment in multi-brand retail, and his promotion of retroactive taxes on certain offshore transactions of foreign corporations, discussed below, support that claim.

Pranab Mukherjee is a savvy veteran of Congress Party politics. As early as 1969, Indira Gandhi secured Mukherjee's seat in the Rajya Sabha, India's upper house of parliament; she also appointed him to his first cabinet post, as deputy minister of industrial development, in 1973. Never a politician with broad popular appeal, Mukherjee remained a trusted Gandhi family loyalist throughout his five decades in Congress Party politics. His unmatched knowledge of parliamentary and administrative procedures—along with his long acquaintance with a range of leaders within the Congress Party and its political opposition—made him perhaps the most important political strategist of the United Progressive Alliance (UPA) governments from 2004 until his resignation to become India's president on July 25, 2012. During that time, no one played a more important role in coordinating government policy, as evidenced by the fact that at the time of his resignation, Mukherjee headed an unprecedented 13 Groups of Ministers and 13 Empowered Groups of Ministers, each of which coordinated government action on important policy issues.

During his tenure as finance minister, Mukherjee became embroiled in controversies that deterred efforts to maintain accelerated growth. One controversy involved UTI Mutual Fund, which until 2006 was the largest mutual fund in India. In February 2011, U. K. Sinha left his post as UTI's chairman to become head of the Securities and Exchange Board of India (SEBI). Pranab Mukherjee and the Ministry of Finance insisted that Jitesh Khosla, brother of Mukherjee's adviser Omita Paul, become UTI's next chairman even though UTI's subcommittee for human relations, which was charged with vetting candidates, had determined that Khosla lacked the requisite experience. T. Rowe Price, which had purchased 26 percent to become UTI's largest shareholder, resisted Khosla's appointment. A standoff ensued, and UTI remained without a chairperson through the end of 2012. During that time, UTI's share of India's mutual fund market steadily shrank, in large part because without a chairperson, UTI was legally prohibited from starting new funds.

While Mukherjee's intervention in UTI suggested that the finance minister might not respect the autonomy of India's financial institutions, his role in the December 2011 failure to adopt a proposal to permit foreign investors to hold majority shares in multi-brand retail companies underscores the important role of politicians in ensuring the advance of reforms. India's retail sector is dominated by small, family-owned *kirana* stores. The 40 million people in households owning *kirana* stores constitute a powerful political constituency that opposes the entry of multinational retail companies like Walmart and Tesco in the Indian market. Yet multinationals can modernize the retail sector, bring needed investment to India's distributional networks, and, by complying with a requirement to purchase at least 30 percent of their goods locally, stimulate the local economy. At the end of November 2011, the UPA cabinet passed a resolution approving legislation to allow foreign majority ownership in the multi-brand retail sector. Passage in parliament required the support of all of the coalition members of the UPA government. Following the cabinet's decision, Mamata Banerjee, leader of the political party Trinamool Congress, stated that her party opposed the measure and that if the UPA tried to pass the legislation, it would withdraw from the UPA government—and in so doing, possibly bring the government down. Pranab

Mukherjee was liaison to the Trinamool Congress. His failure to anticipate Banerjee's opposition and persuade her to compromise or to develop a strategy to circumvent her resulted in a demoralizing defeat in which Mukherjee and the leaders of the Congress Party alienated both supporters and opponents of the reform. The embarrassing policy reversal underscored the political paralysis of the UPA at a time when repeated corruption scandals had already eroded its legitimacy. The fact that his successor as finance minister, P. Chidambaram, was able to spearhead a successful effort to pass the reform less than ten months later is a stark contrast with Mukherjee's tainted tenure.

Finally, in spring 2012, Mukherjee's budget announcement proposed changes in India's tax policy that raised serious concerns about the government's commitment to upholding the rule of law for foreign investors. The key measure, the General Anti-Avoidance Rule (GAAR), would authorize the Indian government to retrospectively tax offshore sales of shares of companies whose value is "substantially" derived from Indian assets. The GAAR was aimed specifically at the telecom giant Vodafone and its US$11 billion offshore acquisition of the Indian telecom Hutchison Essar in 2007. The government claimed that Vodafone owed US$2.6 billion dollars in taxes on the transaction. Mukherjee proposed the measure only after India's Supreme Court ruled against the government's claim in January 2012. Raghuram Rajan, who was serving at the time as adviser to Prime Minister Manmohan Singh, criticized the measure, declaring that "a government that changes the law retrospectively at will to fit its interpretation introduces tremendous uncertainty into business decisions, and it sets itself outside the law."[62] Both the U.S. secretary of the treasury and the U.K. chancellor criticized the GAAR, stating that it raised significant concerns among foreign investors. In response to the widespread criticism of the measure by foreign investors, the government announced that it would delay implementation. It then formed a committee to study the matter.

Fiscal Politics as a Site for Interaction between Mass and Technocratic Politics

A recent International Monetary Fund study insightfully explained that India's growth slump was a product of four factors:
—growth of the fiscal deficit
—high inflation
—high current account deficit
—decline in private corporate investment.[63]

Each of those factors is profoundly shaped by India's fiscal politics which, in turn, is driven by the cleavages between popular and technocratic politics.

The doubling of India's central government fiscal deficit from 2.5 percent of GDP in 2007–08 to an annual average of 5.4 percent during the period from 2008–09 to 2013–14 is in considerable measure a consequence of populist measures taken prior to the 2009 elections. The pre-election budget presented by the government in spring 2008 announced a massive debt waiver program that, according to some estimates, benefited more than 40 million farmers at a cost of 0.7 percent of GDP.[64] The budget also included a 72 percent increase in expenditures for the Mahatma Gandhi National Rural Employment Guarantee Scheme, enough to generate 2.16 billion person-days of employment on public works projects.[65] In the summer of 2008, the central government implemented the recommendations of the Sixth Pay Commission, providing an average pay raise of 21 percent for the central government's 5 million workers and backdating the increase to January 1, 2006. The move cost an estimated US$3.6 billion in 2008–09 and even more in the following year.[66] Total spending on subsidies steadily grew from 1.4 percent of GDP in 2007–08 to 2.6 percent of GDP in 2012–13 before dropping to 2.3 percent in 2013–14.[67] Spending on social welfare may be a worthwhile investment if the funded programs are efficiently implemented and if the state raises revenues to finance the programs. However, the second UPA government was lacking on both counts.[68]

Fiscal politics contributed to India's large current account deficits through two channels. First, the combination of high inflation and financial repression resulted in negative real interest rates on deposits. The consumer price index, which began to increase as early as 2005–06 as a consequence of economic overheating before the global financial crisis, jumped to 12.4 percent in 2009–10 and remained at the elevated average of 9.8 percent from 2010–11 to 2013–14. Motivated by expectations of continued high inflation and negative deposit rates, Indians shifted their savings from financial instruments to gold. Combined with higher prices, the switch increased gold imports from less than US$11 billion in 2005–06 to almost US$57 billion, or 11.5 percent of all imports, in 2011–12. The government therefore imposed quantitative restrictions and increased import duties, thereby reducing the import of gold in the following two years.[69] The second channel from fiscal politics to high CADs was created by oil subsidies, which rose from an annual average of 0.1 percent of GDP from 2004–04 to 2008–09 to 1 percent in 2012–13.[70] By limiting the pass-through of higher global oil prices, the subsidies contributed to the growth of oil imports and a further increase in the CAD.

Finally, India's high fiscal deficits curtailed its growth by reducing corporate investment. From 2003–04 to 2007–08, gross capital formation by the private corporate sector steadily increased from 6.5 percent of GDP to 17.3 percent (see table 4-4) but dropped to just 9.2 percent in 2012–13. Indian households' shift from financial investments to gold reduced the savings available for the corporate sector. In its fight to combat high levels of inflation, the RBI increased interest rates, thereby reducing corporate profits and raising financing costs. At the same time that the government ran high deficits, it curbed public investment and thus diminished incentives for private investment. In 2007–08, the government's capital expenditures were 2.5 percent of GDP; in 2013–14, they were less than 1 percent. Large fiscal deficits, high rates of inflation, and large capital account deficits contributed to the volatility of foreign investment, as manifested by the capital outflows experienced in 2012–13.[71] More generally, these factors, along with the retroactive tax policies announced in spring 2012, contributed to an atmosphere of economic uncertainty that discouraged Indian corporate investment and hampered growth.[72]

The election of Narendra Modi in May 2014 and the advent of the National Democratic Alliance government (NDA), led by Modi's Bharatiya Janata Party, substantially altered the situation. In anticipation of Modi's election, foreign investors increased their investment in India, and the valuation of Indian stock markets rose by 20 percent in the first half of 2014. The rising expectations that have accompanied the new government highlight the impact of politics on economic prospects. Fiscal politics under the NDA government will play a central role in determining India's economic performance. Whether Modi succeeds in aligning India's fiscal politics with its long-term economic interests will be crucial to achieving his administration's economic goals.

Concluding Remarks

India's quick rebound from the global economic crisis can be explained largely by a mix of policies and circumstances that included macroeconomic reforms, which enabled the government to apply a substantial fiscal and monetary stimulus; trade policies that enhanced India's resilience to the crisis by reorienting trade away from the North Atlantic; regulatory intervention to ensure financial stability; and initially supportive but volatile global markets. The rebound was short lived, waning after two years. While difficult international conditions in 2012 hampered a return to rapid growth, India's recent economic downturn highlights the importance of the political process.

Table 4-4. *India's Savings and Gross Capital Formation, 2003–04 to 2012–13*

Measure	2003–04	2004–05	2005–06	2006–07	2007–08	2008–09	2009–10	2010–11	2011–12	2012–13
Total domestic savings	29.0	32.4	33.4	34.6	36.8	32.0	33.7	33.7	31.3	30.1
Household	23.1	23.6	23.5	23.2	22.4	23.6	25.2	23.1	22.8	21.9
Financial saving	11.0	10.1	11.9	11.3	11.6	10.1	12.0	9.9	7.0	7.1
Physical assets	12.1	13.4	11.7	11.9	10.8	13.5	13.2	13.2	15.8	14.8
Private Corporate	4.6	6.6	7.5	7.9	9.4	7.4	8.4	8.0	7.3	7.1
Public sector	1.3	2.3	2.4	3.6	5.0	1.0	0.2	2.6	1.2	1.2
Gross capital formation	26.1	32.5	34.3	35.9	38.0	35.5	36.3	36.5	36.4	34.7
Household	12.1	13.4	11.7	11.9	10.8	13.5	13.2	13.2	15.8	14.8
Valuables	0.9	1.3	1.1	1.2	1.1	1.3	1.8	2.1	2.7	2.6
Private Corporate	6.5	10.3	13.6	14.5	17.3	11.3	12.1	12.8	10.1	9.2
Public sector	6.6	7.4	7.9	8.3	8.9	9.4	9.2	8.4	7.7	8.1

Source: Muneesh Kapur and Rakesh Mohan, "India's Recent Macroeconomic Performance," IMF Working Paper WP/14/68, April 2014, p. 16 (www.imf.org/external/pubs/ft/wp/2014/wp1468.pdf).

Pre-election spending increases in 2008–09 fortuitously coincided with the need for a sizable stimulus in the wake of the global financial crisis. However, the stimulus led to high fiscal deficits and persistent inflation. India's central bank combated those problems by increasing interest rates, but in the context of persistent inflation and historic CADs in 2011–12 and 2012–13, it maintained elevated rates even as growth declined. New policy initiatives launched earlier on might have revived India's growth, but the preceding Congress Party–led ruling coalition was plagued by corruption scandals and had difficulty passing legislation in India's fragmented and contentious parliament. The newly elected NDA government, having campaigned on the promise that its leader, Narendra Modi, will accelerate economic development, must address the challenge of aligning India's contentious democratic politics with its economic interests.

India's experience supports Wise, Armijo, and Katada's claim in chapter 1 that developing countries fashioned relatively successful responses to the global financial crisis by adopting a synthesis of market-based and state-oriented policies. Although there is a convergence on particular policy principles, the synthesis leading to success is likely to vary from country to country. More generally, a growing consensus among analysts of economic development calls for employing rigorous economic analysis to fashion policy regimes that are adapted to local circumstances.[73] This chapter demonstrates that the political process is central to the formulation and implementation of economic development policies. Analyzing the impact of specific policies in particular circumstances is an important part of the challenge of promoting economic development. At least as important is the study of how the political process can be shaped to advance a country's long-term economic interests.

Notes

1. Atul Kohli, *Poverty amid Plenty in the New India* (Cambridge University Press, 2012); Ashutosh Varshney, "India's Democratic Challenge," *Foreign Affairs,* vol. 86, no. 2 (March 2007), pp. 93–106; Ashutosh Varshney, "Mass Politics or Elite Politics? India's Economic Reforms in Comparative Perspective," in *India in the Era of Economic Reforms,* edited by Jeffrey D. Sachs, Ashutosh Varshney, and Nirupam Bajpai (Oxford University Press, 2000).

2. Sudipto Mundle, M. Govinda Rao, and N. R. Bhanumurthy, "Stimulus, Recovery, and Exit Policy: G-20 Experience and Indian Strategy," *Economic and Political Weekly,* vol. 46 (July 16, 2011), pp. 85–94.

3. Reserve Bank of India, *Handbook of Statistics on Indian Economy: 2011–12* (Mumbai: 2012), table 236. For the table, see http://www.rbi.org.in/scripts/PublicationsView.aspx?id=14596; for the entire volume, see www.rbi.org.in/scripts/annual Publications.aspx?head=Handbook+of+Statistics+on+Indian+Economy.

4. Reserve Bank of India, *Report on Currency and Finance: 2008–09* (Mumbai: 2010), p. 234.

5. Arvid Panagariya, *India: The Emerging Giant* (Oxford University Press, 2008), pp. 218–19.

6. Repos are collateralized lending agreements in which banks acquire short-term liquidity by selling securities to the RBI with an agreement to repurchase them back at a predetermined rate and date. Repo rates are the charges imposed by the RBI for the transaction. Reverse repos are agreements in which the RBI borrows funds from banks by lending them securities. The reverse repo rate is the interest rate paid by the RBI for this transaction.

7. Government of India, Ministry of Finance, Department of Economic Affairs, *Report of the Working Group on Foreign Investment,* 2010 (www.finmin.nic.in/reports/ WGFI.pdf).

8. Rakesh Mohan, *Growth with Financial Stability: Central Banking in an Emerging Market* (Oxford University Press, 2011) p. 175.

9. Jayant Varma, "Indian Financial Market Development and Regulation: What Worked and Why?," in *Asian Perspectives on Financial Sector Reforms and Regulation,* edited by Masahiro Kawai and Eswar S. Prasad (Asian Development Bank Institute and Brookings, 2011), p. 262.

10. World Bank, *World Development Indicators: 2012* (http://data.worldbank.org/ data-catalog/world-development-indicators).

11. Philip R. Lane and Gian Maria Milesi-Ferretti, "The External Wealth of Nations Mark II: Revised and Extended Estimates of Foreign Assets and Liabilities, 1970–2004," *Journal of International Economics,* vol. 73 (November 2007), pp. 223–50. Dataset available at www.philiplane.org/EWN.html.

12. Reserve Bank of India, *Handbook of Statistics on Indian Economy: 2011–12.*

13. Ila Patnaik and Ajay Shah, "Why India Choked When Lehman Broke," National Institute of Public Finance and Policy Working Paper 2010–63 (New Delhi: January 2010), pp. 7–10, 17 (www.eaber.org/node/22974); Jayant Varma, "Indian Financial Sector and the Global Financial Crisis," *Vikalpa,* vol 34 (January 2009), pp. 25–34.

14. Reserve Bank of India, *Report on Currency and Finance 2008–09*, p. 226.

15. Ibid., p. 283.

16. Ibid., p. 237

17. Ibid., p. 197.

18. Government of India, Ministry of Finance, *Economic Survey: 2010–2011*, p. 219 (http://indiabudget.nic.in/index.asp).

19. Reserve Bank of India, "RBI Releases 'Quarterly Statistics on Deposits and Credit of Scheduled Commercial Banks: June 2014,'" press release, September 29, 2014 (http://rbi.org.in/Scripts/BS_PressReleaseDisplay.aspx?prid=32190).

20. Richard Herd and others, "Financial Sector Reform in India: Time for a Second Wave?," Economics Department Working Papers 2011, no. 48 (OECD, July 26, 2011), p. 8 (www.oecd.org/eco/workingpapers).

21. Mohan, *Growth with Financial Stability,* pp. 404–05.

22. There was considerable political opposition to privatization. For instance, the 1998 Narasimham Committee on the Banking Sector Reforms recommended that the minimum public sector equity in banks be reduced to 33 percent from 55 percent for the State Bank of India and 51 percent for public sector banks. The government introduced legislation to that effect in parliament, but parliament failed to pass it.

23. Panagariya, *India: The Emerging Giant,* p. 234.

24. Varma, "Indian Financial Market Development and Regulation," pp. 258–59.

25. Reserve Bank of India, *Report on Currency and Finance: 2008–09,* p. 219.

26. Reserve Bank of India, *Handbook of Statistics on Indian Economy: 2011–12,* tables 64, 65.

27. Reserve Bank of India, *Report on Currency and Finance: 2008–09,* p. 232.

28. World Bank, *World Development Indicators: 2014* (http://data.worldbank.org/data-catalog/world-development-indicators).

29. Reserve Bank of India, *Report on Currency and Finance: 2008–09,* p. 251.

30. Ibid., p. 252; Government of India, Ministry of Finance, *Economic Survey of India: 2013–14,* p. 2 (http://indiabudget.nic.in/survey.asp).

31. Engineering goods were the fastest-growing sector of Indian manufacturing exports, rising from 11.9 percent in 1999–2000 to 23.8 percent in 2010–11. The remarkable success of India's engineering goods is a consequence of the country's trade reforms but also earlier industrial policies that laid the foundation for the sector. Although engineering goods exports dropped by 18.7 percent in 2009–10, they rebounded by 84 percent in 2010–11. See Government of India, *Economic Survey: 2011–12,* p. 159.

32. Ibid., p. 168.

33. Reserve Bank of India, *Report on Currency and Finance: 2008–09,* p. 254.

34. Panagariya, *India: The Emerging Giant,* pp. 201–07.

35. Government of India, *Economic Survey: 2011–12,* p. A-71.

36. Indira Rajaraman, "India's Experience of the Crisis and Key Lessons," in *How to Prevent the Next Crisis: Lessons from Country Experiences of the Global Crisis,* edited by Aniket Bhushan (Ottawa: North-South Institute, 2012), pp. 62–63.

37. International Monetary Fund, *World Economic Outlook,* April 2014, table A9, p. 192 (www.imf.org/external/Pubs/ft/weo/2014/01/).

38. Government of India, *Economic Survey of India: 2013–14,* p. 108.

39. Muneesh Kapur and Rakesh Mohan, "India's Recent Macroeconomic Peformance: An Assessment and Way Forward," IMF Working Paper WP/14/68, April 2014 (http://econpapers.repec.org/paper/imfimfwpa/); and Government of India, *Economic Survey of India: 2013-14,* p. 2.

40. Biswajit Dhar and K. S. Chalapati Rao, "India's Current Account Deficit: Causes and Cures," *Economic and Political Weekly,* vol. 49, no.21 (May 24, 2014), p. 42.

41. Ibid., p. 43.

42. Government of India, *Economic Survey of India: 2013–14*, p. 26.

43. Dhar and Rao, "India's Current Account Deficit," p. 42.

44. A 2013 World Gold Council report observed, "The share decline in the official import of gold into India led to an increasing amount of this demand being met by gold imported through unofficial channels." See Dhar and Rao, "India's Current Account Deficit," p. 42.

45. Government of India, *Economic Survey of India: 2013–14*, p. 118.

46. Varshney, "India's Democratic Challenge," pp. 93–106; Varshney, "Mass Politics or Elite Politics?," pp. 222–60.

47. Varshney, "India's Democratic Challenge," p. 100.

48. Varshney, "India's Democratic Challenge," pp. 93–106; Kohli, *Poverty amid Plenty in the New India;* Devesh Kapur, "The Political Economy of the State," in *The Oxford Companion to Politics in India,* edited by Naraja Gopal Jayal and Pratap Bhanu Mehta (Oxford University Press, 2010), pp. 443–59.

49. Varshney, "India's Democratic Challenge," pp. 93–106; Kohli, *Poverty amid Plenty in the New India.*

50. Government of India, Ministry of Finance, *High-Powered Expert Committee Report on Mumbai—An International Financial Centre* (2007) (http://finmin.nic.in/reports/).

51. Government of India, Planning Commission, *A Hundred Small Steps: Report of the Committee on Financial Sector Reforms* (Delhi: Sage, 2009).

52. Y. V. Reddy, "Converting a Tiger: Lessons from India's Gradualist Approach to Capital Account Convertibility," *Finance and Development,* vol. 44 (March 2007), pp. 1–9.

53. Vikas Bajaj, "In India, Central Banker Played It Safe," *New York Times,* June 25, 2009.

54. Y. V. Reddy, *India and the Global Financial Crisis* (New Delhi: Orient Blackswan, 2009).

55. Author's interview of Reddy, Hyderabad, July 10, 2011.

56. "At 7.2%, Inflation is Still High, Says RBI Governor," *The Hindu,* February 11, 2013.

57. Tamal Bandyopadhyay, "What Y. V. Reddy's Book Did Not Say," *Live Mint,* May 11, 2009 (www.livemint.com/Opinion/wZQN4x9fwgOGRu1IzkkFUJ/What-YV-Reddy8217s-book-did-not-say.html).

58. Government of India, *A Hundred Small Steps.*

59. Poonam Gupta, Kalpana Kochhar, and Sanjaya Panth, "Bank Ownership and the Effect of Financial Liberalization: Evidence from India," IMF Working Paper 1150, March 22, 2011 (www.imf.org/external/pubs/cat/longres. aspx?sk=24695.0); Indira Rajaraman and Garima Vasishtha, "Nonperforming Assets of Public Sector Banks: Some Panel Results," *Economic and Political Weekly,* vol. 5 (2002), pp. 429–35.

60. Ila Patnaik and Ajay Shah, "Did the Indian Capital Controls Work as a Tool of Macroeconomic Policy?," National Institute of Public Finance and Policy Working Paper 2011-87 (April 2011) (www.nipfp.org.in/workingpapers).

61. Ila Patnaik and Ajay Shah, "Did the Indian Capital Controls Work as a Tool of Macroeconomic Policy?," *IMF Economic Review,* vol. 60, no. 3 (2012) pp. 439–64 (http://macrofinance.nipfp.org.in/releases/PS2012_CapitalControls.html).

62. James Crabtree, "India Resumes Vodafone Tax Battle," *Financial Times,* May 10, 2012.

63. Kapur and Mohan, "India's Recent Macroeconomic Performance."

64. "PC Budgets for Early Elections," *Business Standard*, March 1, 2008; "Nomura Lowers India FY09 GDP Growth Forecast to 6.8% from 7.2%," *Economic Times*, December 2, 2008.

65. Jagdish Bhagwati and Arvind Panagariya, *India's Tryst with Destiny* (Noida, India: Collins Business, 2012), p. 194.

66. Amy Kazmin, "India Approves Pay Rise for 5M Federal Workers," *Financial Times*, August 14, 2008.

67. Government of India, *Economic Survey of India: 2013–14,* pp. 64–65.

68. Kapur and Mohan, "India's Recent Macroeconomic Peformance," p. 20.

69. Dhar and Rao, "India's Current Account Deficit," p. 42.

70. Kapur and Mohan, "India's Recent Macroeconomic Performance," p. 20.

71. T. N. Ninan, "No Shortage of Money," *Business Standard,* July 11, 2014.

72. Rahul Anand and Volodymyr Tulin, "Disentangling India's Investment Slow-down," IMF Working Paper WP/14/47 (March 2014). Note that factors other than fiscal policy also contribute to economic policy uncertainty. Anand and Tulin also note delayed project approvals and implementation as well as supply bottlenecks; see p. 6.

73. Dani Rodrik, *One Economics, Many Recipes: Globalization, Institutions, and Economic Growth* (Princeton University Press, 2007).

MARK BEESON

5

Southeast Asia's Post-Crisis Recovery: So Far, So Good

Trying to make meaningful generalizations about a group of countries as diverse as those found in Southeast Asia is difficult enough at the best of times. Analysis is made even more challenging by a paradox: a region that was synonymous with economic (and political) failure scarcely a decade ago is now considered one of the few bright spots in a global economy weighed down by a rolling series of crises that have yet to be definitively resolved. The key question about the various economies of Southeast Asia is whether their generally strong rebound from their own earlier crises and their apparent resilience in the face of a severe global downturn can be maintained.

Anyone who has been following economic development in Southeast Asia for a number of years might instinctively answer "Probably not." Southeast Asian states have frequently been buffeted by economic and political forces over which they have relatively little control. After all, these are comparatively small (or very small) economies that are highly exposed to shifts in international economic conditions, and even the head of the International Monetary Fund has described the 2008–09 global financial crisis as the worst since the 1930s.[1] Even though the dependence of Southeast Asia on the crisis-affected markets of Europe and North America has declined somewhat, that is primarily because the region has become more reliant on China.[2] Consequently, the really big question is whether the Chinese economy is now "decoupled" from Europe and especially the United States. Put differently, will China's rise continue and provide a source of continuing growth for the rest of the region?

Although it is impossible to say anything conclusive about the future prospects of a region with such a checkered history, what we can do is identify some of the changes and reforms that have occurred since the last crisis devastated much of Southeast Asia in the late 1990s and consider how they may influence the region's ability to withstand a new downturn. The discussion begins with a very brief snapshot of the region and its economic development that highlights the types of changes and reforms that have taken place over the last ten years or so. Some empirical detail is then presented to illustrate Southeast Asia's current situation, with particular attention given to changing trade and investment links as well as the different circumstances prevailing in some of the region's key economies. Finally, the implications of the changes for Southeast Asia's position as a coherent, institutionalized actor in world affairs are explored.

Southeast Asia in Context

"Heterogeneous" is the adjective most commonly used to describe Southeast Asia,[3] and it is not hard to see why. Just about every conceivable form of political organization can be found in the region, from fully fledged democracies in Indonesia, the Philippines, and (currently) Thailand through "semi-democracies" in Malaysia and Singapore, "communist" regimes in Vietnam and Laos, forms of constitutional monarchy in Cambodia and Brunei, and Burma's infamous military junta.[4] This political variation is matched by vastly different levels of economic development, ranging from Singapore and Brunei, which enjoy some of the highest per capita incomes in the world, to Laos, Cambodia, and especially Burma, which remain extremely poor. While this diversity may delight students of comparative analysis, it makes it difficult to generalize about the politics of the region, let alone its economic prospects. However, it is possible to make two broad observations that help to explain the way that some of the governments of the region have—or have not—been able to respond to crises and manage economic development more generally.

The first observation is that the region as a whole has been profoundly influenced by colonialism, which left its mark on the region's subsequent political, economic, and social development.[5] Not only was economic development "distorted" by the demands of empire, but so too were many Southeast Asian societies: for example, neither the complex ethnic mix that continues to shape Malaysian politics nor the rather arbitrary boundaries that define modern Indonesia can be understood without reference to the legacy of the imperial period. That is not to say that such historical influences are crude determinants of the current position of various countries, but they do help to account for the material circumstances and policy ideas held by policymakers across the region. Vietnam, for example, might be in a rather different position today if it had not had to fight two major wars against extraregional great powers to ensure its reunification and independence.

A second observation, therefore, is that regional development has occurred within a wider geopolitical context determined largely by forces outside the region, which also have had a major impact on the course of political and economic development in the region.[6] Southeast Asian industrialization was comparatively "late," even by East Asian standards, and occurred in the context of an overarching regional division of labor dominated by Japan and to a lesser extent by the other "newly industrializing economies" of Northeast Asia.[7] Nor did the states of Southeast Asia generally have anything like the sort of "state capacity" that distinguished the economic development efforts of their path-breaking counterparts in Northeast Asia. All of this is well known, of course, but merits repetition because we often overlook the precise historical circumstances in which economic activity occurs. In Southeast Asia's case, the apparent resilience of the region in the face of the current global downturn is all the more remarkable given its difficult historical legacy and the impact of the Asian financial crisis of 1997–98. It is noteworthy that part of the region's apparent strength owes something to that earlier episode, discussed below.

The Impact and Legacy of the Asian Crisis

Although some reforms were implemented prior to the Asian financial crisis, the crisis touched off a real transformation of Asian economies. Fifteen years later, it is hard to believe what a traumatic event the "Asian crisis" was. Whether it was strictly an *Asian* crisis, given that its impact was also felt in Russia, Latin America, and even the United States itself following the collapse of Long-Term Capital Management (LTCM), is moot but immaterial in the context of this discussion. What is less debatable is the fact that the economies of Indonesia, Thailand, Malaysia, and South Korea were at its epicenter, and that had important short- and long-term consequences. The most visible and dramatic short-term impact of the crisis was the downfall of the Suharto regime in Indonesia. But throughout Southeast Asia, the domestic foundations of the region's distinctive politico-economic accommodations were shaken and the reputations of its "miracle" economies were dealt what looked to be a fatal blow. Perhaps unsurprisingly, in the aftermath of the crisis a broad regional consensus emerged about the need to avoid repeating the experience in the future. There are many good analyses of the first Asian crisis, and I have no intention of trying to add to that literature.[8] Of greatest significance here in that regard are the sorts of long-term measures that were taken as a result of the political and economic shocks experienced during the crisis.

At the most general level, there was a collective realization that the East Asian region generally lacked institutions with which to manage such crises; as a consequence, it relied heavily on external actors and agencies to provide assistance. That might have been important enough in itself, but when the external actors were the United States and an International Monetary Fund bent on imposing far-reaching structural reforms on regimes judged to be suffering from all the malign effects of "crony capitalism," the recognition of regional vulnerability was all the more acute.[9] Accordingly, one of the most noteworthy legacies of the Asian crisis has been a heightened interest in developing regional institutions.[10] Some of that impetus has been generalized and manifested in the still unresolved contest to determine which piece of the region's burgeoning institutional architecture will prove to be the most consequential. Whether it proves to be China's preferred vision of ASEAN+3 or the increasingly popular East Asian Summit is still not clear, but there is no doubt that the earlier crisis provided a major catalyst for institution building.[11]

Whether or not any of the institutions ultimately prove effective or decisive, it is important to highlight other more specific impacts of the Asian crisis, the most important of which is the amount of policy and analytical attention paid to the possibility of developing new monetary mechanisms with which to insulate the region from future external shocks. The much-discussed Chiang Mai Initiative (CMI) concerning currency swap provisions was the principal manifestation of that attention, although its actual impact remains debatable. As Emmers and Ravenhill point out, when faced with its first major test—in the form of the 2008–09 global financial crisis—"the CMI failed abysmally."[12] What is clear is that in the aftermath of the first crisis, partly as a consequence of a general depreciation-driven expansion of exports and partly as a result of government policy, currency reserves across East Asia have increased dramatically. The scale of China's reserves has understandably attracted the most attention, but in other parts of East Asia, including Southeast Asia, there also has been a noteworthy transformation in the position of a number of key economies. Indonesia, Malaysia, Thailand, and even the Philippines now have substantial and significantly larger reserves than they did on the eve of the Asian crisis.[13] The buildup of those reserves, especially in China's case, has contributed to an ongoing debate about the nature of—and the responsibility for—global imbalances, but as far as their collective vulnerability to externally induced pressures and shocks is concerned, Southeast Asia's most important economies seem to have defensive strengths that they lacked 15 years ago. However, a more detailed examination of the situation in the region reveals a more complex position, with a number of countries continuing to exhibit weaknesses and a collective exposure to changes in the global economy, over which Southeast Asian policymakers have limited influence. The next section provides a more detailed snapshot of some of the region's continuing vulnerabilities.

Surprising Strengths or Enduring Weaknesses?

The so-called global financial crisis (GFC), which was marked by the collapse of Lehman Brothers in 2008, provided a major test of the Asian economies' resilience. Despite being called a *global* financial crisis, in reality the United States, Britain, and more recently the economies of the European Union have been most badly affected.[14] But whatever the current crisis is called, thus far at least, the East Asian economies have emerged relatively well from a downturn as severe as anything seen since the 1930s. Indeed, so impressive has the comparative performance of a number of the East Asian economies been that there has been much talk about the possibility of East Asia generally and China in particular "decoupling" from the United States and acting as an independent center of growth.

When attempting to make sense of the decoupling hypothesis, it needs to be recognized at the outset that the GFC and its aftermath have not been definitively resolved; consequently, trying to make predictions is an even more foolhardy exercise than usual. But while the EU's problems remain unresolved and undermine America's tentative recovery, it is difficult to see how any part of the world, even China, can escape the impact of international economic problems. Indeed, there already are signs that the East Asian economies *are* beginning to be increasingly impacted by economic problems elsewhere.[15] If we add the growing concerns being voiced about China's economic prospects,[16] we can see that there are many sources of uncertainty that make predicting future prospects difficult. Nevertheless, it is worth tracing the evolution of the debate about decoupling because it tells us something important about both the East Asian region as a whole and the Southeast Asian economies in particular. One thing that is clear at the outset is that the relative strength of economies in the region has meant that they have been able to play a surprisingly effective role in stimulating their domestic economies in the face of an external downturn.[17] At the very least, that provides a note-worthy contrast to government efforts in Europe and North America and reinforces the general perception about the world's center of gravity shifting inexorably toward Asia.

It is significant, therefore, that the decoupling debate attracted the most attention at the height of the global financial crisis. The editors' fourth hypothesis, concerning countervailing external conditions, is especially significant in this regard. Southeast Asia benefited from the continued vibrancy of the Chinese economy. Some observers believed that the sheer scale of China's economic development and its growing links with economies outside the traditional "core" economies of the United States and Western Europe meant that it had developed the capacity to act as an independent center of growth in the world economy.[18] Beijing's response to the crisis—a massive and seemingly successful domestic stimulus package—appeared to lend weight to that argument when China's growth was largely unaffected by the downturn in the United States,[19] despite the latter's importance as an export market. The debate about the health of the Chinese economy and its potential impact on the region is of special importance to the economies of Southeast Asia, as their trade ties with China have expanded dramatically over the last few years.[20] Indeed, Southeast Asia's economic ties with China have become so important that they are influencing the broader geopolitical relationship between Southeast Asia, China, and the United States, further complicating ASEAN's policy response as a result.[21]

One of the most important illustrations of how China is using its growing economic leverage to reshape its relationship with Southeast Asia has been the China-ASEAN Free Trade Agreement (CAFTA). As far as China is concerned, Southeast Asia's principal importance is not economic. Because the ASEAN economies represent only a small proportion of China's overall trade, it was possible for China to offer an "early harvest"—a unilateral reduction in tariffs—to ASEAN with no expectation that it would immediately reciprocate. Whatever the merits of CAFTA from the Southeast Asian perspective, as far as China is concerned it has longer-term strategic importance. As Chin and Stubbs point out, "CAFTA has been as much about economic statecraft and geo-economics as purely economics."[22]

CAFTA and the general rise of China are pivotal parts of an emerging regional economy that seems less reliant on developments elsewhere. However, it is worth remembering that in the immediate aftermath of the early phase of the global financial crisis in 2008–09, when Asian economies initially experienced a fairly severe downturn, many dismissed the thesis that trade diversification away from advanced economies would lead to decoupling of those economies and the economies of Asia. Although there has been a marked recovery in East Asia over the last year or so,[23] some of the early criticisms of the decoupling thesis remain valid. For example, Athukorala and Kohpaiboon point out that the trade figures that appear to demonstrate the apparent resilience of regional exports can be deceptive and disguise the fact that "the dependence of East Asia on extra-regional markets (in particular those in NAFTA and the EU) for export-led growth is far greater than is revealed by the standard intra-regional trade ratios commonly used in the debate of regional economic integration."[24] The confusion stems from the nature of intraregional trade and the role played by regional production networks established by Japan and more recently by China. Athukorala and Kohpaiboon argue that because much regional trade is based on the import of parts and components from other East Asian economies for assembly into products that will ultimately be exported to markets in Europe and America, a deceptively positive picture of regional trade emerges that downplays what they see as the continuing importance of extraregional markets. Indeed, some observers argue that production networks and intra-firm "trade" make economic statistics all but meaningless.[25]

Even if the scale of regional trade and self-reliance is exaggerated by the cross-border movement of parts and components for products that will be sent to extraregional markets, regional production networks have become a vital piece of an increasingly integrated regional economy. Two aspects of these networks merit emphasis. First, they are being increasingly driven by the growth of China. That is important enough in itself and helps to account for China's growing political importance in Southeast Asia. However, it is also important to recognize that China is part of a global production network. One of the reasons that Southeast Asia (and China, for that matter) is potentially vulnerable to external shocks is because production is overwhelmingly intended for external markets and often organized by foreign companies.[26] More than half of China's manufacturing exports are derived from foreign-invested enterprises,[27] making regional production networks potentially very sensitive to changes in external demand. Second, for all the additional "efficiency" generated by the establishment of these complex, highly interdependent networks, they have proved to be surprisingly vulnerable to climate-induced interruption. Recent floods in Thailand disrupted production at over 1,000 companies, primarily in the electronics and automotive sectors,[28] revealing the risks associated with cross-border integration and interdependence. Given the array of pressing environmental problems facing East Asia as a whole and Southeast Asia in particular, Thailand's problems and the limited capacity that the government displayed in addressing them suggest that a deteriorating natural environment may add significantly to existing concerns about governance and state capacity.[29]

Nevertheless, the reality at this stage is that the recovery since the beginning of 2010 has been widespread and, despite the problems in the EU and the United States, generally quite impressive.[30] While China may continue to grow more quickly than all other countries in the region, the performance of the ASEAN economies has generally been surprisingly good. Of even more potential importance in the long run is the fact that one of the principal contributors to growth in the region is the economic expansion that has occurred as a consequence of domestic consumption. The region's expanding middle class and the growing numbers of people who have been lifted out of poverty are clearly at the heart of this trend. But a country such as Indonesia also highlights the ambiguous nature of the demographic dividend: certainly living standards have risen, but so have expectations and demands for well-paying jobs. It is not clear at this stage whether Indonesia's government can guarantee the future of its expanding middle class, let alone of those further down the social scale.[31] Still, the current rise in domestic demand is important for two reasons. First, the region as a whole has been widely criticized for relying too extensively on external markets and thereby contributing to the imbalances that cause such international political friction. Second, an expanding domestic market ought to make the region's economies less reliant on the crisis-stricken, potentially protectionist, economies of America and Europe.[32]

In many ways Indonesia is emblematic of how much genuine progress has been made in the region—and not just economic progress. It also illustrates some of the remaining obstacles to development. It is important to remember that, on the positive side of the ledger, Indonesia has made an impressive and sustained transition to democracy in difficult circumstances and with little tradition of political pluralism. That said, the quality of Indonesian democracy attracts a good deal of criticism, as does the pervasive nature of the corruption that continues to plague the political system overall.[33] Nevertheless, Indonesia—Southeast Asia's biggest economy and a member of the G-20—is attracting growing amounts of foreign investment, which is fueling its recent high levels of economic growth.[34] Indeed, many observers believe that if Indonesia maintains its current level of economic development, it has the potential to add another "I" to the BRIC economies.[35] While it seems that

Indonesia's sheer size will underpin its growing geopolitical ambitions, some of its apparent strengths carry inherent weaknesses: demographic and environmental pressures are creating a combustible mix in parts of Indonesia, raising questions about the government's ability to manage profound social changes and rapidly rising expectations.[36] It also is important to note that one of the paradoxes about Indonesia's democratic transformation is that democracy seems to have made it harder to implement domestic policy and to act in concert with other ASEAN states.[37]

However, for all the optimism about the rise of Indonesia and East Asia more generally, it is clear that the level of development in China and a number of other emerging market economies of Southeast Asia is still fundamentally different from that of their counterparts in Europe and the United States. With the exception of Singapore and Brunei, per capita incomes are still significantly lower in most of Asia than they are in the West, and it is simply implausible that the region can provide the sort of market for consumer goods that might benefit the more developed economies, despite the importance of domestic consumption in the region's recent resilience.[38] That leaves a number of the ASEAN economies exposed to shifts in market conditions and government policy elsewhere in the world. Because a number of key manufacturing industries, such as electronics, have played such a crucial part in the industrialization and development of Southeast Asia, its economies remain especially vulnerable to shifts in consumer sentiment.[39]

As a consequence, there is a continuing general perception that East Asia as a whole and the Southeast Asian economies in particular remain exposed to "spillovers" from crises elsewhere. Goldstein and Xie have developed an elaborate taxonomy of trade, investment, debt, deficits, growth, inflation, money supply, and exchange rate volatility measures to try to estimate the region's overall vulnerability to externally generated shocks.[40] Perhaps unsurprisingly, the conclusion of their analysis is that China is the least vulnerable to external shocks, but the fact that the Philippines ranks second *is* a surprise. Given the notorious economic underperformance of the Philippines in the region and its limited state capacity,[41] the value of such an analysis would seem to be limited even if well-intentioned. Rampant corruption, chronic environmental problems, growing inequality, a demographic crisis, and a perennially restive military are among the Philippines's many formidable challenges, which intuitively seem to exceed those of its neighbors.[42] Singapore, which is in the middle of Goldstein and Xie's rankings, appears much more secure at first blush, yet it highlights the potential dangers of reliance on external markets and volatile consumer demand. Indeed, Singapore was badly affected by the initial crisis in 2008, and there are signs that the country, which many regard as a bellwether economy for the international economic system in general, is experiencing another serious downturn. Although it is dangerous to read too much into one set of figures, a 22 percent decline in manufacturing activity on a quarterly basis in 2012 is potentially alarming and certainly worthy of attention.[43]

Investor Confidence

How do external financial players view Southeast Asia? Given the role played by the ratings agencies in recent crises,[44] perhaps their views should not be taken too seriously. Nevertheless, they are plainly an influence on "investor sentiment," broadly conceived, and they provide one measure of how extraregional actors view the region. Malaysia is easily the best regarded of the Southeast Asian economies[45]—no small irony given its highly unorthodox response to the previous Asian crisis, when it flouted the conventional (Western) wisdom and instigated capital controls.[46] The general picture, however, hardly calls for a resounding vote of confidence—an observation that assumes greater significance when we consider the nature of capital flows into Southeast Asia. Potentially footloose portfolio investment—of the sort that played such a destabilizing role in the first Asian crisis as well as in the 1994 Mexican peso crisis, which presaged the Asian financial fiasco—remains the largest source of capital inflow into Southeast Asia's main economies.[47] The rapid outflow of portfolio capital in 2008 provides a suitably graphic illustration of just how volatile and destabilizing such flows have been and can continue to be. Although foreign direct investment has not dried up in the way that some had feared given the rapid rise of China and its capacity to absorb massive amounts of foreign investment,[48] it remains at relatively modest levels. By contrast, overall portfolio investment flows to East Asia generally have increased significantly.[49] The ASEAN 4 are especially exposed to the United States, while the Philippines has received large inflows from the troubled Eurozone economies.

While the parallels with the earlier Asian crisis are noteworthy given the prominent role then played by highly mobile capital and investor sentiment, this time around there are grounds for qualified optimism. Southeast Asia's current account balances and external liabilities are generally in a much healthier position than those of their counterparts in Europe and the United States, allowing governments in the region to play a greater role in stimulating their own economies in the face of an external downturn.[50] Equally important, levels of public debt are, at least by European and Japanese standards, relatively low.[51] Notwithstanding all of these comparative strengths, the Asian Development Bank's overall assessment of the region's exposure to external crises notes that the risk posed by a continuing Eurozone crisis is likely to be "serious" but not as bad as the debacle of 2008–09.[52]

With the noteworthy and somewhat surprising exception of Singapore, the ASEAN 4 economies look to be well placed to withstand any new crisis.[53] Singapore's outlier status does tend to cast doubt on the usefulness of these sorts of predictive exercises given its comparative strengths and high level of economic development and state capacity. The general point is that the relatively small size of most of the Southeast Asian economies—combined with their exposure to and dependence on external economic circumstances over which they have little influence—serves to remind us that their fates are not entirely in their own hands. They remain vulnerable. One way of trying to assess just how vulnerable they are is to highlight some of the economic, political, and social forces whose interaction within individual Southeast Asian countries will affect both the success of internal policy initiatives and the perceptions of external actors.

The "image" of the region is an important influence on investment decisions, and a number of surveys attempt to measure the ease and confidence with which external investors can do business around the world. Southeast Asia receives a fairly mixed score that highlights the inherent limits of trying to generalize about the region as a whole. For example, according to the World Bank's assessment of business regulations, of the 190 countries surveyed, Singapore and Hong Kong are the two easiest places in the world to do business. Other Southeast Asian nations fare less well: Thailand (17) and Malaysia (18) are quite impressive, but Vietnam (98), Indonesia (129), and the Philippines (136) are much less so.[54] One problem that deters business investment is endemic and seemingly inescapable corruption.[55] Transparency International's 2010 annual survey of perceptions of corruption presents a similarly mixed picture.[56] While Singapore is again the outstanding Southeast Asian state, coming in first internationally, others—such as Malaysia (56), Thailand (78), Indonesia (110), Vietnam (116), and especially the Philippines (134)—are much less impressive. Despite seemingly serious attempts to reduce the politics of patronage and cronyism in places such as Indonesia, there are continuing doubts about the government's ability and commitment to the task.[57] Ironically, pressure from external agencies such as the World Bank to decentralize Indonesian governance may have actually contributed to the problem and further undermined the effectiveness of state-sponsored reform initiatives.[58]

One of Southeast Asia's other most pressing problems—and a major disincentive for potential investors—is the parlous state of the region's infrastructure, especially transport and energy infrastructure. Again, Indonesia highlights the challenges: despite much higher levels of investment, in transport in particular,[59] the recent rapid growth of the Indonesian economy has highlighted deficiencies and threatens future development.[60] That reflects in part the unforgiving nature of the region's geography, especially in maritime Southeast Asia. However, it is telling that even in mainland Southeast Asia, the great hope for overcoming the region's perennial transport problems is China, with its proposal to fund a rail network that would link up the region and enhance its attractiveness as an integrated production hub.[61] That would also enhance China's influence, of course, something that is already making some of the Southeast Asian states nervous as they try to balance competing economic and geopolitical interests. Even more immediately unsettling for some of the mainland Southeast Asian states has been China's assertive behavior along the Mekong River, where its dam-building projects threaten the environmental security and sustainability of downstream states.[62] It is emblematic of a number of challenges that Southeast Asian elites must attempt to address if they are to maintain economic stability, let alone take advantage of some of the opportunities emphasized by more optimistic observers.

The Geopolitics of Economic Development

In many ways, the management of the Mekong River illustrates many of the complex, intersecting challenges that confront the governments of Southeast Asia. China's actions with respect to management of the river not only are a reminder of the continuing importance of power politics and the relative weakness of the Southeast Asian states but also highlight the increasingly dire state of the natural environment in the region. The implacable nature of environmental pressures is testing the limits of intraregional cooperation. It is worth briefly reminding ourselves of just how difficult the environmental situation in Southeast Asia is as it can make many of the more esoteric discussions about the merits of comparative economic policy redundant.

More than 40 percent of the population of Southeast Asia still relies on agriculture for a living, and this group is especially exposed to climate change. The recent floods in Thailand and the catastrophic crop losses that accompanied them provided a sobering reminder of just how important food security is to social and political stability and just how uncertain the world's ability to feed a rapidly growing global population actually is.[63] It is also important to remember that notwithstanding all the excitement about the region's economic prospects, about 200 million people in Southeast Asia still live on less than $2 a day.[64] In addition, approximately 500 million Southeast Asians live along its vast coastlines, which are especially vulnerable to likely rising sea levels. More immediately, there are major questions about the sustainability and management of important regional industries, such as logging, which highlight and increase overall environmental pressures. The Asian Development Bank (ADB) recently concluded that

> Southeast Asia is one of the world's most vulnerable regions to climate change impact such as droughts, floods, typhoons, sea level rise, and heat waves. This is because of its long coastlines; large and growing population; high concentration of human and economic activities in coastal areas; importance of the agriculture sector in providing jobs and livelihoods for a large segment of people, especially those living in poverty; and dependence of some countries on natural resources and the forestry sector for growth and development. Climate change poses significant threats to the sustainability of the region's economic growth, its poverty reduction endeavors, the achievement of the Millennium Development Goals, and long-term prosperity.[65]

Such challenges are formidable enough at a national level, but they are made even more complex by the inescapable necessity for cooperation at the transnational level if problems such as climate change and environmental degradation are to be addressed. Thus far the regional track record does not inspire confidence.[66] In the case of Southeast Asia, multiple governance problems tend to reinforce each other and lead some to predict challenges to state authority as a consequence.[67] Compounding the difficulties at the national level is the ineffectiveness of regional institutions in addressing problems that require collective action.

The very diversity of Southeast Asia means that it is possible to find evidence for almost any trend or development and wildly different readings of precisely the same issues. That is true not only of individual countries but also of the region's expanding institutional architecture. For example, some think that ASEAN has exerted an ideational and normative influence over its more powerful neighbors in ways that work to Southeast Asia's collective advantage.[68] Others argue that ASEAN is ineffective and concerned primarily with avoiding disagreement among its members.[69] A good deal is at stake in this debate because the future economic and security prospects of the economically small, strategically weak ASEAN states will increasingly depend on the ability of these states to exercise influence in the Asia Pacific region's growing number of new institutions.

Concluding Remarks

Space precludes exhaustive consideration of the issues confronting Southeast Asia,[70] but a few simple observations can be offered by way of conclusion. First, although a polite fiction is maintained about ASEAN's being "in the driver's seat" when it comes to regional actions, in reality the capacity of the Southeast Asian states to influence the behavior of more powerful East Asian and extraregional states is inevitably limited. The recent U.S. decision to "pivot" back toward Asia is driven by a calculation of U.S. national interests and a concern about the "rise of China,"[71] not by a desire to respond to any collective view of the members of ASEAN, even if such a thing existed. Somewhat paradoxically, it has been precisely the same concerns about China's increasingly assertive behavior that has brought about a degree of consensus in some Southeast Asian capitals, like Hanoi and Manila, about the benefits of a continuing U.S. strategic presence in the region.[72]

The dilemma for much of Southeast Asia, then, is that its economic future is once again dependent on that of an outsider. In this regard it is hardly unique, but what makes Southeast Asia's relationship with China especially challenging is the latter's increasingly assertive behavior in ASEAN's backyard. China's territorial claims in the South China Sea are long-standing, but until recently China's assiduous "charm offensive" appeared to have calmed the fears of its Southeast Asian neighbors.[73] However, China's recent assertive, even aggressive, behavior has undermined that confidence and placed a large question mark over the future relationship between the region's small economies and China, upon which they have become ever more reliant. Many of China's neighbors are becoming increasingly nervous about its strategic intentions.[74]

For a number of Southeast Asia's most important economies—Indonesia, Thailand, Malaysia, the Philippines, and even Vietnam—growing strategic tensions will make the challenge of escaping the so-called middle-income trap all the more difficult.[75] In some ways that is a good problem to have—

becoming a middle-income economy in the first place is no small achievement. The question of perhaps greatest interest to students of comparative political economy is how the different Southeast Asian economies will attempt to keep their respective development projects going. At one level, potentially competing economic and strategic pressures will test ASEAN's capacity to broker regional trade and investment agreements designed to facilitate economic activity—an arena in which it has become dependent on China.[76] China's influence can also be detected in the way that some countries are attempting to accelerate the development process; Vietnam is arguably the country that is most closely mimicking the Chinese development model.[77]

Even before recent crises undermined the credibility of the Washington Consensus, China's rise was diminishing the material and ideational hegemony of Western liberal, capitalist, democratic values, leading some to predict the inevitable triumph of Chinese authoritarianism.[78] It is clear that *if* the continuing economic development of countries such as Vietnam and Indonesia can be sustained, not only will they become more important in material and strategic terms, but the manner in which they achieve development will also say something about which way the winds of ideational influence are blowing. Southeast Asia remains an important laboratory in which many combinations of political and economic development theories have been tried, and some have plainly worked. The question is whether successful approaches can be sustained in a region in which major powers continue to assert themselves and in which daunting external economic forces present as many challenges as they do opportunities.

A complex range of domestic, historical, and geopolitical factors continue to influence economic and political outcomes in Southeast Asia. It is difficult to make generalized observations about the current or future prospects of such a diverse group of countries. Nevertheless, it is worth considering how the Southeast Asian story confirms or refutes some of the observations made in chapter 1 of this volume about the policy responses of elites across the region. In some ways, the relatively small economic scale of a number of the Southeast Asian economies and their specialization in a limited range of manufacturing or resource-based activities mean that they are especially exposed to "countervailing external conditions," as suggested in hypothesis 4. That observation would seem to be even more plausible when we consider the region's historical exposure to a limited number of key markets and trade partners—North America, Western Europe, and now China. Southeast Asia is not unique in this regard, but sheer propinquity in China's case and an uncertain geopolitical environment make this an especially challenging set of circumstances.

But many Southeast Asian leaders have learned from the past and sought to insulate themselves from possible future crises and the vicissitudes of external economic forces. Two further points may be made here: first, even where meaningful reforms have occurred, they have done so under specific circumstances, and the sorts of institutionalized political and economic relationships that were synonymous with state-led developmentalism, "crony capitalism," authoritarianism, or simply "strong" government have not necessarily been swept away. On the contrary, in some places such as Vietnam, Laos, Cambodia, and recently rehabilitated Burma, they have barely begun. The point that emerges from the generally quite impressive recent economic performance in Southeast Asia is that given the overwhelming diversity of individual experiences and circumstances, the common denominator among them must be—at least to some extent—simply that they were in the right place at the right time. It is worth remembering that timing and contingency worked to both the advantage and the disadvantage of Southeast Asia in the run-up to the crisis in 1997–98. In good times, policy errors may not be so costly; in bad times, good policy may not make a decisive difference.

Thus far Southeast Asia has defied the sceptics. Overall economic performance has been surprisingly good, and the balance sheets of most of the region's economies look much healthier than they did in the aftermath of the Asian financial crisis. So far, so good, indeed. The question is this: Can it last? All things being equal, there are now plausible reasons to think that a number of the region's economies—Indonesia, Malaysia, perhaps Thailand—are on reasonably firm economic footing and may ultimately escape the middle-income trap. In the "real world," of course, things are rarely equal. As ever, the Southeast Asian economies are exposed to forces over which they have little control. The key issue here is the ongoing crisis in Europe, which still may get worse before it gets better. There already are worrying signs that the European crisis is indeed beginning to exert a malign influence in Asia.[79] The decisive factor is likely to be the resilience of China's economy and its capacity to act as a regional growth engine. But again, there also are worrying signs that China's economy may not be as strong as some had believed and that there may be limits to how much stimulus the Chinese government can apply this time around.[80]

In some ways, China is Southeast Asia writ large: its development is remarkable but remains dependent on key export markets that are currently subdued or in recession. If nothing else, the current crisis in Europe and the downturn in the United States will be a definitive test of the decoupling thesis. If the region can weather this storm and maintain recent growth levels, its success will represent something of a watershed in global economic history and an unambiguous indicator of just how much has changed in the global economic pecking order. The Southeast Asian countries discussed here may yet play a role in bringing this about and proving the sceptics—like me— completely wrong. I hope that they do.

Notes

1. Hugh Carnegy, "IMF Chief Warns over 1930s-Style Threats," *Financial Times*, December 15, 2011.

2. Mark Beeson, "Asymmetrical Regionalism: China, Southeast Asia, and Uneven Development," *East Asia*, vol. 27, no. 4 (December 2010), pp. 329–43.

3. To simplify an already complex discussion, "Southeast Asia" is taken to refer to the members of the Association of Southeast Asian Nations (ASEAN).

4. See William Case, *Politics in Southeast Asia: Democracy or Less* (London: Routledge Curzon, 2002).

5. Frank B. Tipton, "Southeast Asian Capitalism: History, Institutions, States, and Firms," *Asia Pacific Journal of Management*, vol. 26, no. 3 (September 2009), pp. 401–34; John T. Sidel, "Social Origins of Dictatorship and Democracy Revisited: Colonial State and Chinese Immigrant in the Making of Modern Southeast Asia," *Comparative Politics*, vol. 40, no. 2 (January 2008), pp. 122–47.

6. Mark Beeson, *Regionalism and Globalization in East Asia: Politics, Security, and Economic Development*, 2d ed. (London: Palgrave Macmillan, 2014).

7. Jomo Kwame Sundaram, "Southeast Asian Development in Comparative East Asian Perspective," in *Developmental States: Relevancy, Redundancy or Reconfiguration?*, edited by Linda Low (New York: Nova Science Publishers, 2004), pp. 57–77.

8. See, for example, Stephan Haggard, *The Political Economy of the Asian Financial Crisis* (Washington: Institute for International Economics, 2000).

9. Rodney B. Hall, "The Discursive Demolition of the Asian Development Model," *International Studies Quarterly*, vol. 47, no. 1 (March 2003), pp. 71–99.

10. Mark Beeson, "Crisis Dynamics and Regionalism: East Asia in Comparative Perspective," *Pacific Review*, vol. 24, no. 3 (July 2011), pp. 357–74.

11. William W. Grimes, *Currency and Contest in East Asia: The Great Power Politics of Financial Regionalism* (Cornell University Press, 2009).

12. John Ravenhill and Ralf Emmers, "The Asian and Global Financial Crisis: Consequences for East Asian Regionalism," *Contemporary Politics*, vol. 17, no. 2 (2011), pp. 133–49.

13. World Bank, "Navigating Turbulence, Sustaining Growth," *East Asia and Pacific Economic Update*, vol. 2 (Washington: World Bank, 2011), p. 90.

14. Shaun Breslin, "East Asia and the Global/Transatlantic/Western Crisis," *Contemporary Politics,* vol. 17, no. 2 (April 2011), pp. 109–17.

15. Bettina Wassener, "West's Economic Slump Catching Up with Asia," *Wall Street Journal,* November 23, 2011.

16. Ruchir Sharma, "China Has Its Own Debt Bomb," *Wall Street Journal,* February 25, 2013.

17. See Asian Development Bank (ADB), *Asia Economic Monitor* (Mandaluyong City, Philippines: December 2011), p. 53.

18. Geoff Dyer, "World Economy: The China Cycle," *Financial Times,* September 12, 2010.

19. Nicholas R. Lardy, "The Sustainability of China's Recovery from the Global Recession," Policy Brief PB10-7 (Washington: Peterson Institute for International Economics, 2010).

20. Asian Development Bank, "Asian Development Outlook 2011, Update: Preparing for Demographic Transition" (Mandaluyong City, Philippines: 2011).

21. Evelyn Goh, "Institutions and the Great Power Bargain in East Asia: ASEAN's Limited 'Brokerage' Role," *International Relations of the Asia-Pacific,* vol. 11, no. 3 (September 2011), pp. 373–401.

22. Gregory Chin and Richard Stubbs, "China, Regional Institution Building, and the China-ASEAN Free Trade Area," *Review of International Political Economy,* vol. 18, no. 3 (2011), pp. 277–98.

23. ADB, *Asia Economic Monitor,* p. 3.

24. Prema-Chandra Athukorala and Archanun Kohpaiboon, "Intra-Regional Trade in East Asia: The Decoupling Fallacy, Crisis, and Policy Challenges," Working Paper 177 (Tokyo: ADB Institute, 2009), p. 177.

25. Timothy J. Sturgeon and Gary Gereffi, "Measuring Success in the Global Economy: International Trade, Industrial Upgrading, and Business Function Outsourcing in Global Value Chains," *Transnational Corporations,* vol. 18, no. 2 (August 2009), pp. 1–35.

26. Prema-Chandra Athukorala, "Production Networks and Trade Patterns in East Asia: Regionalization or Globalization?," *Asian Economic Papers,* vol. 10, no. 1 (January 2011), pp. 65–95.

27. Mark Beeson and Shaun Breslin, "Regional and Global Forces in East Asia's Economic Engagement with International Society," paper for the workshop "International Society and East Asia: English School Theory at the Regional Level" (Shanghai: Fudan University, May 26–27, 2011).

28. Ben Bland and Robin Kwong, "Supply Chain Disruption: Sunken Ambitions," *Financial Times,* November 3, 2011.

29. Mark Beeson, "The Coming of Environmental Authoritarianism," *Environmental Politics,* vol. 19, no. 2 (March 2010), pp. 276–94.

30. Alex Frangos and Patrick McGroarty, "Troubles of West Take Toll on Emerging Economies," *Wall Street Journal,* October 14, 2011.

31. Anthony Deutsch, "Insecurity Troubles Indonesia's Middle Class," *Financial Times,* August 2, 2011.

32. Kathrin Hille, "China and the U.S.: Access Denied," *Financial Times,* April 7, 2011.

33.Vedi Hadiz, *Localising Power in Post-Authoritarian Indonesia: A Southeast Asia Perspective* (Stanford University Press, 2011).

34. E. Bellman and I. Sentana, "Foreign Investment Jumps in Indonesia," *Wall Street Journal,* April 23, 2012 (http://online.wsj.com/article/SB10001424052702303592404 577361672344559982.html#mod=djemITPA_t).

35. See Karen Brooks, "Is Indonesia Bound for the BRICS? How Stalling Reform Could Hold Jakarta Back," *Foreign Affairs,* vol. 90, no. 6 (November-December 2011), pp. 109–18.

36. Gudrun Ostby and others, "Population Pressure, Horizontal Inequality, and Political Violence: A Disaggregated Study of Indonesian Provinces, 1990–2003," *Journal of Development Studies,* vol. 47, no. 3 (March 2011), pp. 377–98.

37. Jürgen Rüland, "Deepening ASEAN Cooperation through Democratization? The Indonesian Legislature and Foreign Policymaking," *International Relations of the Asia-Pacific,* vol. 9, no. 3 (2009), pp. 373–402.

38. Dilip K. Das, *The Asian Economy: Spearheading the Recovery from the Global Financial Crisis* (London: Routledge, 2011).

39. World Bank, *East Asia and Pacific Economic Update: Navigating Turbulence, Sustaining Growth* (Washington: 2011), p. 29.

40. Morris Goldstein and Daniel Xie, "U.S. Credit Crisis and Spillovers to Asia," *Asian Economic Policy Review,* vol. 4, no. 2 (January 2009), pp. 204–22.

41. Paul D. Hutchcroft, *Booty Capitalism: The Politics of Banking in the Philippines* (Cornell University Press, 1998).

42. David Pilling, "'Reluctant' Philippine President Plays Down Challenges," *Financial Times,* April 4, 2011.

43. Sarah Mishkin, "Singapore Economy Shrinks in Fourth Quarter," *Financial Times,* January 3, 2012.

44. Adair Turner, *The Turner Review: A Regulatory Response to the Global Banking Crisis* (London: Financial Services Authority, 2009) (http:fsa.gov.uk/pages/Library/ Corporate/turner/index.shtml).

45. ADB, *Asia Economic Monitor,* p. 16.

46. Lena Rethel, "Financialisation and the Malaysian Political Economy," *Globalizations,* vol 7, no. 4 (January 2011), pp. 489–506.

47. ADB, *Asia Economic Monitor,* p. 11.

48. John Ravenhill, "Is China an Economic Threat to Southeast Asia?," *Asian Survey,* vol. 46, no. 5 (September-October 2006), pp. 653–74.

49. ADB, *Asia Economic Monitor,* p. 51.

50. Ibid., p. 53.

51. Ibid.

52. Ibid., p. 55.

53. Ibid., p. 53.

54. World Bank, *Doing Business* (2011) (http://doingbusiness.org/rankings).

55. Howard Dick, "Corruption in East Asia," in *The Routledge Handbook of Asian Regionalism*, edited by M. Beeson and R. Stubbs (London: Routledge, 2012), pp. 186–99.

56. Transparency International, *Corruption Perceptions Index* (Berlin: Transparency International, 2010).

57. Peter Alford, "Jakarta Party Graft 'Inevitable,'" *The Australian*, August 22, 2011; Hal Hill and Monica Wihardja, "Indonesia's Reform Reversal," *Wall Street Journal*, November 29, 2011.

58. Vedi Hadiz, "Decentralization and Democracy in Indonesia: A Critique of Neo-Institutionalist Perspectives," *Development and Change*, vol. 35, no. 4 (2004), pp. 697–718.

59. KPMG, *Global Infrastructure, Trend Monitor: Southeast Asian Transport Edition* (Singapore: 2009).

60. Anthony Deutsch, "Indonesian Boom Highlights Infrastructure Crisis," *Financial Times*, November 7, 2011.

61. "China Coming Down the Tracks," *The Economist*, January 22, 2011, pp. 33–34.

62. Philip Hirsch, "China and the Cascading Geopolitics of Lower Mekong Dams," *Asia-Pacific Journal*, vol. 9, no. 2 (May 2011).

63. Iwan J. Azis, "Food Crisis Looms as New Global Threat," *The Australian*, November 2, 2011.

64. Guanghua Wan and Iva Sebastian, "Poverty in Asia and the Pacific: An Update," ADB Economics Working Paper Series 267 (Mandaluyong City, Philippines: Asian Development Bank, 2011), p.10.

65. Asian Development Bank , *The Economics of Climate Change in Southeast Asia: A Regional Review* (Mandaluyong City, Philippines: 2009), p. 18.

66. Lorraine Elliott, "Regionalizing Environmental Security in Asia," in *The Routledge Handbook of Asian Regionalism,* edited by Beeson and Stubbs, pp. 300–12.

67. Christopher Jasparro and Jonathan Taylor, "Climate Change and Regional Vulnerability to Transnational Security Threats in Southeast Asia," *Geopolitics*, vol. 13, no. 2 (May 2008), pp. 232–56.

68. Amitav Acharya, *Whose Ideas Matter? Agency and Power in Asian Regionalism* (Cornell University Press, 2009).

69. David M. Jones and Michael L. R. Smith, "Making Process, Not Progress: ASEAN and the Evolving East Asian Regional Order," *International Security*, vol. 32, no. 1 (Summer 2007), pp. 148–84.

70. See Mark Beeson, "Living with Giants: ASEAN and the Evolution of Asian Regionalism," *TRaNS: Trans-Regional and -National Studies of Southeast Asia*, vol. 1, no. 2 (July 2013), pp. 303–22.

71. Mark Beeson and Y. Wang, "Irreconcilable Interests, Inadequate Institutions? Australia, China, and the U.S. in an Era of Interdependence," *Asian Survey*, vol. 54, no. 3 (2014), pp. 565–83.

72. Yoree Koh, "Asian Bloc Agrees to Counter China Heft," *Wall Street Journal*, September 30, 2011.

73. Joshua Kurlantzick, *Charm Offensive: How China's Soft Power Is Transforming the World* (Yale University Press, 2007).

74. Robert D. Kaplan, "The South China Sea Is the Future of Conflict," *Foreign Policy,* vol. 188 (September–October 2011), pp. 1–8; Mark Beeson and F. Li, *China's Regional Relations: Evolving Foreign Policy Dynamics* (Boulder, Colo.: Lynne Rienner, 2014).

75. "Tiger Traps," *The Economist,* November 17, 2011 (http://economist.com/node/21536964).

76. Chin and Stubbs, "China, Regional Institution-Building, and the China-ASEAN Free Trade Area."

77. Mark Beeson and Hung Hung Pham, "Developmentalism with Vietnamese Characteristics: The Persistence of State-Led Development in East Asia," *Journal of Contemporary Asia,* vol. 42, no. 4 (September 2012), pp. 539–59.

78. Stefan Halper, *The Beijing Consensus: How China's Authoritarian Model Will Dominate the Twenty-first Century* (New York: Basic Books, 2010).

79. Kathy Chu, "Asia Strains under Euro Crisis," *Wall Street Journal,* May 31, 2012.

80. Bob Davis and Tom Orlik, "Beijing's Growth Tools are Limited," *Wall Street Journal,* May 13, 2012.

ERIC HERSHBERG

6

The Global Financial Crisis
and Latin American Economies

Conventional wisdom concerning the economic turmoil that rever-berated from the United States during 2008 anticipated that the impact of the global financial crisis on emerging economies, including those in Latin America, would be highly negative, as had been the case during previous crises.[1] It turns out that the impact of this external shock varied in both degree and duration across different countries and subregions of Latin America. Several factors were responsible for the differences in outcomes, including domestic economic conditions at the onset of the crisis, the capac-ity and willingness of governments to deploy countercyclical policies, and the sectoral and geographic orientation of trade. Political and ideological factors further conditioned state responses to the crisis, and they remain highly rel-evant in explaining policy variation to this day. Now, five years since the onset of the crisis, it is fair to conclude that most Latin American economies held up surprisingly well. However, the diverse circumstances that enabled much of the region to weather the storm may call into question the capac-ity of Latin America to avoid contagion in the event of a new round of exter-nal shocks. In some countries, internal conditions that are in part the product of the government's response to the crisis may also undermine future economic performance, regardless of the global environment.

Research assistance for this chapter was provided by Sebastian Bitar and Marcela Torres Wong. I am grateful to the volume editors, Carol Wise, Leslie Elliott Armijo, and Saori Katada, and to Robert Blecker, Stephan Haggard, and Injoo Sohn for insightful comments on previous versions. Errors of omission or commission are the responsi-bility of the author.

This chapter explores these issues at the region-wide level, first outlining debates about Latin America's capacity to withstand external crises and examining the impact of the most recent shocks on growth rates and trade. It then examines policy responses that emerged beginning in late 2008, with particular attention given to the role played by countercyclical policies in the Andean countries, including Chile. (The crucial cases of Argentina, Brazil, and Mexico are analyzed in depth in separate chapters in this volume.) The relevance of political and ideological configurations in shaping government policy also are considered. The chapter concludes with an analysis of the Latin American experience in light of the four central hypotheses put forth by the editors in chapter 1 and with an assessment of the sustainability of Latin America's achievements in maintaining growth in a turbulent global environment.

Defying Predictions: All of Latin America Did Not Come Down with Pneumonia

Many seasoned observers anticipated that the emerging economies would suffer the fallout from the U.S. financial crisis more deeply than the advanced economies.[2] Pineda, Pérez-Caldentey, and Titelman argued in March 2009 that the crisis wrought by the bursting of the U.S. subprime mortgage bubble would have the same devastating economic effects on Latin American countries that previous financial crises had unleashed, and they predicted that the particular conditions of each country would not help to mitigate the overall effects of the crisis.[3]

As it turned out, however, the impact of the 2008–09 crisis was far greater and enduring in the advanced economies, while Latin American countries, particularly those in South America, experienced brief downturns and performed much better than in crises such as the 1982 debt shocks. The region did not confront the dramatic balance-of-payments adjustments and banking collapses that were typical in the past.[4] While the impressive growth rates of 2003–07 were abruptly interrupted during 2008 and 2009, by 2010 most of the region was once again growing rapidly. Table 6-1 presents 2007–12 annual growth rates for the region as a whole, with countries grouped by subregion to illustrate regional patterns analyzed later in this chapter.

A widely cited explanation for Latin America's ability to withstand the effects of global instability holds that its governments had learned the right (orthodox) lessons from previous crises and had made the adjustments nec-

Table 6-1. *Latin American Gross Domestic Product, by Subregion*
Percent annual growth

Subregion/country	2007	2008	2009[a]	2010	2011	2012
Latin America and the Caribbean	5.6	4.0	−1.9	6.0	4.3	3.2
South America (ten-country non-weighted average)	6.3	6.1	0.1	6.4	5.8	2.8
Argentina	8.7	6.8	0.9	9.2	8.9	2.0
Bolivia	4.6	6.1	3.4	4.1	5.2	5.0
Brazil	6.1	5.2	−0.3	7.5	2.7	1.6
Chile	4.6	3.7	−1.0	6.1	6.0	5.0
Colombia	6.9	3.5	1.7	4.0	5.9	4.5
Ecuador	2.0	7.2	0.4	3.6	7.8	4.5
Paraguay	5.4	6.4	−4.0	13.1	4.4	−2.0
Peru	8.9	9.8	0.9	8.8	6.9	5.9
Uruguay	6.5	7.2	2.4	8.9	5.7	3.5
Venezuela	8.8	5.3	−3.2	−1.5	4.2	5.0
Mexico and Central America (seven-country non-weighted average)	6.4	3.7	−1.3	4.0	4.7	4.6
Costa Rica	7.9	2.7	−1.0	4.7	4.2	5.0
El Salvador	3.8	1.3	−3.1	1.4	1.5	2.0
Guatemala	6.3	3.3	0.5	2.9	3.9	3.5
Honduras	6.2	4.2	−2.1	2.8	3.6	3.2
Mexico	3.4	1.2	−6.0	5.6	3.9	4.0
Nicaragua	5.0	2.9	−1.4	3.1	5.1	5.0
Panama	12.1	10.1	3.9	7.6	10.6	9.5

Source: ECLAC, *Economic Survey of Latin America and the Caribbean: Policies for an Adverse International Economy* (Santiago, Chile: 2012).

a. Figures for 2009 represent growth at the height of the crisis.

essary to minimize vulnerability to external shocks.[5] Those lessons included reducing inflation to single digits, lowering external debt, dismantling protectionism, maintaining fiscal and monetary discipline, and ensuring liquidity in international reserves and within private banks.[6] Financial variables often are portrayed as especially significant. A review of the extensive economics literature reveals a broad consensus on the importance of four major finance-related factors that helped mitigate the effects of the crisis across most of Latin America: greater exchange rate flexibility; high levels of liquidity; the deepening of domestic capital markets; and a sizable reduction in external debt.

It is noteworthy not only that absolute levels of public debt declined but also that the composition of the debt of Latin American countries shifted during the decade prior to the crisis. Whereas dollar-denominated debt represented about 40 percent of the total at the beginning of the decade, it accounted for less than 20 percent by 2008.[7] Undoubtedly, the significant reduction of public external debt gave governments greater leeway to stabilize private markets. Nonetheless, the declining burden of debt associated with "responsible policies" based on learning through previous mistakes is not an adequate explanation for the region's surprisingly rapid rebound. In contrast with Porzecanski and other scholars,[8] many observers concluded that in much of South America the reduction of external debt was due mainly to the booming terms of trade.[9] Moreover, the exploding demand for raw materials that became apparent in the new millennium, particularly by 2003, and skyrocketing prices for Latin American commodity exports relieved debt burdens even in those countries that had not adopted the orthodox playbook. That was the case in several Andean countries in particular, whereas Mexico—along with most Central American and Caribbean economies—suffered disproportionately despite having stuck closely to the prescriptions of the Washington Consensus.

The notion that sound economic policies would inoculate the region against the effects of crises in the advanced economies was compelling to many Latin American policymakers on the eve of the crisis. Mexican authorities, for example, were convinced that thanks to years of prudent macroeconomic management, the country had overcome its historic vulnerability to external shocks and would prove immune to a serious downturn in the United States.[10] Therefore, even when the U.S. Federal Reserve began easing interest rates rapidly in 2008, Mexican authorities persisted in the conviction that inflation was a greater risk than recession. As Gerardo Esquivel discusses in chapter 8, the Mexican Central Bank held interest rates steady until the harsh effects of the crisis were already resonating throughout the Mexican economy.[11]

While that confidence proved misplaced—table 6-1 shows that Mexico's GDP was flat in 2008, declined by more than 6.5 percent in 2009, and did not regain pre-crisis levels until late 2011—Latin America's prompt overall recovery from the crisis has led some observers to assert categorically that the region's economic fate has been decoupled from that of the United States and the developed economies more generally.[12] Three reasons are frequently cited for this supposed decoupling. The first is the aforementioned adoption of sound macroeconomic policies, a widespread but not universal development. The second and the third reasons—the diversification of trade partners and changes in the value of Latin American exports resulting from both their composition and commodity price trends—are closely intertwined. Together they have brought about improvements in Latin America's terms of trade.

The argument is that trade diversification and the thirst for commodities from China and rising economies elsewhere in Asia have led to a diminished role for the U.S. economy as a main destination for Latin American exports. By this account, Asia's demand for commodities and the manufacturing boom that it has triggered are the principal sources of growth in the world economy, and South America, with its specialization in primary commodities, has cashed in on the dramatic price increases stimulated by rapidly expanding Asian demand over the past decade.[13]

However, the evidence on decoupling from the U.S. economy for Latin America and the Caribbean as a whole is mixed. For example, there has been no significant decoupling of Mexico or most countries of Central America and the Caribbean, where regardless of the prudence of macroeconomic policies and despite a modest but real diversification of Central America's trade over the past two decades, conditions in the U.S. economy remain a crucial determinant of performance. For these countries, the United States is still the predominant destination for exports (nearly 80 percent in Mexico's case) and manufacturing remains more significant than commodities as a percentage of exports (Mexico, because of oil exports, is a partial exception). Moreover, remittances from migrants living in the United States are the key driver of domestic demand in this region, further exacerbating the potential impact of slowdowns in the United States. That was especially evident in 2009–11, when the collapse of the U.S. housing sector and the disappearance of the construction sector jobs upon which millions of immigrants depended led to a sharp decline in the volume of remittances. Interestingly, ECLAC data show that by 2012, when the free fall in construction and housing had subsided, remittances recovered to pre-crisis levels, perhaps contributing to a late but significant recovery in Mexico and parts of Central America.[14]

Developments since the onset of the crisis suggest that decoupling is more of a reality in the Southern Cone and Brazil, where both diversification of trade partners and improvements in the terms of trade are pronounced. The

Figure 6-1. *Latin American–U.S. Trade Dependency Index, 2000–09*

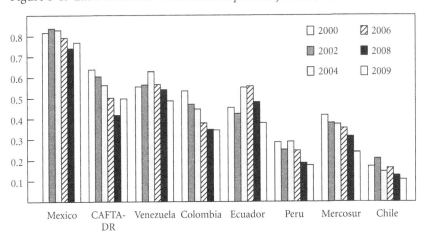

Source: Author's illustration based on data from U.S. Census Bureau, "U.S. Trade in Goods by Country: Argentina, Brazil, Bolivarian Rep. of Venezuela, Chile, Colombia, Costa Rica, Dominican Republic, Ecuador, El Salvador, Guatemala, Honduras, Mexico, Nicaragua, Paraguay, Peru, Uruguay" (www.census.gov/foreign-trade/balance/index.html [October 03, 2014]); and World Trade Organization, "Time Series on International Trade. Reporter: Argentina, Brazil, Bolivarian Rep. of Venezuela, Chile, Colombia, Costa Rica, Dominican Republic, Ecuador, El Salvador, Guatemala, Honduras, Mexico, Nicaragua, Paraguay, Peru, Uruguay. Partner: World" (http://stat.wto.org/StatisticalProgram/WSDBStatProgramHome.aspx?Language=E [October 3, 2014]).

same can be said for most of the Andean countries, with the exception of Venezuela, which is virtually entirely dependent on petroleum exports and where the share of those exports going to the United States has remained at more than 50 percent for the past 20 years.

Bitar and Hershberg have developed a trade dependency index (see figure 6-1) illustrating the degree of intraregional variation in trade dependency on the U.S. market. The index is based on trade with the United States as a percentage of a country's total trade in a given year. As shown in the figure, some countries in Latin America are still extremely dependent on trade with the United States. Both Mexico and the countries belonging to the Dominican Republic–Central America–United States Free Trade Agreement (CAFTA-DR) have diversified their trade modestly, but at the end of the decade all of them still depended on the U.S. market for 60 to 80 percent of their commerce. Several Andean countries—Venezuela, Colombia, and Ecuador—score around 50 percent, although their petroleum exports explain a good part of their reliance on the U.S. market. At the other end of

Figure 6-2. *Destination of Latin American Exports*

Billions of U.S. dollars

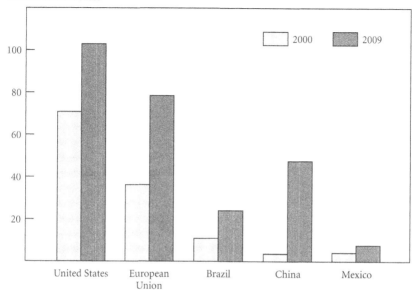

Source: World Trade Organization, "Time Series on International Trade. Reporter: South and Central American Exports (Merchandise). Partner: Brazil, European Union, United States, China, Mexico" (http://stat.wto.org/StatisticalProgram/WSDBStatProgramHome.aspx?Language=E [October 3, 2014]).

the spectrum are the Mercosur countries (Argentina, Brazil, Paraguay, and Uruguay, minus Venezuela), along with Peru and Chile, which during the last decade have further diversified their export destinations and largely overcome any preexisting dependence on the United States.

Latin America as a whole still relies on the United States more than any other single market as an outlet for its products, but as depicted in figure 6-2, export diversification to Europe and Asia has been a prominent feature of the economic landscape in recent years. From 2000 to 2009, the value of China's imports from Latin America quintupled, while the value of U.S. imports from Latin America grew by only a modest 10 percent. The impact of Chinese growth on South America is clear. As a destination for exports, the commodity-thirsty Chinese economy has triggered a reconfiguration of Latin America's extraregional ties.[15] China is also a growing source of foreign investment in the region. ECLAC data show a jump in Chinese investment from US$15.3 billion in 2010 to US$22.7 billion in 2011.

Figure 6-3. *South American Exports to China*

Billions of U.S. dollars

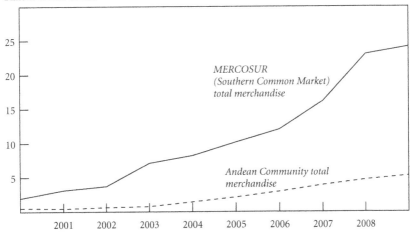

Source: World Trade Organization, "Time Series on International Trade: Selected Regional Integration Units, Andean Community Merchandise Exports, MERCOSUR Exports. Partner: Brazil, European Union, United States, China, Mexico" (http://stat.wto.org/StatisticalProgram/WSDBStatProgramHome.aspx?Language=E [October 3, 2014])

As shown in figure 6-3, however, the Chinese market is not growing in importance at the same pace for all of Latin America. That is not surprising when nearly 90 percent of Chinese imports from Latin America consist of agricultural and mining products.[16] China is now a major destination for exports from Mercosur, but exports to China from the Andean Community[17] are growing more slowly and exports from Central America and Mexico are negligible. Brazil's exports to China, which amounted to 8 percent of total exports in 2008, more than doubled to 17 percent in 2011. While Mercosur's exports to China boomed over the past decade, the increase in trade with China has been much less pronounced for the Andean Community. Peru is the exception. China has invested heavily in Peruvian mining and is a growing source of demand for fishmeal, which is used for feeding livestock.

At the other extreme, the Central American countries rely almost exclusively on exports to the U.S market. The rolling implementation of CAFTA-DR since 2006 has deepened the long-standing pattern of Central American economic dependence on the United States and left these countries with little surplus to sell in alternative export markets (see figure 6-4). Tellingly,

Figure 6-4. *Central American Exports, by Destination*

Billions of U.S. dollars

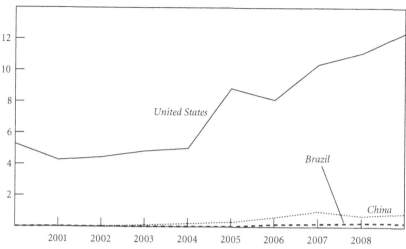

UN Comtrade Database, "Beta Data Extraction Interface. Reporter: Costa Rica, El Salvador, Guatemala, Honduras, Nicaragua, Panama. Partner: Brazil, China, U.S." (http://comtrade.un.org/data/ [October 3, 2014]).

Central American imports of Chinese manufactured goods have experienced a modest downward trend since the middle of the last decade. Although recently elected government officials associated with the leftist "pink tide" in El Salvador, Nicaragua, and for a time Honduras have denounced the agreement while campaigning for office, they have made no efforts to actually revise or exit CAFTA-DR once in office.[18] Reliance on the U.S. market, coupled with high levels of dependency on migrant remittances, helps to account for the especially sharp and comparatively protracted impact of the global financial crisis in much of Central America.

While Asia's growing importance to Latin America is evident, it should not be exaggerated. It is true that the proportion of Latin American exports to Asia increased over 2000–09, from 13 percent to 21 percent for Argentina, 33 percent to 41 percent for Chile, and 20 percent to 26 percent for Peru. In the case of Bolivia, the numbers are impressive: from 2 percent to more than 14 percent.[19] But for Brazil and Colombia, the percentage has remained steady (granted, it is a percentage of a higher overall volume of trade), and for Uruguay, Venezuela, and Ecuador the percentage has actually declined—dramatically in the case of Ecuador.

Table 6-2. *Total Exports for ALADI Members, 2008–09*
Monthly averages, in millions of U.S. dollars

	Exports			
Country	July–September 2008 (1)	January–March 2009 (2)	July–September 2009 (3)	Rate variation (3) / (1)
Argentina	7,123	3,954	4,626	−35.1
Bolivia	638	386	488	−23.6
Brazil	20,072	10,392	13,944	−30.5
Chile	6,199	3,505	4,382	−29.3
Colombia	3,403	2,504	2,789	−18.0
Ecuador	1,892	958	1,355	−28.4
Mexico	26,272	16,763	19,474	−25.9
Paraguay	412	287	258	−37.5
Peru	2,778	1,646	2,236	−19.5
Uruguay	546	360	464	−15.0
Venezuela	11,146	3,382	5,681	−49.0
ALADI	80,482	44,138	55,696	−30.8

Source: Asociación Latinoamericana de Integración [Latin American Association of Integration], "Los Efectos de la Crisis Económica Internacional en el Comercio Exterior de la ALADI [Effects of the International Economic Crisis on the Foreign Trade of ALADI]," Cuarto informe [Fourth report], December 3, 2009 (www.aladi.org/nsfaladi/estudios.nsf/438f22281c05235303256 848005ea465/58a2a3e810fa4c200325768f00650afd/$FILE/2218_3.pdf).

The most recent INTAL data for several Andean countries suggest that an equally important source of diversification since the early 1990s is intraregional trade: the percentage of total trade involving Latin American counterparts increased between 1992 and 2007 from 40 percent to 62 percent in Bolivia; 27 percent to 36 percent in Colombia; 19 percent to 33 percent in Ecuador; and 18 percent to 23 percent in Venezuela (the numbers for Brazil, Chile, and Peru are roughly unchanged).[20] However, the hypothesis that intraregional trade helped to cushion the impact of the crisis is not strongly supported by the performance of intraregional exports during the crisis. For the 11 countries of ALADI, a regional trade association encompassing all of the major economies in Latin America, trade within the region followed a trajectory similar to (albeit slightly less pronounced than) that of trade outside the region.

The data presented in table 6-2 and figure 6-5 leave little doubt that the extent to which Latin America has decoupled from the economic fortunes of the United States should not be exaggerated. Although a full-blown

Figure 6-5. *ALADI: Average Monthly Intraregional Trade Figures,*
January 2007–September 2009

Billions of U.S. dollars

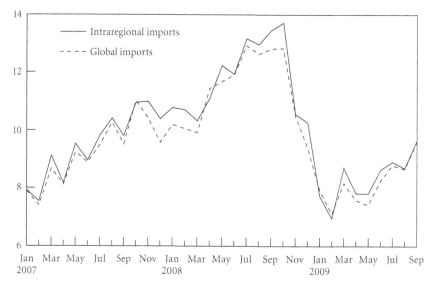

Source: Asociación Latinoamericana de Integración [Latin American Association of Integra-
tion], "Los Efectos de la Crisis Económica Internacional en el Comercio Exterior de la ALADI
[Effects of the International Economic Crisis on the Foreign Trade of ALADI]," Cuarto informe
[Fourth report], December 3, 2009 (www.aladi.org/nsfaladi/estudios.nsf/438f22281c05235303256
848005ea465/58a2a3e810fa4c200325768f00650afd/$FILE/2218_3.pdf).

depression was averted in the United States, the global financial crisis still
had strong negative consequences for Latin America. For example, in all
11 countries of ALADI, the value of exports fell by more than half between
the summer of 2008 and the first quarter of 2009.[21] Less dramatic declines
were experienced in output, employment, incomes, and wealth, although
again, they were comparatively modest and brief in South America.

The degree to which repercussions from the global financial crisis varied
across subregions of Latin America is evident when the depth and duration
of declines in pre-2008 rates of economic growth are examined. The extent
of the divide across regions of Latin America is depicted in table 6-1. South
America fared better than Mexico and Central America, yet for Latin America as a whole the crisis turned out to be the worst regional recession since
the debt crisis of the 1980s, with annual growth rates declining to 0.6 percent during 2008–10.[22] Contagion was extremely pronounced in the core

countries of Central America (excepting Panama and Costa Rica) and in Mexico, where GDP declined by nearly 7 percent in 2009.[23] For South America, with the exception of Venezuela, the impact of the crisis was far weaker than in Central America or Mexico. Decoupling is a reality, but one that holds up quite unevenly across the region.

Divergent Policy Responses

ECLAC has published detailed and fairly comprehensive accounts of the policy measures taken in response to the crisis by governments throughout Latin America and the Caribbean. Drawing on those accounts, Ocampo has differentiated Latin American countries according to which responded to the crisis by adopting full countercyclical measures; which sustained pre-crisis levels of rapid growth and spending; and which adopted procyclical policies.[24] His depiction of the regional landscape during the immediate aftermath of the crisis is presented in table 6-3. To a large extent, although with the significant exceptions noted below, subsequent policy initiatives have not altered the overall picture presented by Ocampo, perhaps because the underlying political economy has remained stable within most countries.

Four factors stand out in table 6-3. First, all of the countries that Ocampo labeled in 2010 as engaging in countercyclical policies had followed the orthodox playbook prior to the crisis. In that respect, the evidence provides support for the contention in much of the literature—and in chapter 1 of this volume—that lessons learned in the past created the fiscal space required for governments to respond proactively to an externally induced downturn. Second, however, a number of countries that had engaged in profligate spending prior to the crisis—and thus do not fit the description of faithful adherents to Washington Consensus prescriptions—continued to do so as the crisis unfolded. Argentina and Venezuela in particular stand out, underscoring the degree to which political and ideological factors have significant policy consequences.

Indeed, it could be argued that "policy learning" in those two countries, following a period of slow growth prior to the commodity boom, led governments to follow precisely the policies that orthodox economists had rejected as no longer viable. Whether the classic macroeconomic populism practiced by the Chávez and Maduro governments in Venezuela and the successive Kirchner administrations in Argentina proves sustainable remains to be seen, and there are plenty of reasons to be skeptical.[25] It is revealing that

Table 6-3. *Characterization of Fiscal Spending*
Percent annual real growth, primary spending

Characterization	2004–08	2009
Countercyclical		
Chile	5.3	14.8
El Salvador	1.8	9.1
Guatemala	1.8	6.4
Paraguay	1.9	28.7
Peru	7.3	12.7
Uruguay	7.8	7.4
Persistent rapid growth of spending		
Argentina	12.1	19.7
Colombia	7.7	10.9
Costa Rica	7.4	12.8
Procyclical		
Bolivia	10.2	−0.8
Brasil	7.7	3.0
Dominican Republic	11.6	−13.3
Ecuador	18.2	5.6
Honduras	7.8	3.5
Mexico	6.7	−4.7
Nicaragua	6.8	−1.1
Panama	11.2	4.2
Venezuela	12.0	−1.0
Average for Latin America	8.1	6.6

Source: Estimates based on ECLAC data in José Antonio Ocampo, "How Well Has Latin America Fared during the Global Financial Crisis?," Iniciativa para la Transparencia Financiera [Initiative for Financial Transparency Series] 56 (2010).

these are the two Latin American countries that have experienced double-digit inflation rates and serious currency devaluations throughout the post-crisis period. Nonetheless, the data on economic growth presented in table 6-1 establish clearly that they succeeded, at least temporarily, in overcoming the consequences of the Great Recession.

The third observation that emerges from revisiting Ocampo's 2010 categorization concerns the critical cases of Brazil and Mexico, analyzed separately in this volume. As chapter 7 makes clear, Brazil did in fact pursue countercyclical policies, contrary to Ocampo's account, and did so aggressively, albeit to uncertain effect. The government's efforts to accelerate growth focused largely on lowering interest rates and loosening credit, but ambitious fiscal measures have been taken as well. Indeed, by early 2013 no fewer than eight separate stimulus packages had been implemented by successive Brazilian administrations in an effort to boost lagging industrial production. The government's granting of tax breaks, state subsidies, easy credit, and even trade barriers signals a decidedly interventionist inclination on the part of the ruling Workers' Party (PT).

Mexico, by contrast, achieved a delayed yet pronounced recovery despite having eschewed the interventionist policies adopted by Brazil and much of the rest of South America. Mexican policymakers had followed highly orthodox policies prior to the crisis and, unlike their counterparts in most South American countries, refrained from enacting countercyclical policies until the crisis was well under way. Even then, the scale of the intervention was modest, reflecting continuity in preferences for limited state interference. Statements by newly elected president Enrique Peña Nieto have signaled interest in emulating Brazil's practice of relying on the National Development Bank (BNDES) to boost investment-fueled growth.[26] Although by mid-2014 that had not yet resulted in tangible measures, it is ironic that such a shift in thinking in Mexico City surfaces at a moment when conventional wisdom in some quarters holds that statist Brazil is lagging behind free market Mexico.

The evidence suggests that until now ideological contrasts in Latin America's two largest economies have invoked very different responses to the crisis, but the combination of Brazil's tepid recovery and Mexico's return to Institutional Revolutionary Party (PRI) rule in 2012 may portend a gradual and unforeseen convergence in the economic policies of both countries. At any rate, there is some evidence that the fiscal stimuli implemented mainly in the South American countries were relatively ineffective in stimulating investment. A 2012 study finds that loosening monetary policy (by cutting interest rates) and channeling credits into the economy via development banks had a countercyclical impact in Latin America but that fiscal policies mattered much less.[27] Finally, with regard to the three Andean cases that Ocampo categorized as of 2012 as procyclical—Bolivia, Ecuador, and Venezuela—the cutback in expenditures that immediately followed the crisis must be placed in the proper context. Dramatically high levels of expansion in spending prior to the crisis constrained Bolivia and Venezuela from immediately boosting expenditures further, and Ecuador pursued continued expansion at a rate considerably slower than before. Yet in all three countries, as in Argentina, governments committed to high growth and redistribution neither entered nor emerged from the crisis with an inclination toward orthodoxy. The ideological predilections of ruling coalitions and their social bases of support go a long way toward explaining policy responses that diverge from the countercyclical trajectories that emerged elsewhere in 2008–10.

There is evidence that the countries that entered the crisis from a position of macroeconomic strength enjoyed broad latitude to respond proactively regardless of the ideological predilections of policymakers and political leaders, although the latter influenced both the nature and speed of responses. The crisis affected all of the Andean countries, but to differing degrees, and policy responses varied considerably. Chile, Ecuador, and Peru experienced a steep drop in export earnings between the last quarter of 2008 and the first quarter of 2009. Chile and Peru also experienced heavy reversals in capital flows during the last quarter of 2008. Despite being hit by those exogenous shocks, neither Chile nor Peru experienced a major financial crisis or a deceleration in economic growth that was worse than what each had already experienced.[28] The same can be said of Colombia. Having pursued highly orthodox macroeconomic policies for extended periods prior to the crisis, all three countries had considerable room to implement countercyclical monetary policies and—in the case of Chile though less so in Colombia and Peru—countercyclical fiscal and social policies.

Bolivia's earnings also were adversely affected by the downturn, but because monetary policy had been loose previously, there was little leeway for a countercyclical policy response. Efforts to counter the crisis instead focused on increases in social expenditures. As for Venezuela and Ecuador, neither country had much room to pursue countercyclical policies. Venezuela was the region's worst performer in terms of growth rate between 2008 and 2010, and its recovery lagged behind that of the other countries despite high oil prices. The Chávez government had failed to maintain macroeconomic equilibrium, with a growing fiscal deficit and an inflation rate exceeded only by those of Argentina.

In Ecuador, dollarization had eliminated the possibility of resorting to exchange rate or monetary policies, and high levels of public debt precluded taking anything more than symbolic fiscal and social policy measures in response to the crisis. But while Ecuador responded to the crisis prudently by lowering tariffs, it also imposed a series of nontariff barriers, including quotas and other World Trade Organization–sanctioned measures, that protected domestic producers and diminished imports by more than 50 percent.[29] With the return of economic growth and significant increases in both income tax collection and royalty rates on petroleum extraction and anticipated mining activities, Ecuador's leftist government has been making up for lost time. By the beginning of 2012, public spending was double the level of 2006, when President Rafael Correa came to office, with the bulk of expenditures allocated to poverty reduction measures (including conditional cash transfers, universal minimum pensions, and housing and energy subsidies). This highly unorthodox approach to economic management not only enabled Ecuador to achieve high growth rates but also provided a foundation for Correa's overwhelming reelection in February 2013.

Long before the crisis, Chile, Colombia, and Peru had adopted flexible exchange rates, which permitted the economy to absorb external shocks without the need to adjust fixed exchange rates, a slow and costly process. During the crisis, Chile and Colombia allowed their currency to increase in value by as much as 50 percent from March 2008 to March 2009, while Peru allowed its currency to increase by 20 percent. In Ecuador, a country where dollarization meant that there was no exchange rate flexibility, official international reserves shrank by 70 percent from March 2008 to May 2009.[30]

Chile, Colombia, and Peru demonstrated the capacity to undertake countercyclical monetary policies.[31] Indeed, a high level of liquidity made it possible for these and most other South American countries to adopt such monetary policies during the crisis (that was also the case in Mexico, although there the adjustment was too little and too late to achieve a rapid rebound). For those policies to be viable, three levels of liquidity were critical: international reserves at the central bank, liquidity of financial intermediaries, and a manageable public debt in terms of average maturity rates and currency composition.[32] For that reason, among the Andean countries, Chile, Colombia, and Peru, unlike Ecuador, were able to adopt a monetary policy that enabled them to avoid the initial spike in interest rates that was characteristic of previous crises.[33] They were able to undertake measures that Ecuador could not, which encompassed both the financial sector—including changes in mandatory bank reserves and provision of liquidity in local currency—and support for the housing market and small enterprises.[34]

Political Correlates of Policy Responses

Policy responses to the crisis were not solely a function of the economic room for maneuver afforded by pre-crisis conditions or of countries' relative exposure to disruptions in trade. Those factors were important, but a comparative look at the measures taken to stimulate growth and insulate citizens from the impact of the downturn highlights the significance of political and ideological considerations in shaping government action. Administrations associated with the political left invariably pursued fiscal stimuli to the extent that they could, and they were more likely to emphasize support for consumption than to rely disproportionately on tax cuts. By contrast, conservative administrations resisted increasing expenditures and were inclined to channel new spending through the private sector. Public debates over the proper course to follow in response to the crisis frequently revealed sharp divisions along ideological lines.

For example, Chile's center-left Concertación government sought to stimulate the economy through a combination of lower taxes and expanded subsidies for both production and consumption. By contrast, Peru, under the more moderate presidency of Alan García, focused stimulus measures almost exclusively on the tax cuts favored by the business sector. And while there was a general technocratic consensus in the rightist government of Colombia about the appropriateness of countercyclical policies, some economists cautioned about the long-term sustainability of the expenditure side of the country's stimulus.[35] In fact, warnings about runaway government spending echoed a line taken by orthodox economists during the country's fiscal battles of the previous decade.[36]

In Chile, the Concertación government's 2009 fiscal stimulus plan consisted of a mix of tax reductions and increased expenditures totaling around 2.8 percent of GDP. The goal was to promote both investment and consumption, ease access to credit, and boost employment.[37] Chile's plan was a classic example of aggressive countercyclical policies made possible by cautious economic management during periods of prosperity. Yet the measures were not uncontested. While in November 2008 Finance Minister Andrés Velasco argued that the best way to deal with the crisis was to apply a strong countercyclical fiscal policy by expanding public spending, Sebastián Piñera, a prominent business leader and Chile's future president, argued for continued austerity, limiting the stimulus to lowering of the value-added tax, as favored by the private sector. Economist Hernán Büchi, who had served as secretary of the treasury in the 1980s during the military dictatorship, bolstered the position that increased spending was not the preferred option. However, Velasco stood firm, arguing vociferously that the absence of public debt afforded room to apply countercyclical fiscal policies.[38] A skeptical business sector was unable to derail the policies espoused by a progressive administration that had been afforded considerable latitude by the careful macroeconomic management of its predecessors.

In Peru, in December 2008 President García announced plans to increase public expenditures by approximately 2.5 percent of GDP in order to maintain economic growth and sustain employment during the crisis. Roughly half of Peru's stimulus package consisted of support for the construction industry, exporters, and small and medium-size enterprises, with the remainder directed largely toward accelerated public investment. Here, as in Chile, prudent macroeconomic management had created space for aggressive countercyclical measures. But unlike Chile's stimulus package, García's package directed only about 5 percent of the new expenditures to social policies and consumption. Moreover, critics in Peru questioned whether the stimulus was in fact a countercyclical policy at all. Peruvian economist Silvio Rendón, noting that the administration's initial budget for 2009 contemplated lower expenditures than that of the previous year, contended that the government was simply using unspent money from the 2008 budget to pad the numbers for 2009.[39] Additional criticism pointed to the program's reliance on public investment in large construction contracts favored by private sector boosters of the government rather than on programs to subsidize consumption, which were typically favored in neighboring countries.[40]

The ways in which ideology and political alliances weighed on policy choices are further evident in the Peruvian government's delay in loosening monetary policy despite having plenty of room to do so. Whereas Chile reduced interest rates quickly as the crisis unfolded in an effort to promote demand, Peru held back, with policymakers openly fretting about inflation risks. The result, according to Peruvian economist Bertrand Delgado, was a far sharper decline in 2009 GDP growth rates in Peru (8.9 percentage points) than in Chile (4.7 percentage points).[41]

Unlike in Chile, in Peru both conservative journalists and the major business associations supported García's package although they insisted that it be coordinated with the private sector. The country's principal labor union, by contrast, was not satisfied with the government's response. The Confederación General de Trabajadores del Perú (General Confederation of Workers of Peru) presented a plan of its own, centered on increasing the minimum wage and cash transfer programs for the poorest, investing in job-creating public works, and bolstering spending on credit for microenterprises.[42] The union proposal gained little traction, however, and was largely ignored by the administration. In contrast to the process in Chile, where legislative action was needed to ratify the Concertación's fiscal stimulus, in Peru the executive was able to bypass the congress and introduce its plan by legislative decree.

Conclusions and the Sustainability of Success

This review of Latin America's timely rebound from the global financial crisis and of how the rebound evolved differently across the region suggests a number of conclusions about the basis of policy responses by governments in the Andes and elsewhere. These conclusions speak directly to several core hypotheses presented in chapter 1 and analyzed over the course of the volume. First, the Latin American experience lends partial support to the hypothesis that macroeconomic reforms originating in policies learned from previous crises afforded governments greater latitude in mitigating the impact of the global financial crisis. The degree to which Latin American countries had pursued an orthodox path prior to the crisis did indeed hinge in large measure on policymakers having learned the "right" macropruden-tial lessons from previous crises. That holds regardless of the characteristics of key political institutions and processes and the sociopolitical coalitions underpinning governments. It is equally clear in the highly institutional-ized party system in Chile and in Peru's "democracy without parties"[43] and in governments on the right as well as those on the left of the ideological spectrum.

However, the extent to which countries had implemented the "right" macroeconomic, financial, and financial sector reforms was a product not only of lessons learned but also of enabling political conditions. In Latin American countries where economic expertise had consistently been in place in relatively autonomous and stable policymaking institutions, the lessons applied were orthodox and the state enjoyed fiscal latitude to respond to the crisis countercyclically if it chose to do so. Among the Andean cases depicted in table 6-3, those countries included Chile, Peru, and to a lesser extent Colombia.

By contrast, the cases of Venezuela, Argentina, and Ecuador, in particu-lar, highlight the degree to which orthodoxy was less relevant and long-standing political structures had weakened or broken down.[44] Arguably, policy learning had taken place in these countries as well, but the lessons that governments derived—wisely or not—were quite distinct from those espoused by the Washington Consensus. Where economic authorities were not insulated from short-term pressures from spendthrift legislatures and executives, there was less space to adopt countercyclical measures when the need arose. In the Andean bloc, that was the case in Bolivia, Venezuela, and Ecuador, although in all three countries spending continued to expand rapidly once the immediate crisis had passed.

This chapter also supports the hypothesis in chapter 1 regarding the potentially beneficial impact of trade diversification. In particular, Latin American countries that had increased commodity exports to China and come to rely less on trade with the United States rebounded more quickly and more fully than those that remained overwhelmingly connected to the U.S. economy. Trade diversification provides much of the explanation for the favorable experience of South America relative to that of Central America and Mexico. However, their divergence was magnified by Mexico's persistence in adhering to an orthodox strategy; South American countries were more likely to loosen both monetary and fiscal policies in response to the crisis.

Moreover, this chapter concludes that the extent to which governments pushed the full range of countercyclical measures advocated by influential experts like Ocampo—that is, how far their efforts to stimulate the economy went beyond the usual tweaking of fiscal and monetary policy—was also a reflection of the sociopolitical coalitions in power. This conclusion holds in large as well as small countries and across subregions of Latin America. To cite but a handful of examples, Brazil, Chile, and El Salvador, which represent progressive governments, contrast with, respectively, Mexico, Peru, and Panama, which represent conservative governments. Indeed, the presence of the left in office is strongly associated with governments responding countercyclically, as in Chile (with the Concertación government) and Uruguay (governed by the left-leaning Frente Amplio), and helps to explain the less likely cases of El Salvador (Mauricio Funes had just been elected) and Paraguay (under Fernando Lugo). Conversely, countries such as Panama, Mexico, and Honduras, with conservative governments in office, were more apt to respond procyclically even if they had the latitude to do otherwise.

In other words, fiscal capacity mattered, but not only in the sense suggested by Ocampo and others. Whereas most analyses emphasize the importance of government spending prior to the crisis—the idea being that comparatively profligate governments had less space to implement countercyclical policies when the crisis hit—evidence suggests that government capacity to secure revenues through taxation was at least as important. Where sociopolitical alliances had blocked states from increasing tax rates to the extent expected given the country's level of development—most notably in Mexico and Central America, where for the most part tax revenues languished below 20 percent of GDP—there was diminished space for meaningful countercyclical policies. That was true even in countries such as El Salvador, where a progressive administration would have intervened more aggressively had the tax base permitted.[45] Conversely, where tax revenues had risen, either modestly (Chile) or substantially (Colombia), policymakers in relatively orthodox governments were able to respond actively to the crisis. Here the issue is not whether governments had adhered to the orthodox playbook but whether they had both the inclination and the political latitude to secure the revenues necessary to react countercyclically.

This chapter documents how the timely rebound in Latin America applies primarily to South America, despite the fact that Mexico did reasonably well from 2011 to 2013, on the heels of a sharp and comparatively prolonged decline preceded by two decades of substandard performance. However, the jury is still out as far as the sustainability of the South American rebound is concerned. Most notable in this regard is Brazil, where growth has slowed dramatically and repeated stimulus initiatives under President Dilma Roussef have not succeeded in arresting the stubborn decline in industrial production. Moreover, the Andean economies have largely failed to diversify beyond commodity exports, and populist experiments in Argentina and Venezuela have triggered alarming macroeconomic imbalances.

China's voracious demand for South America's commodities accounts for a big part of the rapid and initially impressive rebound in South America, but growing doubt about whether China can sustain its own high growth rate raises the question of whether it can continue to drive South American dynamism and thereby offset slowing demand for South American exports from other trade partners. Some observers insist that the demand for and therefore prices of primary commodities exported by South American countries will remain high for the foreseeable future, but Shaun Breslin's contribution to this volume indicates that it is by no means a sure bet. The repercussions of a Chinese slowdown could be mitigated by the fact that agricultural goods accounted for a third to nearly half of all Latin American exports to China between 2008 and 2011.[46] Therefore, Chinese demand for Latin American exports is likely to continue even if the pace of industrial growth wanes.[47] Meanwhile, as European economies continue to languish even as the worst of the euro crisis has ebbed, its adverse impact is readily evident in Latin America, far beyond the Eurozone. The prospect of a renewed contraction in the United States is not out of the question given persistent European stagnation and the inability of the U.S. executive and legislative branches to agree on the basic features of sound fiscal policy. That could have severe implications for all of Latin America. Even though this chapter emphasizes the partial decoupling of South American economies from that of the United States, the recent crisis has made clear that they are by no means immune to developments in the United States. The consequences would be all the more severe if another U.S. recession coincided with a slowdown in Chinese growth.

Seen in this light, Latin America was especially fortunate to have confronted the most recent crisis at a moment when much of the region had been thriving due to the China-driven commodity boom. That lends strong support to this volume's hypothesis regarding the importance of countervailing external conditions—variables that have little to do with whether countries have learned the right lessons, followed the right policies, or constructed particular sorts of domestic political alliances.

Domestic conditions in Latin American countries also will test the region's capacity to sustain the successes of recent years. A decade of impressive growth has created high expectations among citizens of many countries, and governments will be held accountable by electorates that expect them to deliver the goods and deepen advances in the provision of state benefits and services, not to mention reduce the region's long-standing problem of income inequality. In many countries incumbents will be tempted to open the fiscal spigot in advance of key elections, as seen in the run-up to balloting in Argentina, Venezuela, and Ecuador over the past two years. It is entirely plausible that the costs of the political business cycle will impede governments from responding as effectively to the next crisis as they did to the most recent one. There will undoubtedly be occasion to find out, for just as it is human nature to assume that "this time things will be different"— and quite a few politicians wish that to be true—Latin America remains exposed to trends in the global economy. As history shows, those trends are not linear.

Notes

1. Stijn Claessens, M. Ayhan Kose, and Marco E. Terrones, "Recessions and Financial Disruptions in Emerging Markets: A Bird's Eye View," *Journal Economía Chilena*, vol. 13 (2010), pp. 55–84.

2. Ibid.

3. Ramón Pineda, Esteban Pérez-Caldentey, and Daniel Titelman, *The Current Financial Crisis: Old Wine in New Goatskins or Is This Time Different for Latin America?* (Santiago, Chile: ECLAC, 2009).

4. José Antonio Ocampo, "How Well Has Latin America Fared during the Global Financial Crisis?," Iniciativa para la Transparencia Financiera [Initiative for Financial Transparency Series] 56 (2010), p. 1.

5. Arturo C. Porzecanski, *Latin America: The Missing Financial Crisis,* Studies and Perspectives Series 6 (Washington: ECLAC, 2009); Rodrigo Botero and Domingo Cavallo, "The Dog That Didn't Bark: Latin America's Recent Economic Performance in Perspective," *Harvard Business Review* (Summer 2010).

6. Botero and Cavallo, "The Dog That Didn't Bark," p. 16.

7. Porzecanski, *Latin America,* p. 21.

8. Porzecanski, *Latin America*; Botero and Cavallo, "The Dog That Didn't Bark."

9. Ocampo, "How Well Has Latin America Fared during the Global Financial Crisis?"; Eric Hershberg, "Latin America's Left: The Impact of the External Environment," in *Latin America's Left Turns: Politics, Policies, and Trajectories of Change,* edited by Eric Hershberg and Maxwell A. Cameron (Boulder, Colo.: Lynne Rienner, 2010).

10. Gerardo Esquivel, "Mexico: Large, Immediate Negative Impact and Weak Medium-Term Growth Prospects," in *The Great Recession and Developing Countries: Economic Impact and Growth Prospects,* edited by Mustapha K. Nabli (Washington: World Bank, 2010).

11. Ibid., pp. 369–71; see also chapter 8 in this volume.

12. Marcelo Giugale and Otaviano Canuto, *The Day after Tomorrow: A Handbook on the Future of Economic Policy in the Developing World* (Washington: World Bank, 2010).

13. Ibid.

14. ECLAC, *Economic Survey of Latin America and the Caribbean: Policies for an Adverse International Economy* (Santiago, Chile: 2012).

15. ECLAC, *Economic Survey of Latin America and the Caribbean: The Distributive Impact of Public Policies* (Santiago, Chile: 2010).

16. Uri Dadish and Shimelse Ali, "China's Rise and Latin America: A Global, Long-Term Perspective" (Washington: Carnegie Endowment for International Peace, 2012).

17. Defined to include Bolivia, Colombia, Ecuador, Peru, and Venezuela. Venezuela is classified as an Andean economy even though Hugo Chávez opted to suspend Venezuela's participation in the Andean Community following a political rift with Colombia.

18. Hershberg, "Latin America's Left."

19. These figures are from ALADI (Asociación Latinoamericana de Integración [Latin American Integration Association]), "Los Efectos de la Crisis Económica Internacional en el Comercio Externo de la ALADI [The Effects of the International Economic Crisis on the External Trade of ALADI Members]," December 3, 2009.

20. INTAL, *Statistics and Indicators: Rankings* (Washington: International Development Bank, 2013).

21. ALADI, "Los Efectos de la Crisis Económica Internacional," p. 8.

22. Ocampo, "How Well Has Latin America Fared during the Global Financial Crisis?"

23. ECLAC, *La Reacción de los Gobiernos de las Américas frente a la Crisis Internacional* [The Reaction of the Governments of the Americas to the International Crisis] (Santiago, Chile: 2009) (www.cepal.org/publicaciones/xml/2/46422/2012-184-La_reaccion_de_los_gobiernos-WEB.pdf).

24. Ocampo, "How Well Has Latin America Fared during the Global Financial Crisis?," p. 11.

25. Rudiger Dornbusch and Sebastian Edwards, *The Macroeconomics of Populism in Latin America* (University of Chicago Press, 1992).

26. "Mexico Can Be a Global Economic Power: EPN," *Latin News*, November 22, 2012.

27. Tito Belchior Silva Moreira and Fernando Antônio Ribeiro Soares, "Brazil: The International Financial Crisis and Countercyclical Policies," *CEPAL Review*, vol. 106 (April 2012), pp. 169–86.

28. Porzecanski, *Latin America*, p. 17.

29. José Duran Lima and others, "Assessing the Impact of Non-Tariff Barriers during the Global Crisis: The Experience of Argentina, Ecuador, and Venezuela," Working Paper, Department of Economics, Universidad de la Republica de Uruguay; Centro de Investigaciones Económicas (CINVE), and ECLAC International Trade and Integration Division (2010), p. 17.

30. Porzecanski, *Latin America*, p. 24

31. Liliana Rojas-Suárez, "The International Financial Crisis: Eight Lessons for and from Latin America," Working Paper 202 (Washington: Center for Global Development, 2010).

32. Zenon Quispe and Renzo Rossini, "Monetary Policy during the Global Financial Crisis of 2007–09: The Case of Peru," in *The Global Crisis and Financial Intermediation in Emerging Market Economies*, vol. 54, edited by Bank for International Settlements (Basel: 2011), pp. 299–316, p. 299.

33. Ocampo, "How Well Has Latin America Fared during the Global Financial Crisis?"

34. ECLAC, *La Reacción de los Gobiernos de las Américas.*

35. Juan Carlos Echeverry, "Es Sostenible la Política Fiscal en el Mediano Plazo? [Is Fiscal Policy Sustainable in the Medium Term?]" *Debates de Coyuntura Económica (Fedesarrollo)*, vol. 77 (September 2009).

36. Mauricio Cardenas and Valerie Mercer-Blackman, *Análisis del Sistema Tributario Colombiano y Su Impacto Sobre la Competitividad* [Analysis of the Colombian Tax System and Its Impact on Competitiveness] (Bogota, Colombia: Fedesarrollo, 2009).

37. Ministerio de Hacienda del Gobierno de Chile [Chilean Ministry of Finance], *Plan de Estímulo Fiscal* [Fiscal Stimulus Plan] (Santiago, Chile: 2009).

38. "Velasco Apela al 'Yes We Can' de Obama ante la Crisis [Velasco Invokes Obama's 'Yes We Can' in the Face of the Crisis," *La Nación* [Santiago, Chile], November 27, 2008.

39. Silvio Rendón, "Populismo Contracíclico [Countercyclical Populism]," *Grancomboclub.com* (blog), December 8, 2008 (http://grancomboclub.com/2008/12/populismo-contracclico.html); Santiago Roca, "Ciclo Económico y Política Fiscal [The Economic Cycle and Fiscal Policy]," *Actualidad Económica del Perú* [Current Economy of Peru] (http://aeperu.blogspot.com/2011/03/ciclo-economico-y-politica-fiscal.html).

40. Oxfam International, *Pobreza, Desigualdad, y Desarrollo en el Perú: Informe Annual 2008–2009* [Poverty, Inequality, and Development in Peru: Annual Report 2008–2009] (Lima: Oxfam International, 2009).

41. "Las Joyitas del Pacífico [The Jewels of the Pacific]," *America Economía*, 2009 (http://especiales.americaeconomia.com/2010/mejores_ministros_finanzas/joyitas_del_pacifico.php).

42. "CGTP Presenta Su Plan Anticrisis [CGTP Presents Its Anti-Crisis Plan]," *Otra Mirada*, April 7, 2009 (www.otramirada.pe/cgtp-presenta-su-plan-anticrisis).

43. Maxwell A. Cameron and Steven Levitsky, "Democracy without Parties: Political and Regime Change in Fujimori's Peru," *Latin American Politics and Society*, vol. 45 (2003), pp. 1–33.

44. Hershberg, "Latin America's Left."

45. ICEFI, *La Politica Fiscal de Centroamerica en Tiempos de Crisis* [Central America's Fiscal Policy in Times of Crisis] (Guatemala City: Instituto Centroamericano de Estudios Fiscales [Central American Institute of Fiscal Studies], 2012).

46. Osvaldo Rosales and Mikio Kuwayama, *China and Latin America and the Caribbean: Building a Strategic Economic and Trade Relationship* (Santiago, Chile: ECLAC, 2012)

47. I am grateful to Injoo Sohn for pointing this out in his commentary on an earlier version of this chapter.

CAROL WISE *and* MARIA ANTONIETA DEL TEDESCO LINS

7

Macroprudence versus Macroprofligacy: Brazil, Argentina, and the Global Financial Crisis

At first glance, both the trajectories of economic growth in Brazil and Argentina during 2000–10 and the effective responses of the two countries to the 2008–09 global financial crisis appear to closely overlap. Both countries had implemented important market reforms through the 1990s, and each in its own way rebounded successfully from the 2000–03 world recession triggered by the dotcom bust in the United States in the late 1990s and the 9/11 terrorist attacks in New York and Washington in 2001. Although both countries had suffered serious currency crises in the decade prior to the global financial crisis (GFC), Brazil in 1999 and 2002 and Argentina in 2001–02, each had worked its way back to steady growth by late 2003. Moreover, despite high prices and brisk China-driven demand for the raw commodities of both countries since 2003, each has come up against domestic political restraints, economic structural bottlenecks, and slowing growth since 2012. It is there, however, where the comparison between these two South American neighbors quickly begins to unravel.

While Brazil was late to embrace a serious program of inflation stabilization and structural reform, since the launching of the Real Plan in 1994 it has gradually put its macroeconomic house in order. Despite some recent macro-policy missteps, few would dispute Brazil's success in institutionalizing a new pattern of policymaking since the mid-1990s and the importance of political stability in reinforcing its macroeconomic reforms. Argentina is a different story. With the 1991 launch of the Convertibility Plan, which tightly pegged its currency one-to-one to the U.S. dollar, Argentina was more assertive and ambitious in launching a market reform agenda. However, among other things, the difficulty of managing a fixed exchange rate in an era of high capital mobility and failure to maintain fiscal discipline across the federal and provincial governments led to the country's default on some US$100 billion in external debt in late 2001 and the collapse of the Argentine peso in 2002. The ensuing economic chaos provoked a domestic backlash against market reforms and a return to the kinds of populist macroeconomic policies that had characterized Argentina's economic strategies for much of the post–World War II period.[1]

Currently, Brazil is struggling to tackle and complete long overdue structural reforms while maintaining macroeconomic stability. In contrast to Brazil, which has taken a more prudent stance over the past decade, Argentina has largely spent down the fiscal and external surpluses that it had accrued due to a more competitive currency after 2002 and a boom in prices for the country's main commodities. Anxious to address the explosion in poverty and inequality caused by the decade-long Convertibility Plan, Argentine policymakers have engaged in highly expansionary fiscal, monetary, and wage policies. The exchange rate has lost its competitive edge, double-digit inflation is on the rise, and, largely shut out of international capital markets since its unilateral default in 2002, the Argentine government has resorted to import, price, and capital controls. The government's profligacy came to a head in January 2014, when the peso plunged 15 percent, triggering large capital outflows from other vulnerable emerging economies, especially Turkey.[2]

The global financial crisis tested the ability of all 14 of the emerging economies discussed in this volume to both resist and survive the daunting external shocks of 2008–09. What unites these comparatively higher-income countries is the fact that a necessary degree of prior institutional, financial sector, and macroeconomic reform had been implemented by most of them so that almost all were able to rebound quickly. Trade barriers had also been greatly reduced across these countries. Since 2007 both Argentina and Brazil had accumulated ample central bank reserves that enabled them to survive the crisis, and the fiscal accounts of each were basically solid; yet the prolonged slump in the markets of Organization for Economic Cooperation and Development (OECD) countries has sorely challenged the ability of both to sustain high growth over the medium term. Whereas Brazilian policymakers have at least committed to a further round of reforms designed to promote industrial development, productivity, and growth,[3] Argentina has circled back to a 1980s-type strategy of loose fiscal and monetary policy, tossing any semblance of effective inflation control out the window. The difference this time around is the dramatic rise of China in the world economy and its voracious demand for commodities from both Brazil and Argentina. Because of this, Argentina may be able to muddle along with macroprofligacy for some time to come. Still, with economic uncertainty and inflation again on the rise, the "good life" seems to be eluding Argentina yet again.[4]

This chapter first establishes an economic baseline for Argentina and Brazil as they stood going into the global financial crisis and probes the main hypotheses presented in the introduction to this volume concerning the degree and nature of macroeconomic, financial sector, and trade reforms that occurred prior to the global financial crisis. It then examines the policies employed once the GFC struck in 2008–09, seeking to explain how each country was able to fend off the financial contagion that emanated from the U.S. economy. Next it explores the path toward economic recovery for these countries as well as the effect of high commodity prices since 2003 in each. Both countries are plentiful in soybeans, for which prices have nearly doubled since 2000, and Brazil is rich in iron ore, which has seen a quadrupling of prices in the same time period (see table 1-4 in chapter 1 of this volume). Amid this foreign exchange bonanza, Brazil has maintained a macroprudent stance, by keeping inflation low and adopting sound fiscal policies; Argentina, however, has not.

Nonetheless, in both cases the crisis served as an important reality check: first, it highlighted the efficacy of reforms that had been launched in the 1990s in both countries and for the most part continued into the first decade of the 2000s in the case of Brazil; second, it revealed the incomplete nature of the reform agenda and policy implementation within each country. Our analysis suggests that the inroads made with economic reforms prior to the GFC were necessary for surviving it; however, in neither case has the reform trajectory been sufficient to spur high sustainable growth in its aftermath.

Prelude to the 2008–09 Global Financial Crisis: The Macroeconomic Baseline

The data in tables 7-1 and 7-2 confirm the impressive strides that both Argentina and Brazil have made since the implementation of market reforms in the 1990s. On the upside, both countries saw at least a tripling of GDP between 1990 and 2012 and per capita income more than tripled in Argentina and more than doubled in Brazil during the same period. Brazil's foreign reserves rose from US$9.1 billion in 1990 to US$369.5 billion in 2012, while Argentina's reserves increased from US$6.2 billion in 1990 to US$39.9 billion in 2012, after peaking at US$52.2 billion in 2010. On the less positive side, average annual GDP growth rates were respectable but erratic for both countries during the 20 years in question, and Brazil's public debt is still running high, at 80 to 95 percent of GDP. In addition, double-digit inflation has returned in Argentina, after a full decade of single-digit rates through the 1990s (see figure 7-1). The trajectory of the macroeconomic, financial sector, and trade policy reforms that preceded the global financial crisis is summarized below in order to help assess the strength of the explanatory variables set forth in the introductory chapter to this volume.

ARGENTINA. During the 17-year interim between the launch of the 1991 Convertibility Plan and outbreak of the global financial crisis in 2008, Argentina's macroeconomic framework ran the full gamut of neoliberal and developmentalist approaches discussed in chapter 1. Given the hyperinflation of 1989–91 in Argentina, President Carlos Menem (1989–99) chose the most credibility-enhancing strategy available to countries in such a dire situation: a currency board. Under the currency board, the Argentine peso was fixed one-to-one to the U.S. dollar and full convertibility was established between the two currencies. At the same time, Argentina's central bank was required to maintain foreign reserves totaling 100 percent of the domestic monetary base and its discretionary lending policies were sharply curtailed. Because it shifted the burden of responsibility for monetary policy—and to a lesser extent fiscal restraint—to the external sector, the currency board effectively tied the hands of domestic policymakers. If foreign exchange reserves fell, the domestic monetary base would automatically shrink.[5]

Like many of his fellow chief executives in Latin America in the early 1990s, Menem did a neoliberal about-face two years into his first term because the exigencies of combating hyperinflation and preserving the viability of the currency board made that the only rational option.[6] In line with the Washington Consensus, the government pursued liberalization, privatization, and deregulation in tandem up through 1998. Due to its post–World War II history of zero-sum politics and radical policy swings, Argentina had yet to experience a period of "miracle growth" along the lines of that in Brazil or Mexico; however, the initial results of the Convertibility Plan seemed to herald the country's long-awaited miracle. With inflation under control, the reduction of numerous barriers to trade, and the widespread privatization of state enterprises, the Argentine economy grew by 43 percent in the 1990s.[7] Moreover, through 1998 policymakers were able to finesse each of the three financial crises that erupted in the 1990s—Mexico's 1995 "Tequila crisis," the 1997–98

Table 7-1. *Macroeconomic Performance in Argentina, 1990–2012*[a]

Year	GDP growth (annual percent)	GDP, PPP (current billions of international dollars)	GDP percent growth, PPP (based on current international dollars)	GDP per capita, PPP (current international dollars)	Inflation, GDP deflator (annual percent)	Current account balance (balance of payments, current millions of U.S. dollars)
1990	−2.4	175.8	1.3	5,386.6	2,076.8	4,552.0
1991	12.7	204.8	16.5	6,189.7	133.0	−647.0
1992	11.9	234.1	14.3	6,980.6	11.9	−5,547.7
1993	5.9	253.4	8.2	7,456.8	−1.5	−8,205.8
1994	5.8	273.6	8.0	7,950.1	2.8	−10,979.0
1995	−2.8	272.0	−0.6	7,805.0	3.2	−5,117.9
1996	5.5	292.1	7.4	8,279.6	−0.1	−6,769.9
1997	8.1	321.9	10.2	9,014.4	−0.5	−12,138.0
1998	3.9	339.0	5.3	9,382.7	−1.7	−14,482.0
1999	−3.4	332.3	−2.0	9,095.7	−1.8	−11,943.0
2000	−0.8	336.8	1.4	9,121.9	1.0	−8,980.6
2001	−4.4	329.3	−0.3	8,828.7	−1.1	−3,780.4
2002	−10.9	298.2	−9.4	7,919.2	30.6	8,766.6
2003	8.8	331.4	11.1	8,720.9	10.5	8,139.9
2004	9.0	371.4	12.1	9,689.1	9.2	3,211.7
2005	9.2	419.0	12.8	10,833.4	8.8	5,273.7
2006	8.5	469.1	12.0	12,023.1	13.4	7,767.0
2007	8.7	524.5	11.8	13,324.7	14.3	7,354.3
2008	6.8	572.4	9.1	14,413.1	19.1	6,755.8
2009	0.9	584.8	2.2	14,599.0	10.0	8,337.5
2010	9.2	642.9	9.9	15,910.0	15.4	2,830.4
2011	8.9	715.5	11.3	17,554.1	17.3	−5,640.9
2012	6.5	n.a.	n.a.	17,917.4	n.a.	107.0

Source: Inter-American Development Bank (www.iadb.org/en/research-and-data/latin-american-and-caribbean-macro-watch,8633.html) and World Bank (http://data.worldbank.org/country/argentina).
a. PPP = purchasing power parity.

Asian meltdown, and Russia's 1998 currency crash and debt default. In fact, with generous support from and the endorsement of the International Monetary Fund (IMF), Argentina was the first emerging economy to return to international capital markets following the Asian and Russian disruptions.[8]

It was Brazil's 40 percent currency devaluation and subsequent float in January 1999 that threw the biggest wrench into the Convertibility Plan.

Total reserves (includes gold, current millions of U.S. dollars)	Net capital account (balance of payments, current millions of U.S. dollars)	External debt stocks, total (debt outstanding and disbursed, current billions of U.S. dollars)	External debt stocks, long term (debt outstanding and disbursed, current billions of U.S. dollars)	External debt stocks, short term (debt outstanding and disbursed, current billions of U.S. dollars)	Domestic public debt (millions of U.S. dollars, end of period)	Domestic public debt (percent GDP, end of period)
6,222.0	n.a.	62.5	48.9	10.4	n.a.	n.a.
7,462.5	n.a.	65.6	49.6	13.5	n.a.	n.a.
11,447.0	31.4	68.6	50.1	16.1	n.a.	n.a.
15,499.4	32.2	64.6	52.5	8.6	n.a.	n.a.
16,003.2	35.0	75.0	63.7	7.1	19,788.0	7.7
15,979.4	28.4	98.7	71.2	21.3	20,730.1	8.0
19,719.0	101.6	111.3	81.5	23.4	24,197.6	8.9
22,424.6	132.6	126.8	88.9	31.9	28,229.1	9.6
24,855.7	145.8	140.1	103.7	30.9	31,204.3	10.4
26,350.1	298.2	150.0	115.6	29.4	39,403.2	13.9
25,152.1	211.8	147.0	113.2	28.3	46,621.6	16.4
14,555.5	313.0	149.7	115.3	20.0	59,888.4	22.3
10,492.4	812.2	145.6	116.1	14.7	49,715.3	51.8
14,157.2	140.1	161.1	122.8	22.3	76,813.0	60.1
19,659.5	243.6	164.9	123.8	26.4	79,667.7	52.4
28,081.7	177.8	127.4	82.6	34.8	67,703.9	37.3
32,022.2	159.2	118.4	89.6	28.3	80,478.3	37.9
46,149.4	242.2	120.4	100.6	19.2	82,597.1	31.7
46,385.3	361.8	121.8	101.4	19.9	90,241.6	27.7
48,006.9	148.0	126.6	103.6	19.8	92,112.2	30.2
52,207.5	178.0	111.7	94.7	13.8	103,185.4	28.1
46,265.8	136.6	114.7	94.9	16.6	118,378.1	26.7
39,920.3	38.4	n.a.	n.a.	n.a.	n.a.	n.a.

Because Brazil had become its largest trade partner since the launching in 1991 of the Common Market of the South (Mercosur), Argentina plunged into a deep economic recession. In contrast with the aforementioned crises, which had been transmitted through the financial system, the Brazilian devaluation struck Argentina at the level of the real economy, exacerbating weaknesses in the prevailing strategy that had been swept under the carpet. First

Table 7-2. *Macroeconomic Performance in Brazil, 1990–2012*[a]

Year	GDP growth (annual percent)	GDP, PPP (current billions of international dollars)	GDP percent growth, PPP (based on current international dollars)	GDP per capita, PPP (current international dollars)	Inflation, GDP deflator (annual percent)	Current account balance (balance of payments, current millions of U.S. dollars)
1990	−4.3	775.4	9.1	5,181.9	2,735.4	−3,823.0
1991	1.5	813.9	5.0	5,349.7	414.2	−1,450.0
1992	−0.5	827.2	1.6	5,351.2	968.1	6,089.0
1993	4.7	884.7	7.0	5,636.0	2,001.3	20.0
1994	5.3	845.3	−4.5	5,303.4	2,545.4	−1,153.0
1995	4.4	1.0	20.2	6,277.8	72.0	−18,136.0
1996	2.1	1,056.2	4.0	6,427.3	17.0	−23,248.0
1997	3.4	1,112.9	5.4	6,669.8	7.6	−30,491.0
1998	0.0	1,129.0	1.4	6,664.4	4.2	−33,829.0
1999	0.3	1,148.5	1.7	6,679.8	8.4	−25,400.0
2000	4.3	1,223.8	6.6	7,016.6	6.1	−24,224.5
2001	1.3	1,268.0	3.6	7,169.2	8.9	−23,214.5
2002	2.7	1,322.8	4.3	7,378.5	10.5	−7,636.6
2003	1.1	1,366.2	3.3	7,522.0	13.7	4,177.2
2004	5.7	1,484.9	8.7	8,075.8	8.0	11,737.5
2005	3.2	1,582.6	6.6	8,509.4	7.2	13,984.6
2006	4.0	1,698.3	7.3	9,035.6	6.1	13,621.4
2007	6.1	1,854.0	9.2	9,768.6	5.8	1,550.7
2008	5.2	1,993.0	7.5	10,405.1	8.3	−28,192.0
2009	−0.3	2,012.6	1.0	10,414.9	7.1	−24,302.2
2010	7.5	2,179.5	8.3	11,180.2	8.2	−47,322.9
2011	2.7	2,289.0	5.0	11,639.7	6.9	−52,480.1
2012	0.9	2,365.7	3.3	11,747.4	n.a.	−54,246.4

Source: Inter-American Development Bank (www.iadb.org/en/research-and-data/latin-american-and-caribbean-macro-watch,8633.html) and World Bank (http://data.worldbank.org/country/brazil).

a. PPP = purchasing power parity

was the steep overvaluation of the currency under a fixed exchange rate and policymakers' inability to rectify it through higher productivity gains (see figure 7-2); second was the trade-off between inflation reduction and employment creation (Argentina's unemployment rate had skyrocketed into double digits); third was the fact that fiscal restructuring had turned out to be a shell game of sorts, with only very minimal tax reform having occurred in the

Total reserves (includes gold, current millions of U.S. dollars)	Net capital account (balance of payments, current millions of U.S. dollars)	External debt stocks, total (debt outstanding and disbursed, current billions of U.S. dollars)	External debt stocks, long term (debt outstanding and disbursed, current billions of U.S. dollars)	External debt stocks, short term (debt outstanding and disbursed, current billions of U.S. dollars)	Domestic public debt (millions of U.S. dollars, end of period)	Domestic public debt (percent GDP, end of period)
9,199.6	35.0	120.3	94.7	23.7	n.a.	n.a.
8,748.6	42.0	121.3	93.7	26.3	n.a.	n.a.
23,264.5	54.0	129.5	104.6	24.0	n.a.	n.a.
31,746.9	81.0	144.5	112.9	31.3	n.a.	n.a.
38,491.7	173.0	152.8	120.5	32.1	n.a.	n.a.
51,477.3	352.0	160.9	129.6	31.2	n.a.	n.a.
59,685.4	533.0	181.8	145.8	35.9	n.a.	n.a.
51,705.5	568.0	198.9	164.1	34.8	n.a.	n.a.
43,902.1	429.0	242.0	207.3	29.8	n.a.	n.a.
36,342.3	339.0	245.1	206.5	29.2	n.a.	n.a.
33,015.2	272.9	242.5	209.3	30.9	301,995.9	79.0
35,866.4	−33.6	229.9	192.8	28.2	304,898.5	79.5
37,832.1	452.2	231.9	187.2	23.3	239,709.1	74.9
49,297.2	498.9	235.9	182.4	24.6	341,385.6	80.4
52,934.8	341.3	220.6	169.8	25.2	418,392.0	83.4
53,799.2	662.9	188.3	163.8	23.9	540,747.3	86.9
85,842.8	869.0	194.3	173.4	20.3	658,064.6	90.3
180,333.6	768.0	238.4	198.6	39.2	897,568.5	93.2
193,783.3	1,077.4	262.9	225.7	36.6	762,598.0	92.4
238,539.4	1,129.9	281.6	237.3	39.7	1,172,307.0	94.8
288,574.6	1,139.7	352.4	282.4	65.4	1,394,529.4	95.5
352,010.2	1,566.6	404.3	357.7	42.1	1,365,988.6	95.9
369,565.9	−1,876.6	n.a.	n.a.	n.a.	1,383,075.8	64.5

provinces; fourth was the mass of debt that had built up because Argentina became the IMF's "poster child" for neoliberal reform in the 1990s and was able to easily access international capital markets up to January 1999.[9] After three years of recession and policy floundering, the currency board collapsed in January 2002 and Argentina defaulted on some US$100 billion in privately held external debt.

Figure 7-1. *Inflation Rates, Argentina, Brazil, and Mexico, 1996–2013*

Percent

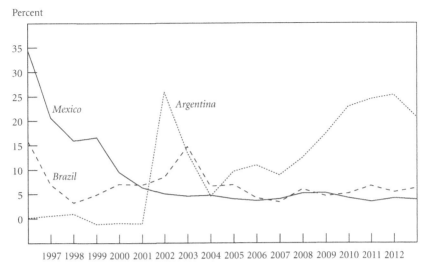

Source: International Monetary Fund, International Financial Statistics, various years. Because of well-known issues with accurate price indices in Argentina, we substitute inflation estimates for 2008–13 from the Economist Intelligence Unit country report after first checking to validate the splice.

BRAZIL. With the liberalization of capital accounts, the opening of foreign investment regimes, and the explosion in stock and bond markets in Latin America, Brazil and other emerging economies in the region (including Chile and Mexico) had moved from fixed to flexible or floating exchange rates by the late 1990s. Like Mexico's in 1995, Brazil's shift to a floating currency was the result of a messy devaluation in January 1999. For both, the realities of high capital mobility in the 1990s meant that there was no going back to an exchange rate peg. Under these new conditions, adopting more flexible exchange rates became the preferred strategy, at least in the Western Hemisphere, for withstanding external shocks and minimizing adjustment costs in terms of output, employment, and inflation.[10]

In Brazil, the shift to exchange rate flexibility was underpinned by the modernization of economic institutions like the Finance Ministry and the central bank. Throughout 2000–10, for example, Brazilian economic officials joined with other countries in the region to control prices by targeting interest rates and inflation rather than by relying on blunter instruments like direct price controls.[11] In addition, Brazil's privatization program was considered one of the most successful in terms of both total revenues and professional execution.

Figure 7-2. *Argentina and Brazil, Real Exchange Rate vis-à-vis the U.S. Dollar, 1990–2012*[a]

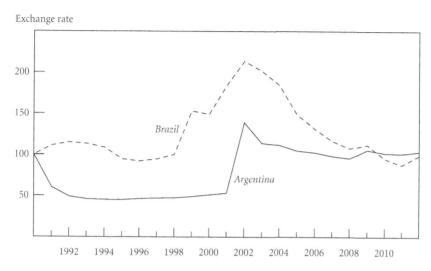

Source: Inter-American Development Bank (www.iadb.org/en/inter-american-development-bank,2837.html).

a. Upward movements in the lines reflect currency devaluation; downward movements indicate currency appreciation.

When the global financial crisis hit in 2008, Brazil was sitting on a stockpile of foreign reserves. Moreover, there was no question as to its institutional and technical capacity to restore macroeconomic stability. In contrast, in Argentina the maintenance of a decade-long currency board had basically relegated the Central Bank of Argentina to the back burner and the post-2002 period saw the politicization of economic policymaking within the bank.

THE ROLE OF THE IMF. The role that the IMF played in Argentina and Brazil is worth noting because of its effect on the macroeconomic baseline in each country. Despite the steep appreciation of the Argentine peso through the 1990s (see figure 7-2), the country's flagrant failure to meet any designated fiscal targets, and the government's half-hearted implementation of structural reforms, the IMF stood by Argentina until the Convertibility Plan met its bitter end in late 2001. However, when the final crash came in early 2002,[12] the Bush administration's newly appointed treasury secretary, Paul O'Neill, made little effort to hide his disdain for the IMF and its largely failed mega-bailout packages in the 1990s, including the massive US$48 billion in loans that had been bestowed on Argentina just a year earlier.[13] Argentina was simply out of cash and had yet to meet the standard of consolidated macroeconomic reforms that constitutes the first hypothesis set forth in the introduction to this volume. Even though the IMF was designed specifically to act as lender of last resort and to provide policy guidance out of a crisis, the IMF, under pressure from the U.S. Treasury, simply bolted from a financial meltdown that was partially of its own making.[14]

Brazil, arguably, benefited from better timing in its interactions with the IMF. When faced with the Asian and Russian crises in 1997–98, IMF and U.S. Treasury officials were convinced that Brazil might be the next economy to implode and that the three crises together would present a systemic threat to global financial markets. The IMF stepped out of its comfort zone to try a more preventive, or proactive, strategy. With the budget deficit running at US$65 billion, the current account deficit at 4 percent of GDP, and the government's outstanding debt at 8 percent of GDP, Brazil received a "frontloaded" IMF package with very vaguely worded conditions. The respite was short-lived: in January 1999 the real came under attack and, with considerable hesitation, policymakers moved to a free-floating currency regime. Brazil's recovery was quicker than the markets had predicted, and the IMF took responsibility for one of its few self-declared successes in the 1990s.

Until 2005–06, the IMF also had a medium-term stand-by agreement with Brazil that focused on macroeconomic restructuring.[15] This fairly orthodox, or "macroprudential," framework centered on fiscal discipline, inflation targeting, and effective management of the floating exchange rate. Under heavy pressure from the IMF, in 2000 the Brazilian congress passed the Law of Fiscal Responsibility, which was essential for reducing the country's deficits and spiraling public debt and for its explicit effort to rein in fiscal outlays by the state governments.[16] Between 1997 and 2002, Brazil's tax base was diversified and tax collection rose from 27.4 percent to 32.8 percent of GDP.[17] This macroprudential pattern has continued under the avowedly leftist Labor Party governments that have presided over the Brazilian economy since 2002. Policymakers within those governments have relied on more interventionist measures to provide social safety nets and implement industrial policy, ostensibly within the confines of the Law of Fiscal Responsibility.

Financial Sector Reform

Although it may be difficult to imagine from the current vantage point, by 1998 Argentina had developed a solid framework for supervising domestic banks and had consolidated the domestic banking system to the extent that it ranked among the most sophisticated in the region.[18] Moreover, during Argentina's Convertibility Plan (1991 to January 2002), full external financial openness had been official government policy. Perhaps the biggest policy U-turn for Argentina has been the deterioration and reversal of financial sector reform following the 2002 meltdown. The previous financial liberalization policy was dramatically reversed under leftist presidents Néstor Kirchner (2003–07) and Cristina Fernández de Kirchner (2007–). Brazil, traditionally more financially interventionist than Argentina and certainly more so during the 1990s, had nonetheless implemented significant liberalization of the domestic financial system from the mid-1990s onward, including through the ambitious Program to Support the Restructuring and Strengthening of the National Financial System (PROER). It continued to modernize its financial sector through 2000–10.[19]

Overall, on the eve of the global financial crisis, neither Argentina nor Brazil could boast that their financial sector was particularly open, especially compared with the financial sectors in Chile, Mexico, and Peru. As can be seen from table 9-4 in chapter 9 of this volume, on a scale of 0 to 1 (with 1 signaling complete liberalization), in 2007 Argentina stood at 0.32 and Brazil at 0.54. Brazil's financial sector was substantially more open than Argentina's, and on the eve of the crisis Brazil also was healthier in terms of several measures of financial performance (see chapter 9).

ARGENTINA. Having stripped the Central Bank of Argentina of its role as lender of last resort under the 1991 Convertibility Plan, the Menem administration was forced to address the weaknesses in the country's banking system. The 1995 Tequila shock, which reverberated throughout Latin America following Mexico's 1994–05 peso crisis, rendered that an urgent task. Accordingly, Menem's economic team undertook a deep restructuring of domestic banks in 1995, with one major result being the heightened participation of foreign banks in Argentina. The combination of foreign ownership and financial sector overhaul positioned Argentina to withstand the successive shocks from Asia and Russia with the usual fiscal and monetary policy tools. It was the 1999 Brazilian devaluation that upset the country's path toward macroprudence, as relative prices quickly shifted against the Argentine peso and drove it up even further (see figure 7-2). The haphazard devaluation and debt default of 2002 were testimony to the inability of policymakers and domestic politics to resolve the country's eternal wars of attrition between different sectors (for example, industry versus agriculture, exporters versus importers), different income groups, and the central government and the provinces.

Despite revolutionary changes in the depth and complexity of financial markets over the past two decades, common wisdom still held that a default along the lines of Argentina's 2002 unilateral debt reduction would consign the country to pariah status. Nevertheless, Argentina seized some desperately needed fiscal relief by declaring a moratorium on its external debt payments. By 2005, amid much IMF bashing and posturing before the country's creditors, President Néstor Kirchner managed to reschedule approximately 75 percent of the outstanding debt on take-it-or-leave terms that represented substantial write-downs for the country's private bond holders.[20] Shortly thereafter, the government tapped into the hefty buildup of central bank reserves and paid off its outstanding debt of US$9.5 billion to the IMF,[21] then turned immediately to the Venezuelan government for financial support. The message was clear: Argentina had defaulted and lived to tell about it, while also pulling the plug on any further IMF policy advice.

The crucial difference between the pre-commodity boom and the current price boom has been Argentina's ability to thrive because of high world prices for its main commodities, driven largely by brisk Chinese demand, and to access funds from nontraditional sources, including direct loans from Venezuela of approximately US$10 billion from 2005 to 2008 and a US$10 billion currency swap with China. Kirchner's maneuvers reduced the debt service burden from 8 percent to 2 percent of GDP. The economy, moreover, grew at an average annual rate of 7 percent from 2003 to 2011. But in 2014 Argentina remained mired in litigation involving an estimated US$25 billion in defaulted sovereign debt still held by creditors who refused to participate in the 2005 debt exchange, and the country is still struggling to access funds in international capital markets.[22] Financial development and reform have taken a back seat since the default because subsequent administrations have focused on debt reduction and the achievement of financial policy autonomy rather than on the implementation of new financial sector reforms. In the end, the record shows that Argentina made very few advances in the way of financial sector reform in the run-up to the global financial crisis. Instead, it gathered some steam from the reforms that had been put in place in the 1990s and found some inventive ways to access capital outside the traditional channels.

BRAZIL. Post-inflationary Brazil saw the failure of a number of banks because the inflation tax no longer sheltered lenders or borrowers from real interest rates. With stabilization, a profound restructuring of markets took place, leading to the privatization of state banks, the strengthening of the federal banks that remained, and the entry of large foreign banks into Brazil. As the arrears of state banks, the private sector, and state government began to pile up, the federal government was forced to intervene. That prompted the Brazilian congress to pass a set of three programs designed to save the banks:

—Program to Support the Restructuring and Strengthening of the National Financial System (PROER), which lasted from 1995 until 1997

—Program of Incentives for State Participation in Banking Activities (PROES), which lasted from 1996 until 1999 but thereafter forbid the use of public funds to bail out private banks

—Program to Strengthen Federal Financial Institutions (PROEF), which lasted from 1999 until 2001.[23]

These programs brought about a remarkable restructuring of the Brazilian financial system, which had been somewhat modernized before price stabilization precisely as a result of the huge gains that banks had made during the times of high inflation. Hoggarth, Reis, and Saporta estimate that the total cost of saving the private banks was about 0.88 percent of GDP and that approximately the same amount was spent on privatizing state government banks. The cost of restructuring the federal banks is more difficult to calculate.[24] Fishlow estimates that the joint costs of these programs was 10.4 percent of GDP, noting that "the expense is much less than the loss from doing nothing. In other countries, saving the financial system had cost a great deal more. The recent Great Recession provides examples."[25]

This comparative analysis reveals deep historical and economic distinctions between the financial systems in Argentina and Brazil. Whereas Argentina spent the initial decade of the twenty-first century severing its ties with the IMF, spending down its fiscal and current account surpluses, and cooking the national statistics on inflation, Brazil towed the line on all three of those fronts. In 2007 and 2008 Brazil received its first investment-grade rating from the top three international credit rating agencies, and in 2009 Moody's further raised Brazil's credit rating, rendering it the first emerging economy to go up a notch since the outbreak of the global financial crisis.[26] Because high interest rates were part of the steady fight against inflation and were necessary in the early part of the first decade of the 2000s as a component of the inflation-targeting strategy, international portfolio capital poured into Brazil. At the same time, the stable economic environment rendered Brazil second only to China as an emerging economy destination for foreign direct investment. The cost of these massive capital inflows to Brazil was a steep appreciation of the exchange rate (see figure 7-2), although with the exception of just one year (2002), the country still ran a trade surplus from

1995 to 2011 (see table 7-2).[27] Still, a number of structural reforms were delayed, setting limits to the long-term growth of the Brazilian economy.

Trade Liberalization and Commercial Policy

Since the onset of market reforms in Argentina and Brazil, both countries have participated actively in the World Trade Organization (WTO), the Latin American Integration Association (ALADI), and Mercosur. In fact, an Argentine appointee currently is secretary general of 11-member ALADI and a Brazilian was appointed director general of the WTO in 2013. Both countries have liberalized trade to an impressive extent and are roughly on par with the average level of trade openness registered by the Asian 7 in 2009.[28] Other countries within the Latin American 7 may be more open (for example, Chile, Peru, and Mexico), but in a cross-regional comparison, Argentina and Brazil are now running neck and neck with China and South Korea.[29] In the 2010s both countries rapidly increased the dollar amount of their trade: Argentina's total trade tripled between 2001 and 2012, and Brazil's more than quadrupled over the same period; both also managed to diversify their trade partners, as shown in table 7-3.

By far the biggest shift in terms of trade is the considerable reduction in each country's total trade with the United States between 2001 and 2012 and the rise of China to become Brazil's top trade partner and Argentina's second-most-important partner, after Brazil. Figures 7-3 and 7-4 track the rise of each country's trade with China, beginning with China's 2001 entry into the World Trade Organization. The data reflect both the severe drop that occurred in Argentine and Brazilian trade with China during the global financial crisis and the rapidity with which China's trade with the two countries recovered, thanks to China's fiscal stimulus, which amounted to nearly 5 percent of Chinese GDP. Although China represented just 7 percent of Argentina's exports in 2012 and 17 percent of Brazil's, the bulk of their exports is in lucrative raw materials (for example, soybeans, iron ore, and oil).

For a full decade, strong Chinese demand for raw materials from countries like Argentina and Brazil has pushed global commodity prices through the roof. For Argentina, with its rich and abundant soybean crops, the commodity price boom that took off in 2003 (see table 1-4 in chapter 1) was a lifeboat back from the brink both in 2002 and during the global financial crisis in 2008–09, although the rebound from the GFC was driven even more by the Brazilian recovery. For Brazil, the quick uptick in commodity exports to China in 2009–10 was an important but not the sole factor in its recovery; Brazil's

Table 7-3. *Top Five Trading Partners, Argentina and Brazil*
Percent of total imports and exports

Argentina

	1995 Imports from	1995 Exports to	2011 Imports from	2011 Exports to
United States	23	8	11	5
Brazil	21	26	28	21
Germany	7	–	5	–
Italy	6	4	–	–
Spain	5	–	–	4
Chile	–	7	–	6
Netherlands	–	6	–	–
China	–	–	14	7
Mexico	–	–	3	–

Brazil

	1995 Imports from	1995 Exports to	2011 Imports from	2011 Exports to
United States	21	21	15	10
Germany	10	5	7	–
Italy	6	–	–	–
Netherlands	–	7	–	5
China	–	–	15	17
Argentina	11	10	8	9
Japan	7	8	–	4
South Korea	–	–	5	–

Source: Economic Commission for Latin America and the Caribbean (ECLAC).

Figure 7-3. *China's Trade with Argentina, 2001–12*

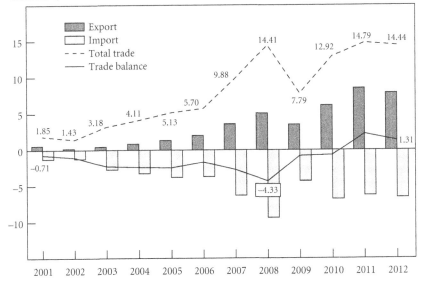

Source: Comprehensive Economic, Industry and Corporate Data (CEIC) (www.ceicdata.com/).

economy is more diversified than Argentina's, and its investment-grade rating means that Brazil is in much better standing in international capital markets. Brazil, in other words, has more room to maneuver than Argentina does on any number of fronts, both domestic and foreign.

However, despite its strong and diverse industrial base, the competitiveness of Brazil's manufacturing sector has slipped in the 2010s. That is due not only to the dominant role that commodity exports have played in promoting Brazil's relatively favorable terms of trade since 2003 but also to the numerous trade policy distortions that both Brazil and Argentina have engaged in within the context of Mercosur. Brazil, in particular, touts protectionist measures within Mercosur as its own brand of "capitalist developmentalism."[30] Nonetheless, Brazilian and Argentine scholars alike argue that this regional trading bloc still matters to its members, despite the fact that it has been limping along since 1998.[31] Table 7-3 shows that in 2011 Brazil was Argentina's most important trading partner and Argentina was third most important for Brazil, after China and the United States.

Figure 7-4. *China's Trade with Brazil, 2001–12*

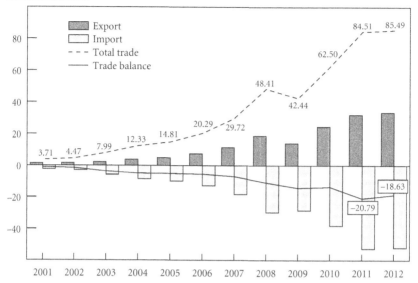

U.S. dollars, billions

Source: Comprehensive Economic, Industry and Corporate Data (CEIC) (www.ceicdata.com/).

Coping with Global Shocks

Both Brazil and Argentina succeeded in responding to severe external shocks with countercyclical economic measures when the GFC hit in 2008–09.[32] According to Prasad and Sorkin, in 2009 Argentina's fiscal stimulus amounted to about 1.3 percent of GDP and Brazil's was around 0.5 percent of GDP (see table 9-3 in chapter 9).[33] In 2008–09 both governments launched a set of strongly expansionary policies (see table 7-4): monetary measures consisted mainly of liquidity expansion through the reduction of reserve requirements combined with extension of credit by public financial institutions; fiscal policy included payment holidays, tax reductions, and even some rebates. While the measures themselves were hardly innovative, the difference this time was that both governments actually had the resources in hand to help cushion the shocks. Although it would be premature to declare the traditional pattern of procyclical crisis responses obsolete in Latin America, it is safe to say that the ability of both Brazil and Argentina to successfully weather the global financial crisis represented a clear break with the past.

Table 7-4. *Responses to the Global Financial Crisis, Argentina and Brazil*

Argentina	*Brazil*
Monetary policy	
Reduction of reserve requirements in dollars and in national currency	Reduction of reserve requirements and reduction of the interest rate spreads for public banks
Provision of liquidity in national currency via the daily repurchase of bonds issued by the central bank, tripling of credit lines to local banks, refinancing of liability issued by the government, and launch of a new plan for mortgage credit	Authorization for BNDES to lend to domestic banks with guarantees based on their credit assets
	Facilitation of rediscount operations with permission to purchase assets of small and middle-size banks
Imposition of measures to deter the sending of capital overseas	Treasury credit transfer to BNDES with reduced fees
	Greater flexibility on the rules for BNDES loans and release of credit lines to states
	Reduction of basic interest rates and BNDES loan fees
Fiscal policy	
Temporary moratorium on fiscal and social obligations, including reduction of employer contributions to employee benefits; elimination of employee payments toward retirement; and payment under the Investment Incentives on Capital Goods and Infrastructure Law of the cost of employee benefits	Tax reductions and lengthening of payment deadlines
	Fiscal rebates of over US$3.5 billion to spur consumption; most benefited sectors: automotive, home appliances, and construction materials
Public works project to construct housing, hospitals, and roads and issuance of bonds to finance the Road Plan (2009–10)	Approximately US$6 billion from the sovereign fund in measures to sustain levels of aggregate demand
Unification of the benefits and grants system under a public regime, with increased state control of and participation in pension fund administration	Expansion of investment expenditures beyond those already planned, amounting to US$4 billion, pushing the total for this budget category to US$20 billion
Incentives for the repatriation of assets	

(continued)

Table 7-4. *Continued*

Argentina	Brazil
Exchange rate policy and foreign trade	
Provision of liquidity in foreign currency through swaps with China's and Brazil's central banks	Provision of liquidity in foreign currency through swaps to importers, swap agreement with the U.S. Federal Reserve worth US$30 billion, and partial easing of reserve requirements
Greater control over the entry of imported products, enlargement of the list of goods requiring a previous import license, reinforcement of import controls, and raising of tariffs	Adoption of nontariff protectionist measures
	Tariff reduction for products with no national competitors
Reopening of maize and wheat exports with reduction of duties on these and on fresh fruits and vegetables	Use of exchange reserves to fund exports
	Possibility for the central bank to lend in foreign currency directly to private banks
Basing the exchange rate on nominal anchor	Exchange rate regime based on a managed float and inflation targeting.
Increasing control over the demand for currency	
Multilateral financing	
Financing agreement with the World Bank worth US$3.3 billion until 2011	
World Bank loan to finance a sanitation project worth US$840 million.	

Source: ECLAC, "A Preliminary Assessment of the Policies Implemented by the Governments of Latin America and the Caribbean in Response to the Crisis" (Lima, Peru: 2010), and authors' revisions based on Economist Intelligence Unit country reports, various issues and years.

Fiscal and Financial Measures

The title of this chapter reflects the overriding difference between Argentina and Brazil: Brazil's more prudent macroeconomic policy versus Argentina's more profligate one. To be clear, the term "macroprudence" has been used to include everything from the management of systemic risks to the specific tools deployed in the quest to maintain low inflation, a stable exchange rate, and a balanced budget. In the 1990s, under the 1991 Convertibility Law, Argentina was almost hyper-prudent—but that approach was dramatically reversed after the collapse of the Convertibility Plan in January 2002, and Argentina has continued to diverge from macroprudential policies since that time.

In contrast, Brazil's macroprudential measures have included tight monetary policies since the launching of the Real Plan in 1994, including high interest rates, a floating exchange rate, and reliance on an inflation-targeting strategy. Moreover, in line with the hypotheses presented in chapter 1 of this volume, Brazil's approach pragmatically combined statist and market-oriented financial policies in response to the global financial crisis. The divergent backgrounds of Argentina and Brazil set the stage for each country's response to the GFC following the crash of Lehman Brothers in September 2008. However, there is one important financial similarity: in neither country were financial institutions especially exposed to the kinds of mortgage-backed securities and collateralized debt obligations that pushed the U.S. financial sector to the brink in 2008–09.

Argentina

Argentina, especially since 2010, has fallen back on a financial policy approach reminiscent of those in the 1960s and 1970s in Latin America, replete with financial repression, capital controls, import licenses, and reliance on central bank reserves to cover its expenditures. As table 7-1 shows, reserves dropped by US$12 billion between 2010 and 2012. Argentina's economic growth since the global financial crisis has largely been a matter of luck, driven by Brazil's recovery and high commodity prices for raw materials produced by both countries (see table 1-4 in chapter 1).

Interestingly, Argentina, in the wake of its 2002 debacle, had succeeded in balancing the budget and achieving equilibrium in its external accounts up to the eve of the GFC. Because it had finessed a restructuring of external debt payments with its creditors, Argentina had ample room to maneuver and, until 2010, the performance of the Argentine economy was such that the country was even able to issue international bonds that year.[34] Nevertheless, Argentina's relations with external investors remained problematic throughout 2000–10. In short, economic policy mistakes have greatly hampered Argentina's ability to benefit from the high levels of global capital liquidity in the post-2003 period (see figure 7-5), making it impossible for the public sector to attract external funds.

In the throes of the 2008–09 crisis, Argentina's president, Cristina Fernández de Kirchner, began to adopt a series of questionable policies that would have been condemned during normal times, including the 2008 nationalization of Argentina's private pension funds—a desperate attempt to rectify government spending, which was beginning to rapidly outpace revenues. At the

Figure 7-5. *Net External Investment Flows, Argentina, Brazil, and Mexico, 1994–2012*

U.S. dollars, billions

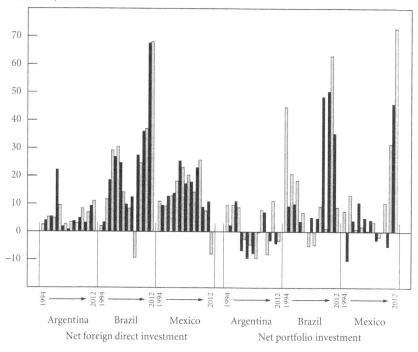

Argentina   Brazil   Mexico   Argentina   Brazil   Mexico

Net foreign direct investment   Net portfolio investment

Source: Economic Commission on Latin America and the Caribbean (ECLAC–CEPALSTAT). See http://estadisticas.cepal.org/cepalstat/WEB_CEPALSTAT/estadisticasIndicadores.asp?idioma=i and http://interwp.cepal.org/sisgen/ConsultaIntegrada.asp?idIndicador=2050&idioma=i.

same time, the government began to manipulate official economic statistics, especially inflation estimates, provoking a formal reprimand from the IMF. Despite the government's insistence that annual inflation is running in the 11 to 12 percent range, we calculate that a more likely range is 20 to 25 percent (see figure 7-1).

Arguably, until 2010 Argentina still had a chance to regain macro-stability with steady growth. Instead, the country's foreign exchange bonanza from high commodity prices prompted a populist-style spending spree that began as a countercyclical response to the GFC and simply kept going. Argentina's business environment has deteriorated rapidly due to the absence of credible statistical indicators, a succession of measures authorized largely by executive decree, and the imposition of capital and exchange controls.[35] On the

Figure 7-6. *Real Interest Rates in Argentina, Brazil, and Mexico, 1994–2013*

Percent

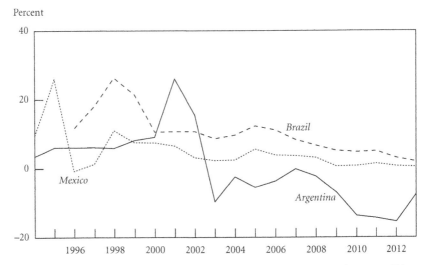

Source: International Monetary Fund, International Financial Statistics, various years. Calculated as the nominal interest rate minus the inflation rate, with interest rates being money market rates for Argentina, Brazil, Mexico, and Peru, deposit rates for Chile, and government securities for Venezuela. As noted earlier, because of well-known issues with accurate price indices in Argentina, we substitute inflation estimates for 2008–13 from the Economist Intelligence Unit country report after first checking to validate the splice.

domestic front, subsidies to control energy prices—combined with a foreign exchange policy that has used the exchange rate as a nominal anchor without any other mechanisms to control inflation—have led to an ever-quickening dollarization of the Argentine economy. The only way forward has been the inflation tax, part of an insidious pattern involving currency appreciation (figure 7-2), negative interest rates (figure 7-6), and high inflation (figure 7-1). Despite the government's tight controls on capital outflows, investors have fled the Argentine market en masse (figure 7-5) while workers and consumers have been left to bear the brunt of the inflation tax.

Brazil

Brazil is a very different story, mainly because the government did more than Argentina to uphold its commitment to the three main pillars of macroeconomic policy during 2000–10 by targeting inflation, adopting a floating exchange rate, and maintaining fiscal balance. In mid-2008 policymakers moved swiftly to control inflation, slow capital inflows, and counter the steep currency appreciation that booming commodity prices had fostered (see figure 7-2). Interest rates were eased, the "financial operations tax" on incoming portfolio inflows was raised to 6 percent (see figure 7-5), and the Brazilian Development Bank became the institutional conduit for channeling credits to both private and public entities. Thus, in Brazil, the bending of institutional rules along the lines of President Fernández de Kirchner's discretionary actions in Argentina has been much less frequent. The Brazilian government stood by its policy of allowing the public banks to be the main expansionary drivers of the economy, which produced an annual growth rate of 7.5 percent of GDP in 2010.

Countercyclical policies, applied accordingly, acted to strengthen domestic markets. Although not completely buffered from global financial turmoil, the Brazilian banking system passed safely through the crisis. Heightened regulation and robust central bank policies to restore credit flows diminished the impact of the liquidity crunch. The stock of international reserves permitted the central bank to defend the national currency in foreign exchange markets, thus preventing a deep and destabilizing depreciation. Later, the currency problem took a very different turn as increased risk tolerance in international markets, poor growth prospects in the developed world, and huge interest rate differentials led to the flooding of the Brazilian market with foreign currencies and a consequent sharp appreciation of the real. Due to Brazil's low domestic savings level (see figure 7-7), foreign direct investment is crucial for economic development, which means that the government must strike a difficult balance between policies that deter speculation and those that attract crucial investments.

Exchange Rate and Trade Remedies

The data in figure 7-2 reflect the extent to which both Brazil and Argentina have struggled with currency appreciation at different times in the 1990s and 2000–10, although there have been some measured competitive gains on this front since the global financial crisis. The new millennium has been anything but ordinary for Argentina and Brazil, and a decade-long commodity price boom has enabled both countries to run hefty current account surpluses since 2003. However, the dynamics underlying both the currency and trade fronts in the two countries are quite different.

Figure 7-7. *Gross Savings as a Percent of Gross National Income, Argentina, Brazil, and Mexico, 1994–2012*

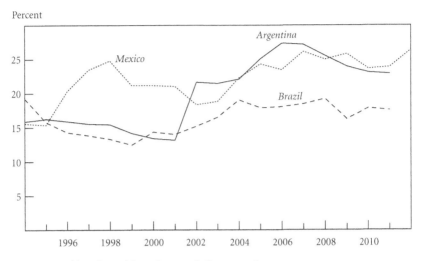

Percent

Source: World Bank, World Development Indicators, various years.

Argentina

Argentina's use of the exchange rate as a nominal anchor, along with administered prices to control inflation (figure 7-1), has been an abject failure. With dwindling reserves and an official exchange rate for pesos now trailing far behind a much higher black market rate, Argentina's currency remains vulnerable to the kind of run that drove it down sharply in January 2014.[36] On the trade side, domestic assumptions during 2000–14 about the benefits to be reaped from trade in Argentina have been misguided. Trade measures imposed by the Kirchner administration, including the requirement for import licenses and taxes on exports of raw materials, have further dampened the economic viability of those operating in the country's tradable goods sector. The growth slowdown since 2012 confirms that Argentina cannot continue to count wholly on exports for its prosperity. Apart from the uncertainties that continue to cloud the international economic environment, the current policy approach simply has too many built-in disincentives.

Brazil

The overvaluation of Brazil's currency since 2008 is a result of the high domestic interest rates (figure 7-2) set to counter inflation and the massive capital inflows (figure 7-5) from profit-seeking investors who continue to flee the negative U.S. interest rates that have been part of the Federal Reserve's "quantitative easing" policies since December 2008.[37] Brazil has effectively managed a floating exchange rate and an inflation-targeting strategy in terms of controlling prices, but the struggle to maintain a competitive exchange rate continues and will require much higher levels of productivity than those that currently exist.

In Brazil, the positive benefits from relatively favorable terms of trade during 2000–10 instilled great faith in the internal market as the engine for growth. Through wage hikes and credit easing by the publicly owned banks, Brazilian policymakers sought to incorporate new sectors of the population into the middle class, and they largely succeeded. However, the foreign exchange bonanza has been a decidedly mixed blessing. First, the flip side of buoyant commodity exports to China has been a flood of Chinese manufactured imports into both Brazil and Argentina, and policymakers in each have not thought twice about raising protectionist trade barriers against China, the rest of the world, and even each other.

In 2011 alone, Brazil initiated 50 anti-dumping investigations against China at the WTO. Second, as shown in figure 7-8, Brazil has seen a decline in the competitiveness of its manufacturing sector since 2000. Domestic debates over the country's "deindustrialization" have become commonplace, although the figures thus far do not entirely support that notion. For example, Jenkins and Barbosa report that only a fifth of Brazil's total manufacturing is exported, half of that to Latin American countries.[38] In fact, the even steeper slowdown of Brazil's economy than Argentina's since 2012 highlights the underperformance of Brazilian manufactured exports and the limits of relying on heightened domestic demand in the absence of further structural reforms, which have been put on the back burner since the decade-long commodity price boom rendered them less urgent.

As the administration of President Dilma Rousseff—who was narrowly reelected for a second term in October 2014—works to stimulate growth through an increasingly aggressive economic policy, there is an air of national remorse over the loss of time and opportunities to enact reforms when growth was more buoyant and international confidence in Brazil allowed for relatively cheap and ample investment opportunities. For example, André Nassif argues that Brazil's thick web of bureaucratic and regulatory barriers and its comparatively higher level of trade protectionism reflect how "the country has sacrificed higher and more productive growth over the past twenty years due to the partial and incomplete nature of its microeconomic reforms."[39] Suffice

Figure 7-8. *Manufacturing RCA for China and Latin American Emerging Markets*[a]

Units

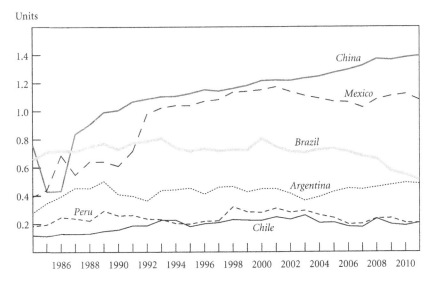

Source: Comprehensive Economic, Industry and Corporate Data (CEIC) (www.ceicdata.com/).
a. RCA refers to Revealed Comparative Advantage Index. If the RCA is > 2.5, an industry's competitiveness is high; 1.25 < RCA < 2.5 is second highest; 0.8 < RCA < 1.25 is weaker; and < 0.8 is weak competitiveness.

it to say that for Brazil as well as for Argentina, the successful rebound of these economies from the global financial crisis has little to do with actual trade policies. In light of the numerous trade distortions that appear for both countries in table 7-4, it could be argued that these countries recovered *in spite of* ongoing trade policy decisions, certainly not because of them.

From Crisis to Recovery to Slow Growth

The slowing of growth from 2012 to the present in both Argentina and Brazil (see tables 7-1 and 7-2) can be accounted for by any number of factors in the external environment, including the slowing of Chinese demand for Latin American commodities as China's own growth dropped from 10 percent of GDP in 2000–10 to around 7.5 percent today. The continued turmoil in world markets and a much longer than expected recovery of the OECD bloc from the global financial crisis have also been a damper on global demand. However, as difficult as these external pressures may be, growth has also slowed rather precipitously due to the huge backlog of structural reforms still pending from the 1990s. It was on this very question of competitiveness and micro-economic restructuring that Washington Consensus reforms based on deeper liberalization and deregulation had been tabled in the late 1990s in Argentina and in the early part of the first decade of the 2000s in Brazil.

A stark reality of this period was the failure of per capita growth and employment creation to keep pace with positive aggregate returns. Those trends were exacerbated by the 2000–03 global recession, not to mention the distributional fallout from Brazil's 1999 financial crisis and Argentina's economic collapse in 2001. Then, seemingly out of nowhere, the commodity lottery struck, and most pending reforms were placed on hold as China suddenly became a key intervening variable in the reactivation of growth in both Argentina and Brazil. Yet despite the slowing of Chinese demand, prices for each country's most abundant commodity exports have remained high by historical standards. Today's growth challenges thus appear to be domestically rooted and related to the weak institutional framework in both Argentina and Brazil for channeling the incoming flow of foreign exchange into domestic savings and much higher levels of productive investment.

To be sure, the lag in saving rates and productive investment is a regional trend, hardly unique to these two countries. For example, when comparing China and the Latin American region, the latter's deficit in terms of gross capital formation (GCF) is glaring. From 2000 to 2008, Latin America's GCF rate averaged less than 19 percent of GDP; conversely, China's average rate was more than double that figure. Argentina, not surprisingly, stands out among the Latin American emerging economies as offering the least hospitable investment environment. Figure 7-9 captures some of this trend, as illustrated by the World Bank's *Doing Business* indicators, which reflect four key measures that are crucial for growth, investment, and competitiveness. As the figure shows, Argentina is ranked abysmally on the "ease of doing business" indicator, although it performs better than Brazil in terms of "getting credit" and "resolving insolvency." In this respect, Brazil's ranking suggests the extent to which this version of the developmental capitalist model is still far too much of a drag on growth.

Although the average South American rate of government spending as a percent of GDP is about 26 percent, Brazil's stands at 40 percent. The private banking sector, meanwhile, has made itself scarce. In 2012, the private sector provided just 12.8 percent of long-term financing, while the state-owned development bank (BNDES) provided around 72.4 percent.[40] Meanwhile, the

Figure 7-9. *Aspects of Doing Business in Argentina, Brazil, and Mexico, Average for 2012–13*[a]

Rank relative to full country set

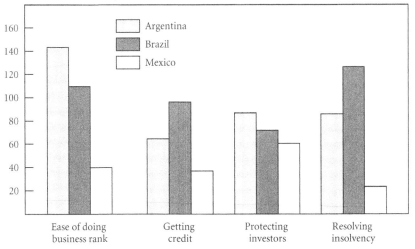

Source: World Bank, *Doing Business* (2012 and 2013) (http://doingbusiness.org/rankings).
a. The higher the score, the worse the performance on a given indicator.

spread between deposit and lending rates in Brazil is one of the highest in the world. Both the spread and the real interest rate premium suggest continued distortions in the banking sector that must be ironed out.[41] In sum, between 2000 and 2012 Brazil's total foreign exchange reserves increased eleven-fold, standing close to US$370 billion at the end of 2012. Capital is therefore abundant but absurdly expensive; private domestic investment and productivity are flat; and, bolstered by an overvalued exchange rate, domestic consumer spending is running at around 62 percent of GDP.

Currently, to speak of Argentina's competitiveness or even a development model proper, is a moot point. Despite our reference to Argentina's economic strategy during 2000–10 as a throwback to the 1970s, it is important to acknowledge that the political economy itself is significantly more modern, cohesive, and developed. Argentina appears today to have relapsed into path dependence, whereby current policy choices are limited by previously existing "institutions that provide disincentives to productive activity."[42] Macroeconomic populism, including financial repression, has thrived on the prolonged commodity price boom. The complementarity of the China-Argentine economic relationship is such that Argentina's commodity exports will be in high demand indefinitely, meaning that the country has a long horizon for muddling through and achieving much less than is warranted by its rich factor endowments.

Conclusion: The Path Forward

Over the past 30 years phenomenal changes have taken place within Latin America's emerging economies. From the 1982 debt shocks to the Washington Consensus, the region's various financial crises, the decade-long commodity boom, the global financial crisis, and now the post-GFC era, perhaps one lesson has held constant: there is simply no substitute for the design and implementation of sound structural reforms, especially within the microeconomic realm. The case of Brazil suggests that macroprudential reforms, along with trade and capital account opening, are perhaps necessary conditions for growth but not entirely sufficient. Argentina, unfortunately, demonstrates how quickly the old inflationary spiral can reappear when policymakers lose sight of these basic fundamentals. Even if the decade-long commodity boom continues, markets have clearly reacted to the need for both countries to revisit the reforms that were shelved amid the foreign exchange windfall of 2000–10.

In this chapter we argue that when compared with the advanced industrial economies, the Argentine and Brazilian economies responded surprisingly well to countercyclical policy stimuli. Moreover, the resilience of the two to the global financial crisis was boosted by loose U.S. monetary policy as well as China's growth and the consequent uptick in demand for commodities. The measures taken were effective in spurring internal markets and hence a steady recovery in growth for both Argentina and Brazil as soon as 2010. Until the 2012 slowdown, the ongoing narrative for these Latin American emerging economies was that they had entered into a prolonged phase of prosperity marked by notable reductions in poverty, expansion of the urban middle class, and consequent strengthening of demand within the domestic economy. The success of both Argentina and Brazil in mitigating the effects of the crisis further fueled expectations that the reform trajectory of each, although markedly different, had matured to the extent that both were now capable of maintaining economic stability despite the uncertainties inherent within the global economy.

However, five years out from the global financial crisis, hindsight suggests that each country has hit its growth frontier and most likely has gone as far as it can in the absence of a further round of reforms. For Brazil, although the institutionalization of key macroeconomic and financial sector reforms in the decade preceding the GFC went a long way toward enabling the country's quick recovery in 2010, the policy "successes" of 2008–09 are fading against the backdrop of today's reform gridlock. For example, without being more assertive in tackling the barriers to higher savings and investment as well as the dense web of state regulation and red tape, the Rousseff administration risks a prolonged period of slower growth. The luck of the commodity draw since 2003 was certainly a factor in Brazil's ability to accrue massive foreign exchange reserves and implement generous fiscal and social outlays; yet policymakers' ability to stick with a macroprudent strategy that has maintained low inflation and a fiscal balance suggests that much more than luck has been at play here.

In the case of Argentina, the administrations that have prevailed since 2003 have exhausted whatever institutional vigor they may have inherited from the macroeconomic reforms and financial sector restructuring under-taken in the 1990s. If anything, policymakers have spent considerable time dismantling any remaining macroprudential policy approaches, although such policies still had enough punch to get the country through the global financial crisis. However, the country's steady gains in per capita growth and income distribution under booming commodity prices and high growth rates during 2000–10 are likely to erode under double-digit inflation. The government's affinity for macroprofligacy, including the burning down of central bank reserves to support current fiscal outlays, suggests that Argentina is in for yet another bumpy ride.

Notes

1. Guido Di Tella and Rudiger Dornbusch, *The Political Economy of Argentina, 1946–83* (London: Macmillan, 1989).

2. Simon Romero and Jonathan Gilbert, "As Argentine Peso Falters, President Keeps a Low Profile," *New York Times*, January 31, 2014, p. A1.

3. Albert Fishlow, *Starting Over: Brazil since 1985* (Brookings, 2011).

4. Manuel Pastor and Carol Wise, "From Poster Child to Basket Case," *Foreign Affairs*, vol. 80, no. 6 (December 2001), pp. 60–72; "Argentina Economy: Digging a Deeper Hole," Economist Intelligence Unit, *ViewsWire*, September 10, 2013, p. 1.

5. Carol Wise, "Argentina's Currency Board: The Ties That Bind," in *Exchange Rate Politics in Latin America*, edited by Carol Wise and Riordan Roett (Brookings, 2000).

6. Susan Stokes, *Mandates and Democracy: Neoliberalism by Surprise in Latin America* (Cambridge University Press, 2001).

7. Juan Corradi, "Prelude to Disaster: Weak Reform, Competitive Politics in Argentina," in *Post-Stabilization Politics in Latin America: Competition, Transition, Collapse*, edited by Carol Wise and Riordan Roett (Brookings, 2003), pp. 125–26.

8. Wise, "Argentina's Currency Board," pp. 103–05.

9. Pastor and Wise, "From Poster Child to Basket Case."

10. Wise, "Argentina's Currency Board," p. 94.

11. Leslie Armijo and John Echeverri-Gent, "Brave New World? Brazil and India's Financial Statecraft in the Changing World Order," unpublished paper, 2013.

12. Paul Blustein, *And the Money Kept Rolling In (and Out)* (New York: Public Affairs Books, 2005).

13. Ibid., pp. 117–18.

14. Michael Mussa, *Argentina and the Fund: From Triumph to Tragedy* (Washington: Institute for International Economics, 2002).

15. Economist Intelligence Unit, "Brazil," Country Report, 4th quarter (London: 2005), p. 8.

16. The U.S. equivalent for this would be some kind of balanced budget law.

17. Fishlow, *Starting Over*, p. 48.

18 Economist Intelligence Unit, "Argentina," Country Report, 4th quarter (London: 1998), p. 8.

19. Fishlow, *Starting Over*, pp. 61–65.

20. Ignacio Labaqui, "Living within Our Means: The Role of Financial Policy in the Néstor and Cristina Fernández de Kirchner Administrations," paper presented at the Latin American Studies Association Annual Meeting, San Francisco, May 2012.

21. Economist Intelligence Unit, "Argentina."

22. Jude Webber, "Argentina Given Month to Make Debt Offer," *Financial Times*, March 2, 2013; Floyd Norris, "The Muddled Case of Argentine Bonds," *New York Times*, July 25, 2014, p. B1.

23. Kurt von Mettenheim, *Federal Banking in Brazil: Policies and Competitive Advantages* (London: Pickering & Chatto, 2010).

24. Glen Hoggarth, Ricardo Reis, and Victoria Saporta, "Costs of Banking System Instability: Some Empirical Evidence," *Journal of Banking and Finance*, vol. 26, no. 5 (2002), pp. 825–55; von Mettenheim, *Federal Banking in Brazil*.

25. Fishlow, *Starting Over*, p. 64.

26. Larry Rohter, *Brazil on the Rise: The Story of a Country Transformed* (New York: Palgrave Macmillan, 2010), pp. 166–67.

27. The real suffered a crisis of confidence in 2002 on the eve of the election of President Luiz Inácio Lula da Silva.

28. As in table 1-2 in chapter 1 of this volume, the Asian 7 countries covered in this study include China, India, Indonesia, Korea, Malaysia, the Philippines, and Thailand.

29. As in table 1-2 in chapter 1 of this volume, the Latin American 7 countries covered in this study include Argentina, Brazil, Chile, Colombia, Mexico, Peru, and Venezuela.

30. We borrow this term from Leslie Armijo, "Equality and Regional Finance in the Americas," *Latin American Politics and Society*, vol. 55, no. 1 (Winter 2013), pp. 95–118.

31. On Brazil, see Eliana Cardoso, "Brazil's Currency Crisis: The Shift from an Exchange Rate Anchor to a Flexible Regime," in *Exchange Rate Politics in Latin America*, edited by Wise and Roett; on Argentina, see Laura Gómez-Mera, *Power and Regionalism in Latin America: The Politics of Mercosur* (University of Notre Dame Press, 2013).

32. Jeffrey A. Frankel, Carlos A. Vegh, and Guillermo Vuletin, "On Graduation from Fiscal Procyclicality," *Journal of Development Economics*, vol. 100 (2013), pp. 32–47.

33. Eswar Prasad and Isaac Sorkin, *Assessing the G-20 Stimulus Plans: A Deeper Look* (Brookings, 2009), p. 5.

34. Arturo Porzecanski, "Should Argentina Be Welcomed Back by Investors?," *World Economics*, vol. 12, no. 13 (July–September 2011), pp. 13–32.

35. Ibid.

36. Romero and Gilbert, "As Argentine Peso Falters, President Keeps a Low Profile."

37. Ben Bernanke, *The Federal Reserve and the Financial Crisis* (Princeton University Press, 2013).

38. Rhys Jenkins, "China and Brazil: Economic Impacts of a Growing Relationship," *Journal of Current Chinese Affairs*, vol. 41, no. 1 (January 2012), pp. 26–29; Rhys Jenkins and Alexandre de Freitas Barbosa, "Fear for Manufacturing? China and the Future of Industry in Brazil and Latin America," *China Quarterly*, vol. 209 (2012), pp. 59–81.

39. André Nassif, "Brazil and India in the Global Economic Crisis," in *The Financial and Economic Crisis of 2008–2009 and Developing Countries*, edited by Sebastian Dullien and others (New York and Geneva: United Nations, 2010).

40. Seth Colby, "Brazil's Second-Best Financial Strategy," *Americas Quarterly*, vol. 7, no. 2 (Spring 2013), pp. 34–35.

41. Alex Segura-Ubiero, "The Puzzle of Brazil's High Interest Rates," IMF Working Paper 12/62 (International Monetary Fund, 2012).

42. Douglass North, *Institutions, Institutional Change, and Economic Performance* (Cambridge University Press, 1990), p. 99.

GERARDO ESQUIVEL

8

Mexico's Recovery from the Global Financial Crisis

Reports from international media outlets as well as multilateral institutions have conveyed the notion that Mexico's economic recovery after the 2008–09 global financial crisis was buoyant. In fact, thanks to such coverage, it is often assumed that Mexico's economic future is bright, and some have recently labeled Mexico "the new China" or an "Aztec Tiger." Others have even predicted that as an emerging economy, Mexico will become "the more dominant economic power in the 21st century."[1] Such interpretations, however, stand in sharp contrast with several recent academic studies that suggest that the Mexican economy continues to be plagued by profound structural problems that must be addressed if the country is to achieve high and sustained economic growth.[2]

These contrasting perspectives have emerged due to the different time horizons taken in analyzing the Mexican economy. Whereas the cautious and critical view employs a long-run analysis, the optimistic view focuses on the short term—more specifically, on the relatively rapid growth rates that Mexico achieved during 2010–12. In that brief period, Mexico's gross domestic product (GDP) grew at an average annual rate that surpassed 4 percent, a rate twice as high as that achieved in the same period among developed economies and similar to that of other emerging economics (EEs), such as Brazil. Not only has the Mexican economy grown fast, but it has done so without upsetting the

The author thanks several participants in the workshop "How Emerging Markets Survived the Global Financial Crisis," University of Southern California, July 2012, for their useful comments.

country's macroeconomic stability: inflation is rather low (close to 4 percent a year) and the fiscal position, in terms of public debt and the budget deficit, is still quite manageable.

Different time horizons alone cannot fully explain the contrast between the two perspectives, however. It is instead the omission of the fact that Mexico was one of the countries most stricken by the global financial crisis (GFC) that leads to the optimistic view. Indeed, this view also overlooks the fact that the Mexican economy started to slow down in 2008, when it grew by only 1.2 percent, and that in 2009 Mexico`s GDP contracted by 6 percent. To put the last number in perspective, that economic contraction was the second largest in Mexico in the last 70 years, topped only by the "Tequila crisis" in 1994–95, when the currency and the banking system collapsed in a matter of days. When the GFC struck, the plummeting of Mexico's growth was one of the largest drops in the entire Western Hemisphere during 2009.

That massive contraction in Mexico's output explains in part the magnitude of the country's quick rebound. For that reason, I start this chapter with the basic premise that no analysis of the Mexican economic recovery is complete without examining the impact of the global financial crisis. How did the Mexican economy perform before the crisis? Why was Mexico so badly affected by it? Could Mexico have averted the crisis? Did macroeconomic policy decisions ameliorate or exacerbate the crisis? Finally, how did Mexico's recovery compare with that of other EEs?

In terms of the four hypotheses laid out in chapter 1 of this volume, Mexico is a bit of an outlier. It is the only Latin American EE in which the shock was felt primarily on the trade side, largely due to its proximity to and overwhelming dependence on the U.S. market, which absorbs some 80 percent of Mexican exports each year. Nevertheless, deep macroeconomic reforms and restructuring of the banking system in the late 1990s positioned Mexico to weather the crisis with ease. As a result of high oil prices throughout most of the 2000s to date, Mexico also was sitting on a healthy buildup of foreign exchange reserves. Remarkably, the neoliberal blinders of frontline technocrats within the Bank of Mexico (the central bank) initially prevailed: policymakers raised interest rates and held back on a fiscal stimulus package for a full year. The dire drop in GDP for 2009 prompted a fiscal stimulus, which led to recovery, but not before the government's initial procyclical response had wreaked the worst of the global financial crisis on the real economy. Conditions in global markets clearly favored Mexico's recovery, even if the initial impulses of domestic policymakers did not.

The chapter first discusses the pre-crisis economic conditions in Mexico.[3] It then analyzes Mexico's experience during the global financial crisis and expands the analysis of post-crisis outcomes with data on per capita output, employment, and poverty. The conclusion discusses the validity of the hypotheses put forward in chapter 1 of this volume with respect to Mexico's experience.

The Pre-Crisis Period

The stage was set for the global boom of 2002–07 by a virtuous cycle of rising world demand for commodities and manufactured goods and rapid economic expansion among the developed countries. Some of the principal beneficiaries of the boom were commodity-producing nations. Among them were several Latin American countries that experienced a strong positive terms-of-trade shock that provided them with additional financial resources and enabled them to achieve their fastest growth rates since the 1970s. For Mexico, however, the pre-crisis global boom was not as favorable as for other resource-rich Latin American countries. The rapid post-2002 expansion of the world economy had only a small positive effect on Mexico's terms of trade, while those of countries such as Bolivia, Chile, Peru, and Venezuela experienced substantial improvement.

Yet the pre-crisis global boom did have at least three positive impacts on the Mexican economy. First, the U.S. economy grew at a relatively rapid pace during 2002–07 (2.8 percent a year). That was a boon to Mexico's economic growth, which, given Mexico's heavy reliance on its trade with the United States, reached 3.3 percent a year during that period. Second, after a prolonged period of relatively low prices, by 2008 the price of oil had reached a historic peak. Oil is Mexico's most important export, and its price skyrocketed from less than US$22 a barrel in 2002 to almost US$80 by the end of 2007. That increase boosted total Mexican export revenues by about US$84 billion during 2003–07. Third, remittances received by Mexican households from abroad surged dramatically. The inflow of remittances, according to official central bank data, increased from less than US$10 billion in 2002 to more than US$26 billion in 2007. As a result, remittances became one of Mexico's most important sources of foreign exchange, even surpassing the income received from tourism-related activities or foreign direct investment (FDI).

The rapid rise in foreign exchange income related to oil price increases and higher remittances put strong appreciation pressure on the exchange rate from 2004 onward. The Bank of Mexico responded to that pressure by increasing its stock of foreign exchange reserves and by sterilizing that increase to combat monetization pressure. Hence, during 2002–07, foreign reserves increased from US$48 billion to more than US$78 billion. That helped strengthen Mexico's external position: for example, the ratio of short-term external debt to foreign exchange reserves declined from 32 percent in 2002 to less than 10 percent in 2007.

Despite the positive factors that existed during this period, Mexico benefited surprisingly little from the pre-crisis global boom. Its average GDP growth remained basically the same as in the previous decade, a fact that can be attributed to the lack of fundamental structural changes in the Mexican economy during those years. Indeed, the Mexican government had made no progress on its structural reform agenda since the late 1990s, a result of the combined effects of reform fatigue and a divided government.[4] Reform fatigue was associated with the disappointing returns on some of Mexico's most important previous reforms, including privatization and pension reform. The enactment and implementation of other long-overdue reforms—for example, fiscal reform and modernization of the energy sector—were further complicated by the inability of the National Action Party (PAN) to obtain a majority voting bloc in Congress throughout its 12-year reign from 2000 to 2012. That made it virtually impossible to reach a political consensus on structural reforms, and only a few relatively minor ones have been approved in recent years.[5]

The rise of strong new players in the global economy, such as China and India, which directly compete with Mexico in terms of products (manufactured goods) and markets (the United States), has also affected the prospects and competitiveness of the Mexican economy. Since China entered the World Trade Organization (WTO) in 2001, it has displaced Mexico as the second-largest U.S. trade partner (Canada still being the largest). However, more important to Mexico's competitiveness is the lack of economic dynamism and relatively low levels of total factor productivity (TFP). Several recent estimates, using a variety of methodologies, have shown that Mexico's TFP growth has been either negative or modestly positive over the past three decades.[6] The lack of economic reforms and the failure to adequately address critical issues such as human capital formation, credit allocation, and investment (both public and private) in large infrastructure projects is also partly responsible for the stagnant productivity in Mexico during that period.

Due to policy decisions made during the global boom period in the early years of the 2000s, Mexico was in a contradictory position when the boom ended in 2007. On one hand, it had strengthened its external position by reducing external debt and increasing foreign exchange reserves. On the other hand, Mexico was in a relatively weakened fiscal position as a result of having financed its current expenditures with oil revenues, which are notoriously volatile and uncertain, for several years.

The Immediate Impact of the Crisis

The outbreak of the global financial crisis had an immediate and far-ranging impact on the Mexican economy. The crisis was transmitted first through the abrupt drop in demand for Mexican exports, which was quickly followed by decreased remittances, tourism, foreign direct investment, external financing, and oil prices and increased exchange rate volatility. Beginning in late 2007, all of those factors converged at once, rendering Mexico the most adversely affected country in the Western Hemisphere, if not the entire developing world.

EXPORTS. Mexico's trade relationship with the United States, which Mexico depends on as a market for nearly 80 percent of its exports, became a key transmission channel. Indeed, the collapse in U.S. demand for durable goods led to a sharp contraction in some of the most important Mexican exports, such as automobiles (–24 percent) and electronic appliances (–19 percent). Likewise, the weakening of the U.S. economy triggered a sharp fall in demand for Mexican oil (–39 percent). As a result, Mexico's foreign trade slowed in 2008 and fell by more than 20 percent in nominal dollar terms in 2009. By mid-2009, the decline in Mexico's total foreign trade had reached almost 35 percent on an annual basis in nominal terms (figure 8-1).

THE REAL ECONOMY. Even before the effects of the decline in U.S.-Mexico trade were fully felt in late 2008 and early 2009, the global crisis had already torn through the real sector of the economy. In fact, the slowdown in U.S. industrial production that began in late 2007 coincided with a similar slowing in Mexican industry, a consequence of the growing integration between and synchronization of the industries of the two countries (figure 8-2). By early 2008, the Mexican industrial sector showed negative year-on-year growth, suggesting that both nations' industries had begun contracting even earlier than trade had.

REMITTANCES. The dramatic reduction in remittances sent by Mexicans living abroad (mainly in the United States) became another channel of shock transmission. Although remittances are far more important for the Central

Figure 8-1. *Annual Growth Rates, Foreign Trade, Mexico, 1992–2013*[a]

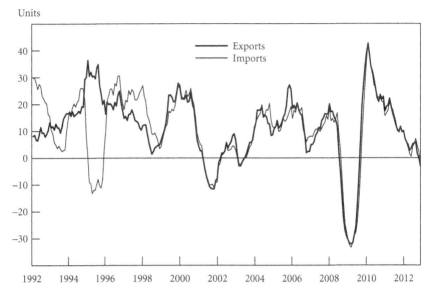

Source: Author's illustration with data from INEGI (Instituto Nacional de Estadística y Geografía), Banco de Información Económica (www.inegi.org.mx/sistemas/bie/).

American and Caribbean countries, Mexico had nonetheless become the second-largest recipient of remittances—which accounted for about 2.5 percent of total Mexican GDP in 2007—in the world. Since the start of the crisis, that flow had begun to steadily diminish; as of early 2010, it was already almost 20 percent lower than two years earlier.

Several studies have shown the close connection between employment indicators in the United States and the level of remittances sent back to Mexico.[7] The connection is close because many Mexican workers who had originally migrated to the United States to work in agriculture had switched to jobs in the then-booming housing sector, where they could earn higher salaries. Because the contraction in the U.S. economy began precisely in the construction sector in August 2007, the amount of remittances going to Mexico was immediately reduced.

TOURISM. Because personal spending on travel and entertainment is highly responsive to changes in income, tourism in Mexico also was affected by the crisis. The number of tourists visiting Mexico from the United States and Europe fell substantially in 2009, by 16.9 percent in the first half of that

Figure 8-2. *Industrial Activity Indexes, Mexico and the United States, 1980–2012*

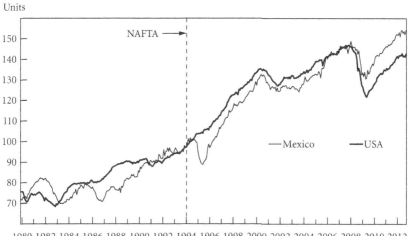

Source: Author's illustration with data from INEGI (Instituto Nacional de Estadística y Geografía), Banco de Información Económica (www.inegi.org.mx/sistemas/bie/) and from the Board of Governors of the Federal Reserve (www.federalreserve.gov/releases/g17/download.htm).

year. The decline was aggravated by the H1N1 flu outbreak that hit Mexico in late April and early May 2009, raising fears of a new pandemic, which then led to an even sharper reduction (–27.6 percent) in the number of tourists coming to Mexico in the April-June period.

FOREIGN DIRECT INVESTMENT. Foreign direct investment and external financing in Mexico also dropped as a result of the global credit crunch and the pullback in financial markets. In 2009, the lack of long-term financing halted several projects, mainly in infrastructure. Multinational corporations postponed or canceled many productive projects due to lack of liquidity. In all, capital inflows diminished by 20 percent, from 2.7 percent of GDP in 2007 to only 2.2 percent in 2009.

OIL PRICES. The collapse of oil prices also has impacted the Mexican economy. The price of Mexican oil, which at its highest had reached $120 a barrel, fell to a third of that in 2009 (although it later experienced some recovery). The decline translated into a substantial fall in income from Mexican oil exports and thus into a large drop in government revenues, 40 percent of which stem from oil sales abroad. Limited capacity in the realm of exploration and development within the state-held oil company (PEMEX) caused a reduction in the level of oil extraction, further reducing public sector revenues. In 2009 the fiscal gap in public finances hit nearly 3 percent of GDP.

EXCHANGE RATE VOLATILITY. Finally, exchange rate volatility increased with the onset of the global financial crisis. In October 2008, right after the collapse of Lehman Brothers, uncertainty around the world triggered a "flight to quality" across all countries—both emerging and developed. That meant that even after massive government interventions in the foreign exchange market, the currencies of many EE countries depreciated by 20 to 30 percent. The average peso exchange rate rose from almost 11 pesos to the dollar in early 2008 to about 13.5 pesos in 2009.

All of these shocks took a toll on domestic demand, particularly on private consumption and gross fixed capital formation. Private consumption in 2009 fell by more than 6 percent from its 2008 level, and fixed capital formation dropped by 10.1 percent over the same period. Total GDP loss during 2008–09, relative to Mexico's potential GDP level, is estimated at close to 11 percentage points. Most of the difference can be explained by a loss in TFP growth equivalent to 8.8 percent of GDP.

Policy Responses

Although the magnitude and severity of the global financial crisis were a surprise to almost everyone, the Mexican government clearly underestimated the situation. Policymakers initially perceived the shocks from the GFC as relatively mild and confined mostly to the financial sector. Local authorities expected the crisis to have a limited impact on the Mexican economy because they believed that the country's financial sector was safe and sound due to stricter regulations put in place during the restructuring of the financial sector following the 1995 crisis. Moreover, they considered the Mexican economy to be relatively immune to the GFC because Mexico had been abiding by strict fiscal discipline and had kept inflation down in the years leading up to the crisis. Because Mexican financial institutions had not dealt in the kinds of high-risk mortgage-backed instruments that had led to the collapse of several U.S. financial institutions, policymakers assumed that the country was safe.

Nonetheless, the global financial crisis was far from being only a financial shock. The crisis also impacted the real sector of the economy through a multiplicity of channels. In the end, the intensity of the shocks transmitted depended, among other things, on the degree of Mexico's economic integration with the U.S. economy. Mexican authorities' erroneous diagnosis of the problem explains their late and timid response to the crisis.

On the fiscal policy front, in the spring of 2008 the Mexican government announced the creation of an infrastructure fund that was intended to have a countercyclical impact. Yet few new financial resources were invested in the fund; most of the financial resources came from existing accounts that were dispersed across different ministries. In addition, the government announced that several existing stabilization funds could be used, if necessary, to maintain the level of public expenditures in the event of lower-than-expected revenues. In late 2008 and early 2009, the Mexican government announced several other fiscal, social, and labor measures to mitigate the negative impact of the GFC. The International Monetary Fund (IMF) estimated that Mexico's fiscal stimulus (that is, the additional increase in aggregate demand due either to increases in government expenditure or to a reduction in taxes) amounted to between 1.0 and 1.5 percent of GDP.[8] However, given the cut in government spending that took place in the second half of 2009, the actual fiscal stimulus was likely even lower than originally estimated.

In cross-country comparisons of fiscal measures implemented to mitigate the crisis, the Mexican government's response was much lower than responses in other emerging economies.[9] Nevertheless, at least the response did not make things worse for the Mexican economy: total government consumption increased in 2009 by nearly 2.3 percent in real terms, helping to cushion the strong contraction in other demand components. Even so, as mentioned before, the increase in spending was rather small and clearly insufficient given the magnitude of the shock affecting the Mexican economy.

On the monetary policy front, the Bank of Mexico responded slowly and timidly to the crisis. In fact, throughout 2008 and in the face of clear signs of further deterioration of the economy, inflationary pressures related to the rapid rise in food prices remained the central bank's main concern. The bank therefore increased the interest rate in the summer of 2008 on three occasions (see figure 8-3), which was exactly the opposite of what other central banks around the world were doing. These policy decisions, which increased the interest rate gap between Mexico and the United States, also contributed to a further rise in foreign portfolio inflows into Mexico. Moreover, these unfortunate policy decisions heightened the vulnerability of Mexico's exchange rate to a sudden stop or reversal of capital flows, which was precisely what happened in September–October 2008, after the collapse of Lehman Brothers.

Figure 8-3. *Target Interest Rates, Mexico and the United States, 2008–09*

Percent

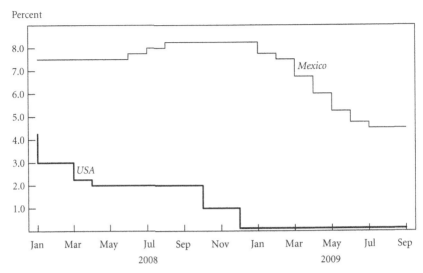

Source: Author's illustration with data from Banco de México (www.banxico.org.mx/estadisticas/index.html) and from the Board of Governors of the Federal Reserve (www.federalreserve.gov/releases/h15/data.htm).

It was not until early 2009, when the recession was already well established in the country and when the target interest rate in the United States was already at zero, that the Bank of Mexico finally started to reduce its target interest rate (see figure 8-3).[10] Even then, it did so in relatively small steps, first by 25 basis points and only later by 75 basis points. All in all, the central bank reduced the interest rate in Mexico from 8.25 percent to 4.5 percent over seven months. But it was too little, too late. By that time, most of the negative effects of the global crisis had already worked their way through the Mexican economy.

Fortunately, the reaction of the Mexican authorities to other aspects of the crisis was more appropriate. For example, following the collapse of Lehman Brothers, the development banks in Mexico intervened to provide liquidity and to maintain fully functioning credit markets amid the worst phase of the financial crisis. Likewise, the Bank of Mexico reacted in a timely manner and implemented a mechanism for a foreign exchange reserve auction, which sold off more than US$10 billion to avoid a large and costly depreciation of the peso, which could have generated serious inflationary pressures.

Figure 8-4. *GDP Growth Rate, Mexico, 1981–2012*[a]

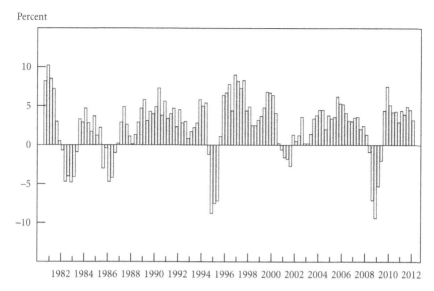

Percent

1982 1984 1986 1988 1990 1992 1994 1996 1998 2000 2002 2004 2006 2008 2010 2012

Source: Author's illustration with data from INEGI (Instituto Nacional de Estadística y Geografía), Banco de Información Económica (www.inegi.org.mx/sistemas/bie/).

Effects on Output and Employment

As discussed, among the world's emerging economies, the Mexican economy was one of those most adversely affected by the global financial crisis. Its GDP contracted by 6.0 percent in 2009, and in the second quarter of 2009 Mexico's GDP fell by more than 9 percent from the previous year's GDP. At that point, the annual contraction was even worse than during the 1994–95 crisis (see figure 8-4).

Employment in Mexico also was hard hit. The open unemployment rate reached 6.3 percent in August 2009 (7 percent in urban areas), its highest level since the 1995 peso crisis. Unemployment climbed steadily beginning in May 2008, when it was at its lowest level in recent years, and by August 2009 the monthly unemployment rate was already 3 percentage points higher than it had been 16 months earlier.

With Mexico's economically active population approaching 45 million in 2009, that suggests that the number of unemployed in Mexico increased by 1.35 million over that 15-month period. According to data from the Mexican

Institute of Social Security (IMSS), the number of jobs in Mexico's formal labor sector had fallen by an average of 400,000 in 2009. Such a contraction represents a decline of almost 3 percent in the total number of formal jobs. The rest of the unemployment number came from the informal sector or from new entrants into the labor force. Many other indicators suggest the extreme weakness of Mexico's labor market at the beginning of 2010. The share of underemployed people, for example, was close to 9 percent of the total economically active population during this time; the usual estimate is around 6 percent. That also suggests than an additional 1.35 million Mexican workers were left underemployed as a result of the crisis.

In summary, the global financial crisis had a very strong negative impact on the Mexican economy. Its impact, which was large by any standard, can be explained by the combination of at least two main factors. The first was Mexico's significant dependence on the U.S. economy on many fronts, including exports, remittances, and tourism, which made it highly vulnerable to U.S. economic conditions. The second was Mexico's delayed and weak policy response, exemplified by its late interest rate reduction and weak fiscal stimulus.

In some sense, then, the impact of the crisis was inextricably linked to previous policy decisions. For example, the impact was partly linked to previous trade reforms, like the North American Free Trade Agreement (NAFTA), which strengthened Mexico's economic ties and trade dependence on the United States without leading to the proper diversification of external trade with other countries or regions.[11] But reforms on the macroeconomic policy front were also to blame, as a very strict inflation targeting system was put in place by the central bank, without any measures designed to address unemployment or output. Furthermore, the Mexican government had tightly adhered to a highly procyclical balanced budget rule. That led first to the spending down of additional revenues received during the oil price boom and second to a downward adjustment of expenditures when oil prices started to contract.

The Economic Recovery and Post-Crisis Outcomes

Did the Mexican economy really rebound quickly in the immediate aftermath of the global financial crisis, as shown in assessments that focus on the short-term rapid growth rates of the 2010–12 period (figure 8-4)? When three different aspects of the recovery—output, labor market performance, and poverty rates—are analyzed from a longer-term perspective, the rebound is

Table 8-1. *Mexico: Pre-Crisis, Crisis, and Post-Crisis Economic Indicators*[a]
Percent

Indicator	2003–07	2008	2009	2010–12
Output growth	3.3	1.2	−6.0	4.4
Export gowth	11.1	7.2	−21.2	17.1
Inflation	4.0	6.5	3.6	3.9
Fiscal balance (percent of GDP)	−0.1	−0.1	−2.3	−2.6
Public debt (percent of GDP)[b]	18.6	18.1	27.3	30.8
Current account balance (percent of GDP)	−0.8	−1.7	−0.7	−0.6
Per capita GDP growth	2.1	0.0	−7.2	3.2
Unemployment	3.6	4.0	5.5	5.2
Job creation (formal sector)	3.0	−0.3	−1.3	4.6

Source: Author's compilation based on data from INEGI (Instituto Nacional de Estadística y Geografía), Banco de Información Económica (www.inegi.org.mx/sistemas/bie/) and from Banco de México (www.banxico.org.mx/estadisticas/index.html).
a. Annual averages.
b. There was an accounting adjustment in 2009.

less clear and the shortcomings of the recovery process, as well as the longer-term effects of the financial crisis, become more visible.

Table 8-1 highlights some of the most important economic variables during the pre-crisis period, the crisis years, and the post-crisis period, revealing several interesting results. First, Mexico's economic performance during the pre-crisis period was good (GDP grew by 3.3 percent a year) but far from stellar. That is, Mexico did not benefit as much from the pre-crisis global boom as some other Latin American countries, which grew at much higher rates (in some cases 5 percent a year or higher). Second, the global financial crisis started to hit Mexico as early as 2008, when growth was clearly slower than it was during the previous year. Third, the recovery of the Mexican economy took place at a relatively rapid rate thanks mainly to exports, which grew at an annual rate of 17.1 percent during the 2010–12 period. Fourth, Mexico's recovery took place amid a relatively stable macroeconomic context: inflation was kept low, the fiscal balance and public debt were still manageable, and the current account deficit was rather small. Finally, formal job creation also grew relatively fast during the recovery, but unemployment was still high compared with unemployment in the pre-crisis period. However, a more detailed look at some specific indicators during the recovery period sheds a slightly different light on the post-GFC dynamics of the Mexican economy.

Figure 8-5. *GDP per Capita, Selected Countries*[a]

Units

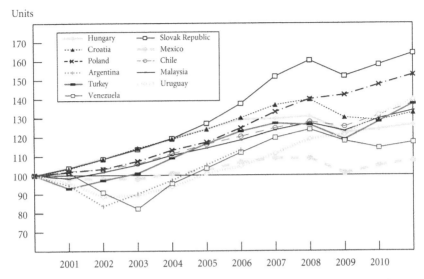

Source: Author's illustration with data from the World Bank, World Development Indicators (http://databank.worldbank.org/data/views/variableselection/selectvariables.aspx?source=World-Development-Indicators).
a. Year 2000 = 100; purchasing power parity data.

Per Capita Output

The type of recovery that Mexico experienced after the global financial crisis can be better understood when the performance of the Mexican economy during the 2000–11 period is put in comparative perspective.[12] To do that, I employ an index of per capita GDP in constant purchasing power parity (PPP)–adjusted dollars and two comparison groups: countries with a similar level of per capita income in 2000 (within a range of +/– US$3,000) and the set of all Latin American and Caribbean countries. In both cases I consider only countries with a population of 3 million or more. Figures 8-5 and 8-6 show the relative performance of the Mexican economy vis-à-vis the two comparison groups.

In figure 8-5, it is evident that Mexico is the poorest performer among the group. Its per capita income was only 8 percent higher in 2011 than it was in 2000, in sharp contrast with that of most other countries in the group, which experienced a per capita GDP increase of anywhere from 20 to 40 percent. Some countries, such as Poland and the Slovak Republic, enjoyed even greater increases. Venezuela scored next to the last in this group, from which it might

Figure 8-6. *GDP per Capita, Latin American and Caribbean Countries*[a]

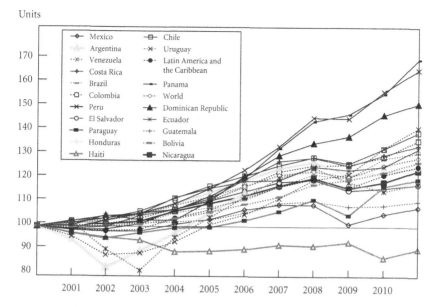

Source: Author's illustration with data from the World Bank, World Development Indicators (http://databank.worldbank.org/data/views/variableselection/selectvariables.aspx?source=World-Development-Indicators).

a. Year 2000 = 100; purchasing power parity data.

be erroneously inferred that Latin America as a region performed worse than the rest of the world in the growth of per capita GDP and that that possibility may somehow explain Mexico's dismal performance.

Figure 8-6 shows per capita GDP for a number of Latin American and Caribbean (LAC) countries, together with averages for the LAC region and for the whole world. The graph shows that the performance of GDP in LAC countries was similar to that of the rest of the world, with an increase in both cases of more than 20 percent in per capita income throughout the period. The figure also demonstrates that Mexico's macroeconomic performance was second to last in the entire LAC region, only above that of Haiti, which suffered a contraction in its per capita income of more than 10 percent due to the great economic, political, and social instability that has afflicted this country for decades. Again, Mexico's macroeconomic performance pales next to that of the rest of its neighbors, which in most cases experienced sizable increases in per capita income.

In sum, figures 8-5 and 8-6 show that from a longer-run perspective, Mexico's post-crisis recovery was rather limited and would have been even if data for 2012 had been included. In fact, by 2012 Mexico's per capita income had just returned to pre-crisis levels, whereas most other countries in figure 8-5 had already achieved that goal by 2011. This analysis shows the importance of taking into consideration the contraction of 2009. In doing so, I conclude that Mexico's recovery is far from being outstanding; it looks quite impressive mostly because the economic contraction during the crisis was so severe.

Labor Markets

The domestic labor market is the second dimension on which Mexico's apparent recovery can be evaluated. The total unemployment rate, for example, almost doubled between 2000 and 2012, jumping from an average of slightly below 3 percent at the beginning of the century to a rate close to 5.5 percent in recent years. This increase took place in steps: the unemployment rate first rose during the 2000–03 recession and then increased again during the 2009 recession; in both cases, it returned to the pre-recession level.

Unemployment is just one aspect of the labor market. A second important consideration is related to the remuneration received by those who have jobs. Available data show that, at least since 2003, wages for contract workers (a subsector of all formal workers) have increased at almost the same rate as prices. That implies that the wages for these workers have remained basically stagnant in real terms for the past ten years. Taking into account all types of workers (including informal workers), the data show that average monthly wages declined by almost 9 percent in real terms between 2007 and 2010.[13] As Freije, López-Acevedo, and Rodríguez-Oreggia put it: "During the crisis, average real wages declined in almost all economic activities and no increase has been recorded during the recovery. Real wages are lower compared to pre-crisis levels."[14] This large decline in real wages has not been fully reversed despite the continuing expansions of 2011 and 2012.

Samaniego points out that Mexico also is in the midst of demographic change, one that implies the need for a faster rate of job creation because of the rapid increase in the labor force.[15] She argues that migration to the United States, which traditionally has been used as a safety valve during economic crises, did not work this time because the crisis originated in the U.S. economy. She suggests that in addition to seeking employment in the informal labor sector, which has increased, those who have recently lost their jobs as well as new entrants to the labor force have followed alternative paths. Among them are the option of returning to rural areas (for those who came to urban areas seeking employment), the "NiNi" phenomenon (young people who neither work nor study [*ni trabaja, ni estudia*]), and crime-related activity.

Poverty

The rise in the poverty rate is one of the clearest examples of the negative effects of the global financial crisis in Mexico. Between 1992 and 2006, Mexico had been able to reduce its total poverty rate (which includes both the moderately and the extremely poor) from 53.1 percent to 42.7 percent of the total population.[16] Similarly, during the same period the extreme poverty rate declined from 21.4 percent to 13.8 percent. However, between 2006 and 2010, both poverty rates increased substantially, a result of the rapid increase in food prices during this period as well as of the economic crisis. While the extreme poverty rate rose from 13.8 percent to 18.8 percent, the total poverty rate increased from 42.7 to 51.3 percent. During this four-year period, official estimates show that some 12 million Mexicans fell into poverty, of whom roughly half were considered extremely poor. These trends failed to improve significantly during the recovery period. Recent estimates provided by the official agency in charge of measuring poverty in Mexico (CONEVAL) show that income poverty increased again between 2010 and 2012, with an additional 3.5 million Mexicans classified as living in poverty.[17]

Conclusions

In summary, I conclude that despite the many economic reforms that the Mexican government has undertaken over the past three decades, the country is still very vulnerable to external shocks, in particular those coming from the U.S. economy through foreign trade. Moreover, the Mexican economy does not have the institutional setup needed to respond effectively to such shocks, since by institutional design—that is, because of the existence of a zero fiscal deficit law and a strict inflation targeting mechanism— it cannot implement countercyclical fiscal and monetary policies that could help to mitigate the impact of the shocks. Instead, the institutional design of the Mexican economy prescribes macroeconomic policies that actually lead to the amplification of external shocks.

The structural reforms undertaken in the previous decades have been mostly of the neoliberal type (according to the terminology suggested by Wise, Armijo, and Katada in this volume), and they did facilitate the relatively rapid recovery of the Mexican economy following the global financial crisis. In particular, the macroeconomic stability framework (low inflation, a flexible exchange rate, low public debt, and low fiscal and current account deficits)—together with the trade openness policies of the mid-1980s and early 1990s—was crucial in promoting an export-led recovery in the aftermath of the crisis. That does not mean, however, that the Mexican economy is actually excelling. Rather, it has just recently returned to its pre-crisis per capita income level.

The Mexican case partially supports some of the alternative explanations put forward by Wise, Armijo, and Katada in chapter 1 of this volume. However, my analysis demonstrates that some measures that could have facilitated resistance to the crisis have in some cases actually led to more vulnerability. That is the case with respect to hypothesis 3, which posits that prior trade reforms could have led to export diversification, thereby increasing crisis resistance—in this case rendering the Mexican economy less vulnerable to the U.S. market. For Mexico, however, the exact opposite has been true, since Mexico's foreign trade is still insufficiently diversified and highly concentrated in a single market (the U.S. market). Hypothesis 2, as it relates to prior banking reforms, fits the Mexican case a bit better, as the deep banking reforms undertaken in the aftermath of the mid-1990s Tequila crisis did lead to the recapitalization of the financial sector and the improvement of the financial regulatory framework. Those reforms were critical for avoiding a financial or banking crisis in Mexico immediately after the global financial crisis. In this regard, the lessons from previous crises were clearly learned and banking reforms certainly contributed to the stability of the economy.

Similarly, the strategic financial statecraft hypothesis (hypothesis 2) also applies, although on a more limited scale. In fact, the Mexican government has focused for a long time on building up foreign exchange reserves to enhance cooperation with international multilateral institutions that can guarantee credit lines and to lend increased credibility and stability to the country's flexible exchange rate regime. But when the global financial crisis struck, Mexico's foreign reserves still were not sufficient to counter volatility in the foreign exchange market. First, because the magnitude of the entry and exit of capital flows has been rather large in recent years; second, because Mexican policymakers decided against implementing any kind of capital control measures.

Two other hypotheses put forward in chapter 1 are relevant to the economic recovery in Mexico. Prior macroeconomic reform (hypothesis 1) was indisputably useful in Mexico's economic recovery. As discussed above, macroeconomic stability was a fundamental characteristic of the post–Tequila crisis recovery period. At the same time, the external situation and the fact that the world economy was characterized by high commodity prices and low interest rates in core economies during most of the first decade of the 2000s (hypothesis 4) played only a minor role in Mexico`s recovery. If anything, the external forces may have helped Mexico only through the role that they played in promoting the U.S. economic recovery.

All in all, I would argue that the numerous reforms that Mexico undertook prior to the global financial crisis were still not enough to reduce the country's macroeconomic vulnerability when the U.S. economy began to implode in 2008. Mexico badly needs to implement additional reforms in order to enhance macroeconomic stability, starting by diversifying international trade and changing the country's institutional macroeconomic policy framework to allow greater room for countercyclical fiscal and monetary policies. Such reform could be achieved by moving toward a more flexible inflation targeting scheme and implementing a structural fiscal balance rule instead of the balanced budget rule that it is currently in place.

Notes

1. See, for example, "The Rise of Mexico: Special Report," *The Economist,* November 24, 2012; Adam Thomson, "Mexico: Aztec Tiger," *Financial Times,* January 30, 2013; Chris Anderson, "Mexico: The New China," *New York Times,* January 26, 2013; Thomas L. Friedman, "How Mexico Got Back in the Game," *New York Times,* February 23, 2013; Thomas L. Friedman, "Is Mexico the Comeback Kid?," *New York Times,* February 26, 2013; Kenneth L. Rogoff, "Mexico Breaking Good?," *Project Syndicate,* March 6, 2013; Shannon O´Neil, "Mexico Makes It: A Transformed Society, Economy, and Government," *Foreign Affairs,* vol. 92, no. 2 (March-April 2013), pp. 52–63.

2. See the following for discussions on Mexico's long-run economic growth: Daniel Chiquiar and Manuel Ramos Francia, "Competitiveness and Growth of the Mexican Economy," Working Paper 11 (Mexico: Bank of Mexico, November 2009); Gerardo Esquivel and Fausto Hernández Trillo, "How Can Reforms Help Deliver Growth in Mexico?," in *Growing Pains in Latin America,* edited by Liliana Rojas-Suarez (Washington, D.C.: Center for Global Development, 2009), pp.192–235; Juan Carlos Moreno-Brid and Jaime Ros, *Development and Growth in the Mexican Economy: A Historical Perspective* (Oxford University Press, 2009); Javier Arias and others, "Policies to Promote Growth and Economic Efficiency in Mexico," Working Paper (Cambridge, Mass.: National Bureau of Economic Research, February 2010); Gordon Hanson, "Why Isn't Mexico Rich?," *Journal of Economic Literature,* vol. 48 (2010), pp. 987–1004; Timothy J. Kehoe and Kim J. Ruhl, "Why Have Economic Reforms in Mexico Not

Generated Growth?," *Journal of Economic Literature,* vol. 48 (2010), pp. 1005–27; Timothy J. Kehoe and Felipe Meza, "Catch-Up Growth Followed by Stagnation: Mexico, 1950–2010," Working Paper 17700 (Cambridge, Mass.: National Bureau of Economic Research, December 2011).

3. The next two sections are slightly modified and updated versions of Gerardo Esquivel, "Mexico: Large, Immediate Negative Impact and Weak Medium-Term Growth Prospects," in *The Great Recession and Developing Countries: Economic Impact and Growth Prospects,* edited by Mustapha K. Nabli (Washington: World Bank, 2010), pp. 359–404.

4. See Esquivel and Hernández Trillo, "How Can Reforms Help Deliver Growth in Mexico?," on the first issue and Fabrice Lehoucq and others, "Political Institutions, Policymaking Processes, and Policy Outcomes in Mexico," Working Paper R-512 (Washington: Inter-American Development Bank, September 2005), on the second issue.

5. In early 2013, with a new administration in place, there was another wave of so-called structural reforms (in areas such as education, telecommunications, and the financial sector, among others). Those reforms, however, have not yet been implemented, and it is not even clear that they are as deep and far-reaching as necessary.

6. See Ebrima Faal, "GDP Growth, Potential Output, and Output Gaps in Mexico," Working Paper (Washington: International Monetary Fund, May 2005); Rodrigo García-Verdú, "Demographics, Human Capital, and Economic Growth in Mexico: 1950–2005," Working Paper (Washington: World Bank, June 2007).

7. See, for example, the study summarized in "Mexico: Selected Issues," IMF Country Report 10/70 (Washington: International Monetary Fund, March 2009).

8. International Monetary Fund, "Mexico: Staff Report for the 2008 Article IV Consultation" (Washington: January 2009); International Monetary Fund, "Mexico: Staff Report for the 2008 Article IV Consultation, Supplementary Information" (Washington: February 2009).

9. *Estudio Económico de América Latina y el Caribe 2008–2009* [Economic Study of Latin America and the Caribbean 2008–2009] (Santiago de Chile: CEPAL, 2009); Organization for Economic Cooperation and Development, *Economic Outlook Interim Report* (Paris: OECD, March 2009).

10. Ben Bernanke, *The Federal Reserve and the Financial Crisis* (Princeton University Press, 2013).

11. Robert A. Blecker and Gerardo Esquivel, "NAFTA, Trade, and Economic Development," Working Paper 24 (Washington: American University, Department of Economics, 2009).

12. Data come from the World Development Indicators of the World Bank; 2011 is the last year for which data are available for all countries.

13. For more details on the labor market impact of the crisis in Mexico, see Samuel Freije, Gladys López-Acevedo, and Eduardo Rodríguez-Oreggia, "Effects of the 2008–09 Economic Crisis on Labor Markets in Mexico," Working Paper 5840 (Washington: World Bank, October 2011).

14. Ibid.

15. Norma Samaniego, "El Empleo y la Crisis: Precarización y Nuevas Válvulas de Escape [Employment and the Crisis: Job Deterioration and New Escape Valves]," *Economía UNAM*, vol. 7, no. 020 (May 2010), pp. 47–70.

16. All figures mentioned here are official data on income poverty provided by the Consejo Nacional de Evaluación de la Política Social [National Council for Evaluation of Social Policy] (CONEVAL), the institution in charge of measuring poverty in Mexico (www.coneval.gob.mx/Medicion/Paginas/Ingreso-Corriente-per-capita.aspx).

17. Ibid.

LESLIE ELLIOTT ARMIJO, CAROL WISE, *and*
SAORI N. KATADA

9

Lessons from the Country Case Studies

This book investigates an unexpected outcome: the quick rebound of most emerging economies around the Pacific Rim (which we define expansively to include Brazil, Argentina, and India) from the 2008–09 global financial crisis. The previous seven chapters delved into economic policy choices and outcomes in key countries. In this concluding chapter we combine insights from those country case studies with quantitative data on 14 emerging economies in Asia and Latin America. We begin with a brief roundup of the findings from the case studies; we then revisit the four hypotheses laid out in chapter 1 to explain the quick rebound in the countries analyzed.

In general, the lessons from the country case studies suggest that one reason why these emerging economies (EEs) recovered much more quickly from the 2008–09 global financial crisis (GFC) than they did from crises during the previous three decades was the near universal willingness of governments to implement standard, Keynesian, countercyclical policies in response to a shock that originated unexpectedly from the richest industrial economy in the world. There were at least two components to this greater willingness to implement stimulus policies in 2008–09. First, pro-market structural reforms undertaken prior to the GFC (often in response to previous international financial crises and frequently imposed by fiat from abroad) had indeed improved the underlying fiscal, monetary, and banking sector fundamentals in many developing economies around the Pacific Rim. In other words, the macroeconomic conditions in those countries gave most governments the fiscal leeway and hence the policy space needed to implement countercyclical policies.

Second, governments in many of these EEs had learned from previous crises that two closely related pitfalls were to be avoided at all costs. The first was a run on the currency, which governments prepared for by building up their foreign currency reserves and moving away from the mostly fixed exchange rates of earlier eras. More flexible currencies, combined with greater willingness to intervene to support the exchange rate, did indeed fend off the usual currency crises associated with large external financial shocks. The second situation to be avoided, if at all possible, was the need to borrow from international financial institutions (IFIs), which could then be expected to impose conditions on borrowing governments—conditions that almost inevitably were at odds with governments' wishes.

A Quick Review of the Country Findings

In the introductory chapter we suggested that the ability of the emerging economies as a group to resist the initial financial contagion of the global financial crisis depended—as a necessary if not sufficient condition—on the extensive macroeconomic, financial sector, and trade reforms implemented by these governments since the early 1990s. We also observed that countervailing factors in the international environment during 2000–14 had, on balance, favored both the economic resistance of the EEs to financial contagion in 2008–09 and their recovery in the wake of the crisis. The combination of prior market reforms and fortuitous countervailing factors provided unprecedented policy leeway, especially in the Latin American cases, to pragmatically tackle the challenge of the GFC in more flexible, nondoctrinaire ways. The country case study evidence generally supports this conclusion.

China has come a long way since launching its more market-oriented economic reforms in the late 1970s, transitioning from a highly state-controlled economy to a bona-fide emerging economy by the advent of the 2000s. But Breslin cautions that China's market economy is a far cry from the neoliberal model earlier advocated by the Washington Consensus. The government still maintains vast influence over prices, particularly those for the factors of production. Despite a decrease in the number of state-owned enterprises, strategically important sectors still remain in the hands of the military and state bureaucracy. Moreover, public sector banks control most financial intermediation and still respond to official pressure, despite their greater use of commercial criteria to assess loans. Nonetheless, the 1990s and the 2000–14 period saw some significant reforms, such as recapitalization of the banks and the reduction of bad bank debt. Fiscal reform allowed the central government to regain fiscal control, permitting China to run a budgetary surplus by 2007. With little debt at the national or household level, this boosted government and household consumption. The country, moreover, had accumulated the astonishing sum of close to US$2 trillion in foreign exchange reserves by the time that the global financial crisis hit.

In South Korea, the Asian financial crisis (AFC) was the catalyst for deep financial sector reform. During the Korean economic miracle from the late 1960s through the 1990s, policymakers liberalized financial markets slowly in order to avoid the vulnerabilities to which rapid liberalization would expose the economy. The AFC forced Korea to turn to the International Monetary Fund (IMF) for a rescue package, an experience that simultaneously enforced market-oriented reforms and instilled a determination among politicians and economists across the political spectrum to never again allow conditions imposed from abroad to dictate crucial policy reforms. Although Korea had always been relatively cautious in its macroeconomic policymaking, Stallings shows that it became even more so after the AFC. For example, policymakers shifted from a fixed to a more flexible exchange rate, partly to forestall the kinds of excessive volatility typically associated with rapid financial and capital account liberalization. Banks were recapitalized and bank regulations strengthened.

Echeverri-Gent argues that despite India's limited financial sector reform prior to the global financial crisis, the country's fiscal, monetary, and foreign exchange positions as of 2008 were reasonably robust. India reformed its monetary policy approach in the 1990s and cut the fiscal deficit after 2003. The liberalization of India's foreign exchange market, which had proceeded incrementally in the 1990s, provided flexibility in the value of the rupee. That, in turn, allowed India's central bank, the Reserve Bank of India (RBI), greater scope to manage inflows of foreign capital and to intervene strategically in the foreign exchange market.

In contrast, Beeson's discussion of the Southeast Asian countries confirms that the level of pre-crisis reform across these countries was quite uneven. In fact, with the possible exception of the larger economies such as Indonesia and Thailand, the ability of domestic policy reforms to head off a significant international financial crisis was quite limited. Still, two pre-crisis shifts in the economic structure of most Southeast Asian countries bear mentioning. First, governments across Southeast Asia gleaned the same lesson from the AFC as policymakers did in the rest of East Asia: that they needed to build up foreign exchange reserves in order to survive financial contagion. Second, the 2000–14 period saw economies throughout Southeast Asia becoming more dependent on China, so much so that China's economic performance would become perhaps the most important determinant of how those economies responded to externally generated crises. In this instance, China's ability to successfully weather the global financial crisis was a boon to its much smaller regional neighbors.

In comparing the Latin American emerging economies with those in Asia, Hershberg notes the following themes. First, the majority of countries in both regions had reasonably good macroeconomic fundamentals going into the crisis. While that also had been true for some East Asian countries prior to the Asian financial crisis, it emphatically had not been the case for most Latin American countries before the 1982–83 debt crisis. Second, financial liberalization, including external opening, was much more extensive in most countries in Latin America than in their East Asian counterparts. Third, while both regions saw a substantial buildup of foreign exchange reserves for insurance reasons, the buildup was greater in East Asia than in either Latin America or India. Finally, most Latin American countries, with the exception of Mexico, are mainly commodity exporters, while most emerging economies in Asia are commodity importers. Interestingly, due to China's rising demand for commodity imports during 2000–14, the South American economies have become less engaged with the United States both politically and economically. This greater distancing from the U.S. market served the South American countries well in surviving the financial shocks of the GFC, in contrast to Mexico, which relies heavily on the U.S. market.

Other significant factors are highlighted by Wise and Lins in their chapter on Brazil and Argentina, including the substantial bank restructuring and recapitalization that followed the end of hyperinflation in both countries in the mid-1990s. In Brazil, in 2000–14 policymakers made a conscious decision to substitute domestic for foreign debt, even if the amount of public debt remained high. In Argentina, what stands out is the extremely dramatic, even draconian, fiscal and monetary policies embodied in the Convertibility Plan, implemented in 1991, although those policies were loosened considerably in the wake of Argentina's 2001–02 financial meltdown. Finally, Esquivel's analysis of Mexico suggests that external factors—including a strong U.S. economy, rising petroleum prices, and high levels of remittances—played a strong role in Mexico's favorable pre-crisis conditions, which included an improvement in the balance of payments, significant exchange reserves, and positive fiscal accounts (see table 9-1).

Table 9-1. *Summary of Country Cases*

Country	Prior reforms	Crisis transmission	Crisis response
China	Bank recapitalization Expanded foreign exchange reserves Increased space for private sector	Trade	Fiscal and monetary expansion, relying on state banks
South Korea	Bank liberalization and recapitalization Expanded foreign exchange reserves	Mainly financial	Fiscal and monetary expansion
India	Trade liberalization and diversification Modest financial liberalization Expanded foreign exchange reserves	Mainly financial (reduced capital inflows; Indian firms lack credit) Falling remittances from abroad	Monetary expansion Exchange rate flexibility Emergency capital controls to halt excessive inflows
Brazil	Macroeconomic stabilization Bank recapitalization Substitution of domestic for foreign debt Expanded foreign exchange reserves	Mainly financial (Brazilian transnational firms lack credit)	Fiscal and monetary expansion, using state banks Emergency capital controls to halt excessive inflows
Argentina	Macroeconomic stabilization, partly reversed from 2002 Expanded foreign exchange reserves	Financial (massive capital flight)	Amplification of previous expansion Emergency capital controls to halt outflows
Mexico	Macroeconomic stabilization; integration with U.S. economy	Trade; remittances from abroad	Initially procyclical monetary policy, reversed in 2009

Source: Authors' illustration.

Each of the country chapters also analyzes the main transmission mechanisms of the global financial crisis. For emerging economies heavily dependent on exports to the United States—including both China and Mexico among the larger countries—the general slowdown of the U.S. economy led to an abrupt fall in demand for imports from these countries and hence a trade shock. There was a direct financial shock from the GFC for most of the other emerging economies examined, although in almost all cases it was buffered by the buildup of foreign exchange reserves. In some countries, including South Korea, Brazil, and India, the major financial jolt came as hard-hit financial institutions in the United States and other advanced economies failed to renew working capital and credit lines for trade financing for EE firms doing business abroad—which was much the same transmission mechanism as in the earlier emerging market crises of the 1980s and 1990s. However, the underlying reasons for the credit shock differed. In the crises of the 1980s and 1990s, a loss of faith in emerging economies sparked the credit drawback, but in 2008–09 it reflected instead a loss of capability among the lending institutions of the global North. Among the cases reviewed in this volume, the sudden drop in remittances from nationals who had migrated to wealthy countries to seek employment was especially acute in Mexico, Central America, and India.

With regard to responses to the global financial crisis, it is clear that virtually every country considered in this volume implemented some form of countercyclical macroeconomic policies, at least eventually. That would not have been possible in the absence of a cushion of some sort, whether in the form of relatively low public debt and deficits, high foreign exchange reserves, or a high investment-grade rating due to a sound record of reform prior to the crisis. Countries such as Mexico, South Korea, Brazil, and Singapore received access to emergency foreign currency swap lines opened by the U.S. Federal Reserve Bank or jointly by China and Japan through the Chiang-Mai Initiative.[1] In addition, the countries themselves were proactive. For example, Brazil, India, and Argentina unabashedly resorted to emergency capital controls.

Among the major cases profiled, only Mexico failed to respond rapidly to the global financial crisis, as policymakers there believed that prior market-oriented reforms and a neoliberal macroeconomic policy stance would insulate them from its effects. Moreover, because the country's financial sector was sound due to consolidation and stricter regulation, the government considered it immune. When the GFC hit the real sector with full force, those assumptions could not have been less accurate. Mexico's late fiscal stimulus was relatively small, and because of worries about rapid food price increases at home, the Mexican monetary authority actually increased interest rates, which were not reduced until early 2009. Intervention by the Mexican development banks did provide some liquidity and enabled credit markets to function during the worst of the crisis, and high foreign exchange reserves enabled the government to avoid a costly currency depreciation.

Nonetheless, each of the volume's contributors expresses reservations about the future economic fate of the emerging economies examined here, despite their victory in surviving the global financial crisis relatively unscathed. For example, China's post-GFC economic strategy has reverted to allowing the state to use its political leverage over commercial banks to direct loans to favored borrowers. About two-thirds of China's overall net growth in 2009 emerged from increases in already high and often inefficient investment spending. In both Brazil and India, as discussed by Echeverri-Gent, there were ongoing policy debates between market liberalizers and those favoring a strong economic leadership role for the state. The latter seemingly prevailed, as state banks had proved their worth in quickly implementing countercyclical policies. But by 2013, India had moved decisively toward further economic and financial liberalization, whereas in Brazil the economic role of the national development bank (BNDES) continued to expand throughout 2013, generating concerns about increasingly inefficient forms of investment. Argentina is perhaps the most worrisome case. Since its early 2002 debt default, the country has been basically shut out of international capital markets, while the GFC has forced the government to draw down central bank reserves at a precipitous rate.

The discussion now returns more explicitly to the four composite hypotheses presented in chapter 1. How, in the end, do we assess these different explanatory themes?

Hypothesis 1: Good Macroeconomic Fundamentals Improve Crisis Resistance and Response

Our introductory chapter suggested that the ability of the Pacific Rim emerging economies to resist the initial financial contagion from the global financial crisis had much to do with the extensive macroeconomic reforms undertaken by most of them, beginning in the late 1980s in Latin America and somewhat later in Asia. Going into the 2008–09 crisis, most of the larger EEs considered here did indeed have "good numbers." Governments, in general, had implemented what neoliberals regard as prudent macroeconomic reforms in response to earlier crises, even when their initial effects were politically

Table 9-2. *Inflation in Asia and Latin America, 1980–2009*
Percent of GDP, period means

Country	1980–84	1985–89	1990–94	1995–99	2000–04	2005–09
China	2	8	11	4	3	4
India	9	8	11	7	5	6
Indonesia	14	8	8	24	9	13
Korea	12	6	9	5	3	2
Malaysia	4	1	4	4	3	3
Philippines	20	9	11	8	5	5
Thailand	6	4	5	4	2	4
Argentina	279	855	445	0	12	13
Brazil	130	488	1,674	26	10	7
Chile	19	23	17	4	5	6
Colombia	24	26	30	16	7	6
Mexico	54	82	17	23	10	5
Peru	82	725	1,472	8	3	4
Venezuela	13	31	37	50	27	20

Source: World Bank, *World Development Indicators: 2011* (http://data.worldbank.org/ products/wdi).

unpopular. Their macroeconomic fundamentals enabled these EEs to avoid the destabilizing effects typically wrought by external financial contagion.

The three most common indicators of macroeconomic status—inflation, external debt, and public or government debt—reflect a dramatic improvement in EEs' macroeconomic performance since 1990. The gains are especially visible in Latin America. Table 9-2 shows that during the early 1990s, three of the seven largest Latin American economies still had average annual inflation rates that ran into triple or even quadruple digits. By the early years of the 2000s, all but Venezuela were within striking distance of the inflation rates in the advanced economies. Asian countries that struggled with inflation—for example, South Korea and the Philippines—also reduced it significantly over the time period shown in the table. In Asia, only Indonesia continues to lag on this indicator.

External debt as a percentage of GDP shows similar declines in both Latin America and Asia (figure 9-1). In fact, across these EEs, external debt was at its lowest level in decades when the crisis hit. Asia's debt peaked following the Asian financial crisis of 1997–99 and has since continued on a downward slope. Latin America's debt burden peaked in the late 1980s; after rising somewhat in the early years of the 2000s, it has fallen to its lowest level since 1980.

Figure 9-1. *External Debt Stocks in Latin America and Asia*[a]

Percent of GDP

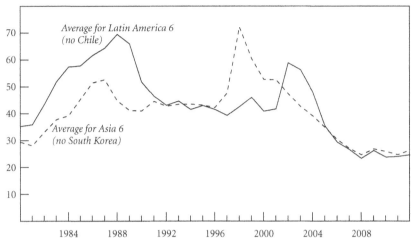

Source: World Bank, *World Development Indicators: 2011* (http://data.worldbank.org/products/wdi).
a. Unweighted means of seven large Latin American economies and six large Asian ones (South Korea is not included).

Levels of foreign debt in both regions were and have remained well below the 90 percent mark that Reinhart and Rogoff consider likely to jeopardize economic stability.[2] As mentioned earlier, not all of that debt was actually retired, as some governments, particularly in Latin America, substituted domestic for foreign borrowing as a means of reducing their foreign exchange risk.

Public debt around the Pacific Rim was also running at reasonable levels on the eve of the 2008–09 crisis and even fell afterward. Figure 9-2, which reflects regional weighted means, shows that the ratio of public debt to GDP in Latin America has remained about 20 percentage points above its level in developing Asia. However, since the turn of the twenty-first century, the level of public debt across these EEs has been notably lower than that registered in the major advanced industrial countries.

Although the contribution of prior macroeconomic reform to the quick rebound was clearly important and very likely essential, reform alone does not provide a sufficient explanation for the resistance to and recovery from the 2008–09 crisis among major emerging economies. One reason to doubt that good macroeconomic fundamentals are sufficient in themselves comes from

Figure 9-2. *Public Debt*[a]

Percent of GDP

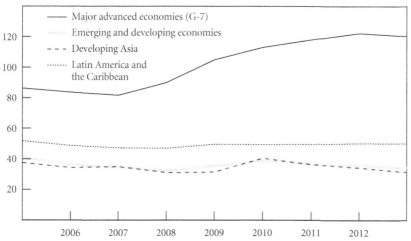

Source: "General Government Debt Stock," World Bank, *World Development Indicators: 2011* (http://data.worldbank.org/products/wdi).

a. Weighted means for each group.

a look back at the Asian financial crisis. In 1997–99 many East Asian countries, including Indonesia, Thailand, and South Korea, had good macroeconomic fundamentals; nonetheless, they were devastated by financial contagion. The larger global political economy arguably played a decisive role: in previous financial crises, even EE governments that possessed ample fiscal or monetary resources implemented the procyclical austerity policies forced on them by the international financial institutions, which were controlled by the major advanced industrial countries.[3]

In contrast, when the global financial crisis hit the emerging economies in early 2008, policymakers in most of them drew down international reserves, loosened fiscal policy, and lowered reserve requirements for domestic banks. Table 9-3 suggests that China's stimulus efforts were on par, both in absolute terms and as a share of domestic GDP, with the stimulus packages implemented by the United States, Germany, and Japan.[4] Moreover, other major East Asian countries contributed as much proportionately to their stimulus efforts as did the remaining G-7 economies. India, Argentina, Brazil, and Mexico had less room to maneuver in terms of the size of their respective stimulus packages, but they did contribute modestly, including in ways that are not

Table 9-3. *Macroeconomic Stimulus Packages*

Country	Policy interest rate cut (percent, to March 2009)	Fiscal stimulus (U.S. dollars, billions)	Fiscal stimulus (percent of GDP)
Canada	3.50	43.6	2.8
France	(ECB)[a] 1.50	20.5	0.7
Germany	(ECB) 1.50	130.4	3.4
Italy	(ECB) 1.50	7.0	0.3
Japan	0.40	104.4	2.2
United Kingdom	2.00	40.8	1.5
United States	3.50	841.2	5.9
China	2.16	204.3	4.8
Korea	2.00	26.1	2.7
India	2.50	6.5	0.5
Indonesia	2.50	12.5	2.5
Malaysia	1.25	...	...
Philippines	0.50	...	...
Thailand	2.50	...	...
Argentina	...	4.4	1.3
Brazil	1.00	8.6	0.5
Chile	1.25	...	...
Mexico	0.25	11.4	1.0

Sources: Interest rate cuts from S. Khatiwada, "Stimulus Packages to Counter Global Economic Crisis: A Review," Discussion Paper (Geneva: International Institute for Labour Studies, 2009), pp. 10, 12; fiscal stimulus from Eswar Prasad and Isaac Sorkin, "Assessing the G-20 Stimulus Plans: A Deeper Look" (Brookings, March 2009), p. 5 (www.brookings.edu/research/articles/2009/03/g20-stimulus-prasad).

a. ECB = European Central Bank.

measured in table 9-3, such as the direct expansion of credit through state banks. The smaller countries in both East Asia and Latin America piggy-backed on the countercyclical policies of their larger neighbors, as explained by Beeson (chapter 5) and Hershberg (chapter 6).

Overall, we conclude that prior macroeconomic reform was a necessary—but not entirely sufficient—factor in the timely rebound of the emerging economies from the global financial crisis. Below we explore financial and trade reforms, other dimensions of national policy environments that permitted EE governments greater policy space than they had enjoyed in the recent past.

Hypothesis 2: Stronger Banks and Financial Sector Reform Enabled Crisis Resistance

Our second hypothesis emphasized the role of prior financial sector reforms in promoting crisis resistance. As noted earlier, many of the emerging market crises of the 1980s and 1990s had been twin crises: first a run on a country's currency when a fixed exchange rate had lost all credibility, then a domestic financial panic when too many savers attempted to withdraw their bank funds at the same time. How important were prior financial sector reforms for EE resistance to and recovery from the global financial crisis?

Neoliberal financial reforms have several distinct dimensions, including international and domestic financial liberalization and deregulation as well as harmonization of domestic financial regulations toward the global financial governance norms embodied in international agreements such as the various Basel Accords on bank regulation. Financial liberalization is said to lead to greater financial depth (a higher ratio of financial assets to GDP) and better performance outcomes, such as fewer nonperforming loans and adequate liquidity in the national economy. In the aftermath of the acute financial crises of the 1980s and 1990s, emerging economies on both sides of the Pacific instituted substantial reforms to liberalize their financial sectors. In Latin American EEs such as Argentina and Mexico, the 1980s debt crisis was the trigger for the reforms. Despite Argentina's abrupt reversal of its liberalization effort in 2002, most Latin American governments have persevered with financial sector reform.[5] Banking deregulation, financial deepening, and the move to floating exchange rates had taken root throughout most of Latin America by the early years of the 2000s.

In Asia, countries that had implemented IMF structural adjustment programs in the throes of the Asian financial crisis—including South Korea, Indonesia, and Thailand—dramatically reduced their nonperforming loans through the 2000–14 period and liberalized domestic finance. South Korea, an OECD member since 1996, has been ranked as having Asia's most liberal financial sector since the government removed all ceilings on foreign shareholding in 1998 and liberalized all capital account transactions in 1999.[6] The discussion by Stallings in chapter 3 of this volume confirms that Korea's financial sector reforms were profound, resulting in a stronger banking sector with greater legal and regulatory oversight. By 2004, nonperforming loans accounted for only 1 percent of all credit. The Korean government also accepted dramatically increased foreign entry into retail commercial banking as part of its effort to import "best practices" from the advanced industrial countries. Under the influence of the IMF, South Korea also introduced a flexible exchange rate policy to better manage domestic financial liberalization.

Of course, not all Asian countries were eager to implement financial reforms along the lines of those recommended by the Washington Consensus. As Breslin observes in chapter 2 of this volume, although China's banking sector is still heavily state owned, improvements that began in the 1990s have led to bank recapitalization and the reduction of bad debt. Echeverri-Gent emphasizes in chapter 4 that in India even basic financial reforms, such as liberalizing private entry into banking and loosening interest rate controls, have remained quite controversial. Similarly, among the Southeast Asian countries considered by Beeson in chapter 5, Indonesia, which stands at one end of the spectrum, has instituted a much more liberal bank regulatory framework than has Malaysia, which is famous for its continued use of capital controls. In fact, there was a great deal of variation among the 14 large Asian and Latin American emerging economies considered here in terms of financial policy reform and financial outcome variables on the eve of the GFC.

In order to sort out the role of prior financial reforms, we need some reliable comparative financial information on the major EEs, which would allow us to judge how much each individual country had reformed according to some absolute standard rather than simply in relation to the earlier financial policy scenario within the country. Table 9-4, which contains comparative information on our 14 EEs, provides context by including similar statistics for the G-7 countries. The first column assesses how financially open each country was on the eve of the global financial crisis. The indicator is a composite "financial policy openness index," which we constructed as the mean of three measures that track de jure capital controls, foreign bank entry into the domestic retail banking market, and domestic financial liberalization, especially the absence of barriers to entry for new banks. Not surprisingly, the G-7 countries were the most financially open, Latin American countries were not far behind, and the Asian emerging economies were the least liberalized. This index also reminds us that however much China and India may have reformed their financial sectors relative to previous conditions in those countries, when viewed within the international context, both financial systems remain heavily state dominated.

The contrasting developmentalist approach toward financial sector reform posits that countries that employed "strategic" financial levers—including reliance on state banks, capital controls, intentional diversification of international lenders, accumulation of large foreign exchange reserves, and creation of

Table 9-4. *Financial Liberalization, Depth, and Performance, 2007*

Country	Liberalization Financial Policy Openness Index[a]	Depth Financial assets/GDP	Domestic performance Nonperforming loans/ total loans	Credit to private sector/GDP
Canada	0.66	4.93	0.7	1.57
France	0.69	3.37	2.7	0.99
Germany	0.69	3.34	2.6	1.05
Italy	0.64	3.05	4.6	0.96
Japan	0.69	6.77	1.4	0.97
United Kingdom	0.85	4.70	1.6	1.74
United States	0.64	4.63	2.9	2.02
G-7 mean[b]	0.69	4.40	2.4	1.33
China	0.14	0.44	6.2	n.a.
India	0.19	2.62	2.5	0.43
Indonesia	0.60	1.28	4.1	0.23
Korea	0.81	3.35	0.7	1.01
Malaysia	0.45	4.66	6.5	1.01
Philippines	0.31	1.92	4.5	0.28
Thailand	0.36	2.98	5.7	0.83
Asian 7 mean[b]	0.41	2.46	4.3	0.63[c]
Argentina	0.32	1.02	2.7	0.13
Brazil	0.54	2.53	2.0	0.43
Chile	0.88	2.42	0.8	0.80
Colombia	0.49	1.15	3.3	0.36
Mexico	0.72	1.22	2.7	0.20
Peru	0.71	1.38	2.2	0.19
Venezuela	0.40	1.29	1.9	0.18
Latin American 7 mean[b]	0.59	1.57	2.2	0.33
Emerging economies 14 mean	0.50	2.02	3.25	0.44[c]

Sources: Our Financial Policy Openness Index is the mean of three measures (re-normed to a common scale): the 2007 score on "overall restrictions [on international financial integration] index," from M. Schindler, "Measuring Financial Integration: A New Data Set," *IMF Staff Papers*, vol. 56, no. 1 (2009), pp. 222–38; the 2005 figure for "fraction of the banking systems assets in banks that are 50 percent or more foreign owned," from J. Barth, G. Caprio, and R. Levine, "Bank Regulation and Supervision Dataset" (2008) (http://econ.worldbank.org/WBSITE/EXTERNAL/EXTDEC/EXTRESEARCH/0,content MDK:20345037~pagePK:64214825~piPK:64214943~theSitePK:469382,00. html); and the 2007 score for "domestic financial liberalization," from G. Kaminsky and S. Schmukler, "Short-Run

(continued on page 216)

bilateral or multilateral currency swap lines—coped with the financial crisis much better. Once the banking sector is fully liberalized—particularly if it becomes dominated by foreign private banks, as in the case of Mexico and to a lesser extent Chile and South Korea in the early twenty-first century—the central government has less control over the choices and activities of the domestic financial sector.[7]

It is not a straightforward matter, in either theory or practice, to distinguish "developmentalist" financial approaches from old-fashioned "financial repression," whereby financial markets are severely distorted and become inefficient due to excessive government manipulation.[8] To a great degree, that judgment is in the eye of the beholder. We also do not attempt to approximate the relative strength of developmentalist financial levers in each country; instead, we include in table 9-4 a single succinct index that summarizes where these EEs stand on a continuum that runs from closed to open in terms of a given EE's financial sector. Nonetheless, we may conclude that Asian governments, on average, have had a wider range of financial levers at their disposal than have the Latin American governments, while state control of financial levers is lowest in the advanced industrial economies.[9] For example, in 2005, based on the unweighted means for each group, public sector institutions' share of total bank assets averaged 35 percent for the Asian 7 and 19 percent for the Latin American 7.[10] Those figures stand in sharp contrast to the mean share of state-owned banks in the G-7 countries, which was less than 8 percent over the same period.[11] Asian EEs also have tended to rely more on capital controls and have built up larger foreign exchange war chests than have their Latin American counterparts. The two Asian giants, India and China, still maintain high levels of control in their respective financial sectors.[12] On a scale ranging from 0 (most closed) to 1.00 (most open), the mean financial sector openness score for the Asian 7 in 2005 was only 0.24 and would have been much lower

Pain, Long-Run Gain: The Effects of Financial Liberalization," IMF Working Paper 03/34 (2003) (updated by World Economic Forum, *The Financial Development Report 2009*). The figures for "Financial assets/GDP" and "Credit to private sector/GDP" are from Thorsten Beck and A. Demirguc-Kunt, "Financial Institutions and Markets across Countries and over Time: Data and Analysis," World Bank Policy Research Working Paper 4943 (May 2009), drawn from columns AM and L, respectively, in the spreadsheet that reports their dataset. "Nonperforming loans/total loans," is from World Bank, *World Development Indicators: 2011* (http://data.worldbank.org/products/wdi).

   a. Index runs from 0.00 to 1.00, most statist to most financially open.
   b. Regional means are unweighted.
   c. Mean excludes China.

without outlier Korea, which scored 0.88 on this measure.[13] The more market-oriented Latin American 7 had a mean financial sector openness score of 0.69.

What stands out then is a set of more statist Asian countries, particularly China and India, and a group of more financially open Latin American countries, notably Chile and Mexico. Financially liberal South Korea is the outlier in Asia, and financially closed Argentina and Venezuela are the outliers in Latin America. Table 9-4 also reports on some other key variables often used to measure financial sector health—including financial depth, nonperforming loans as a share of total loans outstanding, and level of credit extended to the private sector. We assess these dimensions as they stood on the eve of the global financial crisis. When we aggregate the groups by region, it appears that there is no clear relationship between a high degree of financial liberalization (or the reverse) and any of these measures of national financial health. For example, on average, the more financially liberal Latin American EEs had shallower domestic financial systems and extended less credit to entrepreneurs and citizens, but they also had lower rates of nonperforming loans. In contrast, the more developmentalist Asian EEs had greater financial depth and extended more credit to private borrowers, but they had larger shares of nonperforming loans, which often are an indication of financial problems further down the line. In terms of individual countries, relatively neoliberal South Korea and Chile, followed by relatively interventionist India and Brazil, had the best composite profiles, sitting at, or better, than the EE mean on all three performance indicators.

Another measure of financial policy space—or the potential ability of a country to intervene to regulate or move countercyclically against volatile capital flows—is the size of a country's foreign exchange war chest. Because of the lessons that EE policymakers had drawn from earlier crises, countries throughout the Pacific Rim had much larger foreign exchange reserves at their disposal when the 2008–09 crisis hit than they had during earlier financial emergencies.[14] Once again, the Asian countries as a group were most interventionist, the Latin American countries were somewhat developmentalist, and the advanced democracies had the least state involvement in their domestic financial markets. As shown in figure 9-3, the foreign exchange reserves of most Asian governments, especially China, were larger, both absolutely and relative to the home economy, than those of major Latin American governments. The foreign exchange reserves of the advanced industrial countries, except Japan, have remained small by comparison.[15]

Figure 9-3. *Foreign Exchange Reserves: 2000–09*[a]

U.S. dollars, billions

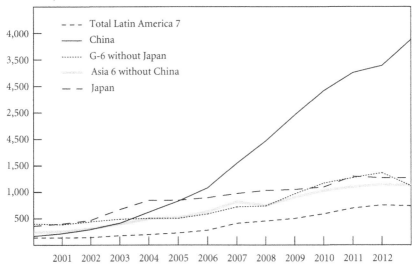

Source: World Bank, World Development Indicators, various years (http://data.worldbank.org/products/wdi).
a. Reserves excluding gold.

In sum, the banking and external financial sectors of these 14 large EEs as a group had been liberalized and modernized substantially in comparison with those sectors during the bad old days of financial repression in the 1960s through the 1980s. At the same time, many countries—particularly in Asia but also including Argentina, Brazil, and Venezuela in South America—opted to retain an array of "interventionist" instruments, including state banks and large foreign exchange reserves that could be employed for defensive financial statecraft. When international financial contagion seriously threatened these EEs in 2008–09, none of them suffered a financial meltdown or a notorious "twin crisis" of simultaneous forced currency devaluation and domestic banking collapse—despite widespread fears that they would.

We judge that the pragmatic combination of liberalizing financial sector reforms in the two decades prior to the global financial crisis and careful and sometimes heterodox financial management during the GFC enabled policymakers in these countries to respond effectively to this daunting external shock.

Hypothesis 3: Trade Deepening and/or Diversification Improves Crisis Outcomes

A third policy dimension to which EE resilience could be attributed is that of prior trade reforms. The link between trade policy and the ability of EEs to survive a spreading international financial crisis is important, although less direct than the link between survival and the causal factors in our first two hypotheses. Economists across most of the ideological spectrum posit strong links between trade liberalization and increased trade integration as well as between trade integration and economic growth; many also attribute the emerging economies' gradual approximation to the status of the mature industrial economies ("convergence") primarily to the more open markets for world trade that have existed since World War II.[16] The debate continues over whether and how governments should intervene to promote exports or to diversify export products and markets.[17]

The wave of market reforms that began in the late 1980s and early 1990s in emerging economies around the Pacific Rim resulted in substantial trade liberalization as well as increased growth led by trade. Kose and Prasad note that emerging market countries "as a group now have the highest average trade openness ratio," about 80 percent.[18] An index of "trade freedom" prepared by the Heritage Foundation shows that trade became more open in the early twenty-first century in all three regions depicted in table 9-5. On an index running from 1 to 100, with 100 representing full liberalization of a country's trade policies, countries in all three groups (G-7, Asian 7, Latin American 7), with the exception of Venezuela, became more commercially open. The greatest movement toward trade opening within the G-7 (more than 10 points on the scale) occurred in Canada; within the Asian 7, China, India, Indonesia, and the Philippines made notable headway on this index; and within the Latin American 7, Chile, Brazil, Mexico, and Peru led the way in trade liberalization.

What about trade diversification, which has been a consistent goal of emerging market policymakers regardless of their ideological bent? In terms of trade product concentration, the G-7 and Asian 7, whose exports already were more diversified than those of the Latin American 7, saw little change in 2000–14 (see table 9-6). Because of Latin America's heavy reliance on commodity exports, the regional mean concentration rose in 2000–14, although only Chile and Venezuela ended with significant increases in product concentration. In terms

Table 9-5. *Trade Liberalization*[a]

Country	Trade policy openness		
	2000	2009	Change 2000–09
Canada	77.4	88.2	+10.8
France	77.8	80.8	+3.0
Germany	78.0	85.8	+7.8
Italy	77.8	80.8	+3.0
Japan	81.0	82.0	+1.0
United Kingdom	77.8	85.8	+8.0
United States	78.4	86.8	+8.4
G-7 mean[b]	78.3	84.3	+6.0
China	42.6	71.4	+28.8
India	19.6	51.0	+31.4
Indonesia	66.0	76.4	+10.4
South Korea	69.2	70.2	+1.0
Malaysia	68.8	78.2	+9.4
Philippines	64.6	78.6	+14.0
Thailand	73.2	75.6	+2.4
Asian 7 mean[b]	57.7	71.6	+13.9
Argentina	62.0	70.0	+8.0
Brazil	51.0	71.6	+20.0
Chile	70.4	85.8	+15.4
Colombia	63.8	72.4	+8.6
Mexico	63.0	80.2	+17.2
Peru	67.8	79.4	+11.6
Venezuela	65.6	59.6	−6.0
Latin American 7 mean[b]	63.4	74.1	+10.7

Sources: "Trade policy openness" is "Trade freedom," from the Heritage Foundation (www.heritage.org/index).

a. Index runs from 1 to 100, least to most trade policy openness.

b. Regional means are unweighted.

of trading partner concentration, each regional grouping as well as almost all of the individual countries diversified their export markets. The most prominent result that emerges from bilateral trading partner data (not shown in the table) is that Canada and Mexico are hugely dependent on the U.S. market, more so than any other countries in the table. A number of smaller Latin American and Caribbean countries (not shown in the tables in this chapter but discussed in chapter 6) have welcomed the opportunity to engage in long-term commodity export contracts with China, seeing it as an opportunity to

Table 9-6. *Trade Concentration*[a]

Country	Export product concentration			Export market concentration		
	1995–99	2006–09	+/–	1995–2000	2006–09	+/–
Canada	13.0	14.9		82.5	76.2	
France	6.6	7.3		26.4	17.9	
Germany	8.9	9.9		22.6	15.2	
Italy	5.5	5.5		25.9	16.1	
Japan	13.0	14.9		33.1	22.3	
United Kingdom	7.8	9.9		24.3	18.7	
United States	8.3	7.0		28.2	20.9	
G-7 mean[b]	9.0	9.8	+0.8	34.7	26.7	–8.0
China	7.4	9.6		35.3	20.6	
India	13.8	14.2		25.5	16.2	
Indonesia	14.3	12.9		31.3	23.0	
South Korea	14.8	15.7		26.8	24.7	
Malaysia	19.4	18.6		32.3	22.4	
Philippines	33.4	34.6		40.4	29.3	
Thailand	10.0	9.1		29.8	16.9	
Asian 7 mean[b]	16.1	16.4	+0.3	31.6	21.9	–9.7
Argentina	13.5	14.5		32.0	22.8	
Brazil	9.0	10.7		26.3	17.6	
Chile	29.3	39.0		26.8	19.6	
Colombia	26.4	25.2		42.9	32.9	
Mexico	12.4	16.4		85.4	71.4	
Peru	23.1	24.9		30.2	23.3	
Venezuela	54.5	91.1		56.6	37.9	
Latin American 7 mean[b]	24.0	31.7	+7.7	42.9	22.2	–20.7

Sources: World Bank, "World Trade Indicators 2009–10" (http://info.worldbank.org/etools/wti/3a.asp?pillarID=1&)

a. Indices run from 1 to 100, least to most trade concentration.

b. Regional means unweighted.

escape from their historically large and asymmetrical dependence on the United States. Moreover, a number of Southeast Asian countries, which look quite diversified in terms of markets in the aggregate data, actually engage in high levels of intra-firm trade and intermediate components production. This means that ultimately they are just as dependent on selling to North American and European markets as they were in the last two decades of the twentieth century.

Despite these caveats, table 9-6 suggests that most Pacific Rim developing countries, as well as the major advanced industrial economies, diversified their trading partners a bit. Few, however, expanded their mix of exports, and major Latin American countries became more concentrated in the export of commodities. Yet the absolute levels of trading partner diversification did not differ notably across the three groups of countries, thus presumably eliminating partner diversification as an explanation for why the recovery of the emerging economies was better than that of the advanced industrial countries. More subtly, we note that since the 1990s there has also been a concomitant rise in South-South trade across the two emerging regions of the Pacific Rim, much of it promoted by government policies. This explosion in EE trade across the Pacific possibly quickened the recovery of these countries from the global financial crisis. For example, Kose and Prasad calculate that intragroup trade among emerging economies, the so-called South-South trade, had "increased nearly fivefold over the last five decades, from less than 9 percent [of their total trade] in 1960 to slightly more than 42 percent in 2008."[19] In particular, rapid Chinese economic growth has led to higher demand for natural resources and intensification of regional trade integration in Asia and Latin America. Major South American countries that were once heavily dependent on the U.S. market now split their trade in varying amounts between China, the United States, the European Union, and their Latin American and Caribbean neighbors.[20]

While there seems to have been clear positive results from prior macroeconomic stabilization (hypothesis 1) and financial reforms and strengthening (hypothesis 2), the contribution of prior trade reforms (hypothesis 3) to the quick rebound is, at the very least, indirect. This is not to say that trade did not play a role in the rebound: for EEs like Argentina, Brazil, Chile, and Peru, the recovery of Chinese demand, in particular for primary commodity exports, was a key factor in their ability to overcome the 2008–09 crisis.[21] However, as compelling as the claim may be that prior trade liberalization mattered, we cannot demonstrate such a link. Moreover, the evidence on trade diversification is sufficiently ambiguous that we probably can discount it as an important explanation for the surprising resilience of Pacific Rim EEs to the global financial crisis.

Hypothesis 4: Emerging Economies Escaped the Crisis due to Favorable Global Conditions

The policy variables discussed so far were more or less under the control of national governments. Yet other aspects of the international economic environment might have tipped the scales disproportionately in favor of a swift recovery in emerging economies. Hypothesis 4 suggests that it was not principally hard-won policy reforms that protected the major EEs around the Pacific Rim from being sucked into the financial maelstrom initially generated by dodgy subprime mortgages in the United States. Instead, the relatively mild effects that EEs experienced were largely the result of the commodity lottery and the luck of the draw for countries with an abundance of the raw materials (petroleum, natural gas, iron ore, copper, tin, fishmeal, soya beans) for which Chinese demand was voracious during 2000–14. Buoyant commodity prices and the exceedingly low interest rates in the G-7 countries are the two international variables mentioned most frequently. The argument about commodity prices applies most vigorously to Latin America, especially South America, where several countries are significant exporters of commodities (petroleum, copper, soya, iron ore, wheat) whose prices have hovered at historical highs for nearly a decade (see table 1-4 in chapter 1). Table 9-7 shows that if we take 2000 as the base year, in which all country ratios are set to 100, then the terms-of-trade ratio (export prices/import prices) had fallen in both the G-7 (to 97) and the Asian 7 (to 92) but had risen dramatically in the Latin American 7 (to 148) just as the global financial crisis was erupting in 2008.

Between 2000 and 2008, there were notably large increases in the windfall benefits flowing to oil-exporter Venezuela (with a terms-of-trade ratio of 250 in 2008) and copper-exporter Chile (with a terms-of-trade ratio of 165) and smaller increases in other Latin American countries, such as Mexico (106) and Brazil (110). Asian countries include those for which the terms of trade improved modestly, such as Indonesia (124) and India (117), and those experiencing large adverse shifts in their terms of trade (which reflect their position as commodity importers but probably are due also to exchange rate interventions), including Japan (62), South Korea (62), and China (75). Although governments in countries with soaring terms of trade during the first decade of the 2000s justifiably worried about deindustrialization—as high commodity demand led to exchange rate overvaluation and uncompetitive prices for manufactured exports, the so-called resource curse phenomenon—being an exporter of an essential commodity with fairly inelastic demand was clearly a boost in terms of coping with the immediate shocks from the global financial crisis. Table 9-7 suggests that further increases in their terms of trade through 2008–10 facilitated the swift recovery in countries such as Brazil, Chile, Peru, and India.[22]

Table 9-7. *Terms-of-Trade Shifts in 2000–09*[a]

	2008	2010
Canada	126	119
France	98	98
Germany	100	103
Italy	95	99
Japan	62	68
UK	105	103
US	92	97
G-7 mean[b]	**97**	**98**
China	75	77
India	117	127
Indonesia	124	127
Korea	62	68
Malaysia	104	100
Philippines	67	69
Thailand	94	98
Asian 7 mean[b]	**92**	**95**
Argentina	133	127
Brazil	110	125
Chile	165	204
Colombia	138	134
Mexico	106	105
Peru	137	153
Venezuela	250	216
Latin American 7 mean[b]	**148**	**152**

Source: "Net Barter Terms of Trade," from World Bank, World Development Indicators (http://data.worldbank.org/products/wdi).

a. Base year, 2000. A score of greater than 100 means that a country's terms of trade have "improved" or the prices of its exports have risen relative to the prices of its imports.

b. Regional means are unweighted.

Global interest rate movements also eased adjustment in many emerging economies. Ironically, G-7 crisis management, led by the United States, necessarily constituted an extension of the same loose fiscal and monetary policies that had benefited EEs throughout 2000–14. In conjunction with a stimulus package that amounted to close to 6 percent of GDP (see table 9-3), the U.S. Federal Reserve Bank maintained near-zero real interest rates from December 2008 through the time of this writing.[23] Other G-7 countries followed a similar strategy of "quantitative easing," pushing highly mobile capital flows out of the advanced economies and toward EE markets with faster growth and relatively higher returns. Although most EEs also reduced their policy interest rates at the height of the crisis, only in Argentina and Venezuela did rates dip below the near-zero levels of Japan, the United States, the United Kingdom, and the Eurozone.[24] Thus, in marked contrast to interest rate policies during other international financial crises in the recent past, those in the advanced industrial countries during the GFC facilitated the adjustment process in many emerging economies.

At least two highly influential factors in the international economic environment thus enabled the relatively mild crisis and quick recovery experienced in many emerging economies around the Pacific Rim. The level of world prices is not, of course, a policy variable that governments in EEs can control—or count on. The "tapering" of the U.S. Fed's policy of quantitative easing, announced in mid-2013 and begun later that year, has already caused strains in EEs that had relied on maintaining high levels of private capital inflows during the crisis and thereafter.[25] However, as of late 2014 it still appeared that interest rate differentials—and therefore incoming capital flows—would favor the emerging economies into the medium term, as U.S. employment data continued to dictate a low interest rate policy on the part of the U.S. Fed for some time to come.

Final Thoughts

Our exploration of policy choices and outcomes around the Pacific Rim during the global financial crisis suggests the following tentative conclusions, summarized in table 9-8. First, there seems to be no doubt that prior macroeconomic reform, which ensured low inflation and reasonable levels of public and external debt, was extremely helpful to all of the Asian and Latin American countries in surviving the immediate shocks of the crisis. In fact, even in those countries (such as Argentina) in which there had been some backsliding from earlier stabilization efforts, domestic macroeconomic patterns were sufficiently stable to enable the government to take short-term countercyclical measures without the risk of exacerbating the crisis.

Second, prior banking and financial sector reforms undoubtedly were helpful in preventing financial crises. But there is no evidence that more liberalized domestic or international financial regulations were superior to policies that gave primacy to the buildup of large foreign exchange reserves (to avoid attacks on the national currency) or to reliance on public banks to channel liquidity

Table 9-8. *Evaluating Explanations for the Surprising Resilience of Emerging Economies*

Hypothesis	Comments
1. Prior (neoliberal) macro-economic reforms	Most large emerging economies had previously enacted reforms, which were helpful, likely even essential.
	Good macroeconomic fundamentals were insufficient. For example, they did not protect countries during the Asian financial crisis.
2. Prior financial reforms (neoliberal and/or developmentalist)	Prior bank cleanup was helpful, but the most liberalized financial systems have not performed the best.
	Defensive financial statecraft (adequate foreign exchange reserves, possibly public banks) was helpful, but too much intervention is problematic.
3. Prior trade reforms	Trade liberalization generally promotes growth, and trade diversification can reduce vulnerability.
	We found no direct relationship of prior trade reforms to either crisis resistance or quick recovery.
4. Countervailing international conditions	Fortuitous conditions (high commodity prices, low interest rates in developed economies) also mattered, although commodity prices hurt some Asian emerging economies.

quickly to the private nonfinancial sector. Third, while prior trade liberalization likely boosted growth and trade diversification would seem to reduce a country's vulnerability to sudden shifts in global demand, it is hard to specify a direct relationship between trade reforms and the ability of a country to survive an acute financial crisis. The country in this study in which the lack of trade diversification had the most harmful effect was Mexico, which was hit hard by the slowdown of the U.S. economy. Fourth, international factors (particularly high commodity prices throughout 2000–14 and low interest rates in the core economies) tended to work in favor of the major emerging economies, although heavy commodity importers such as China benefited much less.

At least as important as any of the factors initially hypothesized was effective crisis policymaking in most of the countries studied, with some exceptions noted previously. That conclusion leads us back to competing economic ideologies—the other big theme with which we began this volume. It appears that institutional innovations and policy learning from the experience of coping with previous crises enabled emerging market policymakers across the Pacific to effectively weather the GFC and its rocky aftermath. Despite different reform trajectories in Asia (gradual reform, higher growth since the 1980s) and Latin America ("big bang" market reforms following previous crises but lower growth until the advent of the 2000s), the economic indicators for these EEs are converging more closely than ever before. In other words, while there is considerable variation in the choice of economic restructuring programs, the timelines involved, and the actual policies employed, the bulk of countries in our database appear to be approaching the same destination.

We also proposed in our introductory chapter that long-standing policy labels such as "neoliberal" and "developmentalist" are becoming less relevant. In 2000–14 policymakers in these countries stepped outside their usual comfort zones and embraced a combination of market-based and state-oriented policies. Policy convergence was most relevant for financial sector reforms. In analyzing longer-run macroeconomic and institutional reform patterns, two groupings emerge. For example, Chile, Mexico, and Korea all relied more heavily on a market-based reform strategy while still tweaking some strategic levers (capital controls, buildup of foreign exchange reserves) along the way; China, India, and Brazil came down much more heavily on the side of state-led reform strategies, with market reforms embraced at the margin but implemented nonetheless.

Another thesis has emerged in the course of writing this book: we suggest that it was precisely their policy and ideological flexibility—combining longer-run macroeconomic and institutional reform with increased confidence to engage in innovative and pragmatic approaches—that enabled these countries to cope effectively with ongoing global challenges, including high levels of capital liquidity in the 2000s. The management of volatile capital flows—both inward and outward—has been the most obvious challenge for all concerned but especially for the South American cases in our sample. The track record thus far reflects a strong commitment to combat currency appreciation and inflationary pressures, with the shadow of earlier financial crises a constant reminder of the costs of not succeeding. However, as the EU continues to sort out its own banking and debt crises and the U.S. Federal Reserve remains committed to a low interest rate policy, many of these Pacific Rim EEs will continue to attract unusually high capital inflows. Therefore, we expect that the kinds of strategic levers that we have discussed throughout this volume—mildly heterodox policy choices that even IMF staffers have begun to recommend[26]—will become increasingly common, even within the more market-oriented countries in our sample. Obviously, there are outliers, especially on the Latin American side, and the weights that can be assigned to our causal variables differ considerably across countries and regions. Nevertheless, the overall pattern that emerges is one of greater flexibility in crossing over conceptual boundaries and policy approaches.

Notes

1. Saori N. Katada and Injoo Sohn, "Regionalism as Financial Statecraft: Pursuit of a Counterweight Strategy by China and Japan," in *Financial Statecraft of Emerging Powers: Asia and Latin America in Comparative Perspective,* edited by Leslie E. Armijo and Saori N. Katada (London: Palgrave Macmillan, 2014), pp. 148–61.

2. Carmen Reinhart and Kenneth Rogoff, *This Time Is Different: Eight Centuries of Financial Folly* (Princeton University Press, 2009).

3. Joseph Stiglitz, *Globalization and Its Discontents* (New York: W.W. Norton, 2002); Paul Bluestein, *The Chastening: Inside the Crisis That Rocked the Global Financial System and Humbled the IMF* (New York: Public Affairs, 2003).

4. S. Khatiwada, "Stimulus Packages to Counter Global Economic Crisis: A Review," Discussion Paper (Geneva: International Institute for Labour Studies, 2009).

5. Barbara Stallings with Rogerio Studart, *Finance for Development: Latin America in Comparative Perspective* (Brookings, 2006); F. J. de Carvalho and F. E. de Souza, *Brazil in the 2000s: Financial Regulation and Macroeconomic Stability* (Buenos Aires: CEDES, 2011).

6. Yong-Chool Ha and Lee Wang Hwi Lee, "The Politics of Economic Reform in South Korea: Crony Capitalism after Ten Years," *Asian Survey,* vol. 4, no. 6 (2007), pp. 894–914; T. Kalinowski and Hyekyung Cho, "The Political Economy of Financial Liberalization in South Korea: State, Big Business, and Foreign Investors," *Asian Survey,* vol. 49, no. 2 (2009), pp. 221–42.

7. Arguably, one reason for the recent subprime mortgage crisis in the United States was the degree to which actors in the private financial sector simply made their own rules while regulators and political authorities believed that any problems would be resolved by market discipline.

8. Manuel Pastor and Carol Wise, "Goodbye Financial Crash, Hello Financial Eclecticism: Latin American Responses to the 2008–09 Global Financial Crisis," *Journal of International Money and Finance* (2015, forthcoming).

9. Of course, other types of monetary and financial capabilities besides those discussed here are enjoyed by countries whose home currencies are international reserve currencies, whose private institutions dominate global banking and securities markets, or who enjoy disproportionate influence in the international financial institutions.

10. Larger countries also tended to have more interventionist financial sectors than smaller countries, with the largest shares registered in the biggest economies in our sample: India (74 percent), China (69 percent), Brazil (45 percent), and Indonesia (38 percent). See J. Barth, G. Caprio, and R. Levine, Bank Regulation and Supervision Dataset, 2008 (http://econ.worldbank.org/WBSITE/EXTERNAL/EXTDEC/EXTRE SEARCH/0,,contentMDK:20345037~pagePK:64214825~piPK:64214943~theSitePK: 469382,00.html).

11. This figure would be even lower if Germany—with a 40 percent share of public banks, the single outlier—were removed from the sample.

12. Also see S. Shirai, "Banking Sector Reforms in India and China: Does India's Experience Offer Lessons for China's Future Reform Agenda?," Japan Bank for International Cooperation Institute Discussion Paper 2 (Tokyo: 2002); C. Roland, "Banking Sector Reforms in India and China: A Comparative Perspective," paper prepared for the Harvard Project for Asian and International Relations Conference, Singapore, August 8, 2006; and A. Walter, "Chinese Attitude towards Financial Regulatory Cooperation: Revisionist or Status Quo?," in *Global Finance in Crisis: The Politics of International Regulatory Change,* edited by Eric Helleiner, S. Pagliari, and H. Zimmermann (London: Routledge, 2009).

13. See M. Schindler, "Measuring Financial Integration: A New Data Set," *IMF Staff Papers*, vol. 56, no. 1 (2009), pp. 222–38.

14. On the use of foreign exchange reserves and other instruments of financial statecraft by emerging powers, see Leslie Elliott Armijo and Saori N. Katada, "Theorizing the Financial Statecraft of Emerging Powers," *New Political Economy* (forthcoming) (www.tandfonline.com/doi/full/10.1080/13563467.2013.866082).

15. For evidence of the diverse types of potential financial power resources possessed by different contemporary major and intermediate powers, see Leslie Elliott Armijo, Laurissa Muehlich, and Daniel C. Tirone, "The Systemic Financial Importance of Emerging Powers," *Journal of Policy Modeling* (forthcoming) (www.science direct.com/science/article/pii/S016189381300104X).

16. See Gavin Kitching, *Seeking Social Justice through Globalization: Escaping a Nationalist Perspective* (Pennsylvania State University Press, 2001); Jagdish Bhagwati, *In Defense of Globalization* (Oxford University Press, 2007); World Bank, *Emerging Stronger from the Crisis: East Asia and Pacific Economic Update*, vol. 1 (Washington: 2010); and Arvind Subramanian and Martin Kessler, "The Hyperglobalization of Trade and Its Future," Working Paper 13-6 (Washington: Peterson Institute for Economics, July 2013), p. 3.

17. Dani Rodrik, *One Economics, Many Recipes: Globalization, Institutions, and Economic Growth* (Princeton University Press, 2007).

18. M. A. Kose and E. S. Prasad, *Emerging Markets: Resilience and Growth amid Global Turmoil* (Brookings, 2010), p. 41.

19. Ibid., p. 46.

20. Many Latin American governments now worry about their trade dependence on China. See, for example, Juan Carlos Gachúz, "Chile's Economic and Political

Relationship with China," *Journal of Current Chinese Affairs*, vol. 41, no. 1 (2012), pp. 133–54, and Ruben Gonzalez-Vicente, "The Political Economy of Sino-Peruvian Relations: A New Dependency?," *Journal of Current Chinese Affairs*, vol. 41, no. 1 (2012), pp. 97–131.

21. Carol Wise and Yong Zhang, "China and Latin America's Emerging Markets: Debates, Dynamism, Dependence," paper presented at the International Studies Association Meetings, Buenos Aires, July 23–26, 2014.

22. See Hanh Nguyen, Martin Stuchtey, and Markus Zils, "Remaking the Industrial Economy," *McKinsey Quarterly* (February 2014), pp. 1–37. The international commodity price boom is not over, and it may last until the major EE resource-importers, including China and India, have advanced much further in their quest to have the level of industrial development in their countries converge with that of the advanced economies.

23. Ben Bernanke, *The Federal Reserve and the Financial Crisis* (Princeton University Press, 2013).

24. Pastor and Wise, "Goodbye Financial Crash, Hello Financial Eclecticism," p. 36.

25. "'Fragile Five' Countries Face Taper Crunch," *Financial Times*, December 17, 2013.

26. Gurnain Kaur Pasricha, "Recent Trends in Measures to Manage Capital Flows in Emerging Economies," *North American Journal of Economics and Finance*, vol. 23, no. 1 (2012), pp. 286–309.

Contributors

LESLIE ELLIOTT ARMIJO
Hatfield School of Government,
Portland State University

MARK BEESON
Political Science and International
Relations, University of Western
Australia

SHAUN BRESLIN
Department of Politics and
International Studies, University
of Warwick

JOHN ECHEVERRI-GENT
Department of Politics, University
of Virginia

GERARDO ESQUIVEL
El Colegio de México

ERIC HERSHBERG
Department of Government,
American University

SAORI N. KATADA
School of International Relations,
University of Southern California

MARIA ANTONIETA DEL TEDESCO
LINS
University of São Paulo, Brazil

BARBARA STALLINGS
Watson Institute for International
Studies, Brown University

CAROL WISE
School of International Relations,
University of Southern California

Index

ADB. *See* Asian Development Bank
Advanced industrial countries, 216,
217–18, 222, 225. *See also* Global
financial crisis of 2008–09; *individual
countries and regions*
AFC (Asian financial crisis). *See* Asia
Africa, 84
Ahluwalia, Montek, 89
Aizenman, Joshua, i–viii
ALADI. *See* Latin American Integration
Association
American Recovery and Reinvestment
Act (U.S.; 2009), 36
Amplio, Frente, 142
Andean countries, 124, 126, 127–28, 130,
132, 137, 138, 143
Argentina: banks and banking in, 151,
157, 158–59, 168, 178, 205, 208, 218;
commodities in, 17–18, 148, 149–50,
160, 162, 168, 169, 175, 176, 178; crises
in, 4, 148–49, 151–52, 153, 159, 168,
175, 213; debt default of, 149, 155,
159–60, 208; economic issues in,
134–35, 143, 148–59, 167–70, 172,
174–78, 206, 208, 217; exchange rates
in, 149, 151, 154, 169–70, 172; foreign
exchange reserves in, 218; foreign
investment in, 168, 169f, 175; global

financial crisis of 2008–09 and, 18 –19,
136–37, 159, 162, 206, 208, 218; gross
savings of, 172f; growth in, 4, 148, 149,
150, 151, 160, 168, 172, 174–77, 178;
interest rates in, 170, 225; policy
learning in, 19, 134, 141–42; political
issues in, 141–42, 144, 148, 151, 157,
159; reforms in, 18–19, 148–50,
154–55, 157–60, 165–69, 174–75,
177–78; response to the global
financial crisis of 2008–09 and, 134,
136–37, 148–49, 159, 162, 165–70,
173–74, 177–78, 206–07, 222; stimulus
package in, 19, 165, 211–12; taxation
in, 154–55, 170, 172; trade in, 18, 129,
131, 153, 162–64, 172, 173–74, 176–77,
222. *See also* Central Bank of Argentina; Convertibility Plan; Emerging
economies; Latin America; International Monetary Fund; South America
Argentina–other countries and regions:
Asia, 131; Brazil, 152–55, 162, 164, 168;
China, 148, 149–50, 160, 162, 164f, 173,
175, 176–77; U.S., 162; Venezuela, 160
Armijo, Leslie Elliott, 1–24, 202–230, 231
ASEAN. *See* Association of Southeast
Asian Nations
ASEAN+3, 105

ASEAN 4, 111, 112

Asia: Asian financial crisis of 1990s, 1, 6, 15, 151–52, 209, 210–11, 213; commodities and, 127, 205; economic issues in, 107, 209–10, 213, 217, 225; foreign exchange reserves in, 217–18; global financial crisis of 2008–09 and, 4, 8, 11, 106, 107–08, 225; Latin America and, 131; reforms in, 21, 213–16, 227; regional production networks in, 108; trade in, 61, 84, 108, 131, 205, 222, 223. *See also* Emerging economies; Pacific Rim; *individual countries and regions*

Asia–East: Asian financial crisis of 1997–98 and, 105, 205; currency reserves in, 105; East Asian Summit, 105; economic issues in, 5, 106–07, 110, 205; environmental issues in, 109; foreign exchange reserves in, 204, 205; global financial crisis of 2008–09 and, 8; growth in, 106; macroeconomic reforms in, 8; portfolio investment in, 111; response to the global financial crisis of 2008–09, 106, 108; stimulus packages in, 211, 212; trade in, 7, 105, 108. *See also* Emerging economies; *individual countries*

Asia–Northeast, 104

Asia–Southeast: Asian financial crisis of 1997–98 and, 104–06, 117, 204; China and, 102, 107, 108, 115, 116–17, 204–05; colonialism in, 103; economic issues in, 102, 103–06, 110, 111–14, 115, 116–17; environmental issues in, 109, 113–14; foreign exchange reserves in, 204; global financial crisis of 2008–09 and, 16; growth in, 118; infrastructure of, 113; institutional architecture of, 114–15; investor confidence and, 111; political issues in, 102, 103, 104, 108, 114, 116–17; reforms in, 104, 117, 204; trade in, 17, 107, 110, 116–17, 221–22; U.S. and, 115. *See also* Association of Southeast Asian Nations; Emerging economies; *individual countries*

Asian Development Bank (ADB), 53, 112, 114

Asian financial crisis (AFC). *See* Asia

Asian 7, 162, 179n28, 216, 217, 219–20, 223

Asociación Latinoamericana de Integración. *See* Latin American Integration Association

Association of Southeast Asian Nations (ASEAN): China and, 107, 116; countries belonging to, 16–17, 24n37; economic issues in, 109, 110, 114–16; global financial crisis of 2008–09 and, 17; policy learning by, 17; political issues in, 110; response to the global financial crisis of 2008–09, 107, 109; stimulus package of, 17; trade in, 17, 107; U.S. and, 115. *See also* Asia; Asia–Southeast; *individual countries*

Banerjee, Mamata, 92–93

Bank for International Settlements, 56, 66

Bank of Japan, 65

Bank of Korea, 55, 65–66

Bank of Mexico, 126, 182, 184, 189–90, 192

Bank Recapitalization Fund, 65–66

Basal Accords, 213

Beeson, Mark, 16, 17, 102–22, 231

Bharatiya Janata Party (India), 95

Bolivia, 131, 132, 136–37, 142, 183

Bombay Stock Exchange (BSE; India), 79

Bond Market Stabilization Fund, 65–66

Brazil: Argentina and, 152–55, 162, 164; Asia and, 131; banks and banking in, 156, 160–61, 171, 173, 175–76, 205, 208, 218; China and, 130, 148, 149–50, 162, 164, 173, 175; commodities in, 17–18, 148, 149–50, 162, 164, 171, 173, 175, 178; crises in, 4, 148, 158, 175, 207; economic issues in, 136, 149–59,

161–64, 167–78, 206, 208, 217–18; exchange rates, 156, 158, 161, 168, 170, 171, 172–73; foreign currency swap lines and, 207; foreign investment in, 161, 169f, 171, 172–73, 175, 178; global financial crisis of 2008–09 and, 10, 18, 19, 156–57, 159, 162, 206, 218; gross savings of, 172f; growth in, 4, 19, 135–36, 143, 148, 150, 151, 171, 173–78; interest rates, 156, 160, 161, 170f, 171, 172–73, 176; political issues in, 142, 148, 161; reforms in, 18, 19, 21, 148, 149, 150, 159, 160–62, 165–67, 173, 174–75, 177–78, 227; response to the global financial crisis of 2008–09 and, 135–36, 143, 148–49, 158, 165–74, 177, 206–07, 222, 224; stimulus packages in, 136, 165, 211–12; taxation in, 158, 160, 171; trade in, 127, 129–31, 153, 161–64, 165f, 173–74, 207, 219, 222–24; U.S. and, 127, 162, 164, 207. *See also* Emerging economies; International Monetary Fund; Latin America; Real Plan; South America

Brazilian Development Bank (BNDES; O Banco Nacional de Desenvolvimento Econômico e Social), 19, 136, 171, 175, 208

Breslin, Shaun, 13, 25–47, 143, 231

Britain, 106, 225. *See also* Europe; European Union; Eurozone

Brunei, 103, 110

BSE. *See* Bombay Stock Exchange

BSE Sensitive Index (Sensex), 79

Büchi, Hernán, 139

Burma (Myanmar), 103, 117

CAFTA. *See* China-ASEAN Free Trade Area

CAFTA-DR. *See* Dominican Republic-Central America-United States Free Trade Agreement

Cambodia, 103, 117

Canada, 184, 219, 220–21

Caribbean countries: China and, 221; commodities and, 221; economic issues of, 195; global financial crisis of 2008–09, 18, 126; remittances from abroad to, 185–86; trade and, 221; U.S. and, 127. *See also* Emerging economies; Latin America; *individual countries*

Central America: global financial crisis of 2008–09 and, 18, 131, 133–34; remittances from migrants in the U.S. and, 127, 131, 185–86, 207; taxation in, 142–43; trade in, 127, 130–31, 142; U.S. and, 127, 130. *See also* Emerging economies; Latin America; *individual countries*

Central Bank of Argentina, 157, 159

Chancellor, Edward, 40

Chiang Mai Initiative (CMI), 105, 207

Chidambaram, P., 93

Chile: Asia and, 131; banks and banking in, 216; commodities in, 17–18; economic issues in, 137, 139–40, 217; exchange rates in, 138, 156; global financial crisis of 2008–09, 18, 137; interest rates in, 140; political issues in, 139–40, 141, 142; reforms in, 17, 18, 21, 227; response to the global financial crisis of 2008–09, 138, 139–40, 141, 142, 143, 222, 224; stimulus package in, 139; taxation in, 143; trade in, 18, 129, 131, 162, 183, 219–24; U.S. and, 129. *See also* Emerging economies; Latin America; South America

Chi Lo, 30

China: banks and banking in, 29, 30, 31, 32, 35, 36–38, 42, 203–04, 208, 214; commodities and, 11–13, 143, 148, 160, 173–77, 221, 223, 227; corruption in, 33, 38, 42; currency reserves of, 105; domestic politics in, 15; earth-quake in, 36; economic issues in, 25–43, 62, 102, 106–10, 116–18, 175, 203–04, 206, 208, 217; employment in,

35; environmental issues in, 32, 34, 113; exchange rates of, 27–28, 31–32; foreign exchange reserves, 31–32, 204, 218; foreign investment in, 111; global financial crisis of 2008–09 and, 13, 15, 25–27, 28, 29–30, 162, 206; government control of land in, 28; growth in, 4, 11, 21, 26, 28, 30, 32–41, 74, 143, 174, 208, 222; infrastructure of, 113; land use rights, 38–39, 42, 43n10; local developmentalist state, 37–42; local investment platform companies (LIPCs), 37–39; nonstate sector in, 26, 28; political issues in, 107, 116; prices and price controls, 28; reforms in, 13, 21, 25, 27–34, 41–42, 203–04, 214, 227; regional production networks of, 108; response to the global financial crisis of 2008–09, 32–41, 42, 107, 109, 206; state developmentalism, 26, 27–32, 35–41; state-owned enterprises (SOEs), 28–29, 30; stimulus package of, 13, 15, 17, 25, 26–27, 36–37, 41, 49, 107, 162, 211; township and village enterprises (TVEs) in, 27; taxation in, 30, 31, 33, 34, 37; trade in, 12, 13–18, 25–27, 30, 33–35, 37, 40–42, 49, 108, 117–18, 143, 162, 184, 207, 219, 221–23. *See also* Asia; Asia–East; Emerging economies; Mekong River; People's Bank of China

China–other countries and regions: Argentina, 148, 160, 162, 164f, 173, 175, 176–77; ASEAN+3, 105; Asia, 222; Brazil, 130, 148, 162, 173, 175; Caribbean countries, 221; Korea, 62; Latin America, 129–30, 143, 221, 222; Mexico, 130; South America, 143; Southeast Asia, 107, 115; U.S., 184, 207

China-ASEAN Free Trade Area (CAFTA), 17, 107

China 2030: Building a Modern, Harmonious, and Creative High-Income Society (report; World Bank), 41

Chinese Academy of Social Sciences, 39

Chinese Communist Party (CCP), 13, 35–36, 38

Citibank, 58

Citicorp, 2

Climate change, 113–14

CMI. *See* Chiang Mai Initiative

Colombia: Asia and, 131; economic issues and, 137; exchange rates in, 138; global financial crisis of 2008–09, 18, 137; political issues in, 139, 143; reforms in, 18; response to the global financial crisis of 2008–09, 138, 141, 143; stimulus package of, 139; taxation in, 143; trade in, 18, 128, 131; U.S. and, 128. *See also* Emerging economies; Latin America; South America

Commercial Bank Law (China; 1995), 29

Commodities: iron ore, 150, 162, 223; oil, 162, 223; price trends, 12t, 226–27; soybeans, 150, 162, 223; wheat, 223. *See also* Emerging economies; Oil; *individual countries and regions*

Common Market of the South. *See* Mercosur

Concertación (Chile),139, 141, 142

Confederación General de Trabajadores del Perú (General Confederation of Workers of Peru), 140–41

Congress Party (India), 91, 93, 97

Convertibility Law (Argentina; 1991), 167

Convertibility Plan (Argentina), 148, 149, 151, 152–55, 157, 159, 167, 205

Correa, Rafael, 138

Corruption, 13; China, 33, 38, 42; India, 93, 97; Indonesia, 109; Philippines, 110; Southeast Asia, 112

Costa Rica, 134

Delgado, Bertrand, 140

Development Research Center (China), 41

Doing Business indicators (World Bank), 175, 176f

Dominican Republic-Central America-United States Free Trade Agreement (CAFTA-DR), 128, 130–31

Echeverri-Gent, John, 16, 74–101, 231
ECLAC. *See* Economic Commission for Latin America and the Caribbean
Economic Commission for Latin America and the Caribbean (ECLAC), 127, 129, 134
Economic issues: bursting of U.S. dotcom bubble (2000), 2, 148; capitalism, 26; causes of financial crises, 6; commodity prices, 2, 3, 8, 11, 12t, 127; credit card, personal, and mortgage debt, 2; developmentalism, 25–26, 216; financial crises, 3–4, 68; financial liberalism, 217; financial market deregulation, 2; fiscal spending, 134, 135t; free trade, 10; global growth, 3; Great Depression of the 1930s, 3; government manipulation, 216; gross domestic product (GDP), 3, 4, 5t, 194f, 195f; growth, 3–4, 5t, 127; hedge funds, 3; interest rates, 2, 8, 11; neoliberalism, 26; policy reforms, 6–7, 8; political process and, 97; stimulus funds, 10; swap lines and agreements, 65, 67, 82, 87, 105, 160, 207, 216; world recession of 2000-03, 148, 175. *See also* Emerging economies; Global financial crisis; Trade issues; *individual countries and regions*
Economic issues–hypotheses: emerging economies escaped the crisis due to favorable global conditions, 10, 223–25, 226–27; macroeconomic fundamentals and crisis resistance and response, 208–12; stronger banks and financial reforms enabled crisis resistance, 8–10, 213–19, 226; trade deepening and/or diversification improves crisis outcomes, 10, 219–22, 226
Economies. *See* Emerging economies
Economist, The, 40, 49–50

Ecuador: exchange rates in, 138; global financial crisis of 2008–09 and, 137; growth of, 138; policy learning in, 141–42; political issues in, 141–42, 144; response to the global financial crisis of 2008–09, 136, 137–38; trade in, 128, 137; U.S. and, 128. *See also* Emerging economies; Latin America; South America
EEs. *See* Emerging economies
El Salvador, 131, 142–43
Emerging economies (EEs): banks and banking in, 213–16, 218; borrowing from IFIs by, 203, 211; capital flows of, 21, 227–28; economic issues of, 209, 213–19, 225, 227; exchange rates of, 188, 203, 213; financial crises of 1980s and 1990s, 1, 6, 9, 10, 202, 207–09, 211, 213; foreign exchange reserves of, 203, 207, 217; growth of, 3, 4; interest rates and, 224–25; recovery of, 203; reforms in, 10, 177, 202, 203, 213–19, 225; stimulus policies of, 202; trade in, 10, 203, 207, 219–22. *See also individual countries and regions*
Emerging economies–global financial crisis of 2008–09, 188, 207; banks and banking in, 211; commodities and, 223, 226–27; favorable global conditions and, 223–25; loose monetary policies and, 11, 211; missing crisis of, 7–11, 219; policy learning and, 11; political issues, 208–09; recovery of 2010–12 from, 1–2, 3, 7, 8–11, 222; reforms and, 8–10, 208–09, 210, 212, 213, 223, 227; response to global financial crisis of 2008–09, 189, 202, 210; trade and, 222, 223, 226–27. *See also* Pacific Rim; *individual countries and regions*
England. *See* Britain
Esquivel, Gerardo, 19, 20, 126, 181–201, 231
EU. *See* European Union

Europe: crises in, 117, 118, 143; economic issues in, 107, 109, 111, 143–44; trade in, 17. See also *individual countries*
Europe–Eastern, 1, 84
Europe–Western, 7, 11. See also *individual countries*
European Union (EU), 21, 60, 106, 222, 228. *See also individual countries*
Eurozone, 111, 112, 143, 225

Fang Cai, 35
FDI. *See* Foreign direct investment
Federal Reserve (U.S.), 2, 3, 21, 126, 173, 225, 228
Federal Reserve Bank (U.S.), 207, 225
Fernández de Kirchner, Cristina, 159, 168, 171
Financial Services Modernization Act of 1999, 2
Financial Supervisory Commission (FSC; Korea), 56
Financial Supervisory Service (Korea), 66
Fiscal Responsibility and Budget Management Act (FRBM Act; India; 2003), 77
Foreign direct investment (FDI), 10, 12. *See also individual countries and regions*
Foreign Exchange Management Act (India; 1977), 81
Foreign Exchange Regulation Act (India; 1974), 81
FRBM Act. *See* Fiscal Responsibility and Buget Management Act
FSC. *See* Financial Supervisory Commission
Funes, Mauricio, 142

GAAR. *See* General Anti-Avoidance Rule
Gandhi, Indira, 91
García, Alan, 139, 140
General Anti-Avoidance Rule (GAAR; India), 93
Germany, 12, 13, 67, 211. *See also* Europe; European Union; Eurozone

GFC. *See* Global financial crisis
Glass-Steagall Act of 1933, 2
Global financial crisis of 2008–09 (GFC): advanced industrial economies and, 4, 5t, 11, 124, 211, 225; banks and banking and, 216; crisis recovery (2010–12) , 5–6, 8–9, 216, 222; crisis resistance, 8, 9t; emerging economies and, 1–2, 3, 5t, 97, 149, 225; interest rates and, 224–25; origins and spread of, 3; policy learning and, 2, 10, 11, 20, 97; policy responses to, 138–39; political issues and, 139; reforms and, 20, 149, 216, 222; severity of, 3, 149; stimulus packages and, 212t; trade and, 149, 222; U.S. and, 3, 7, 11; Western Europe and, 7, 11. *See also* Economic issues–hypotheses; Emerging economies–global financial crisis of 2008–09; *individual countries and regions*
Goldman Sachs Group, 2
Great Britain. *See* Britain
Great Recession. *See* Global financial crisis of 2008–09
Group of 7 (G-7), 53, 211, 213–17, 219–20, 223–25

Haiti, 195
Heritage Foundation, 219
Hershberg, Eric, 17, 18, 123–47, 231
Honduras, 131, 142
Hong Kong, 30, 112
HSBC, 58
Huang Yasheng, 27
Hutchison Essar (Indian telecom), 93

IBK. *See* Industrial Bank of Korea
ICICI Bank (India), 90
IMF. *See* International Monetary Fund
IMSS (Instituto Mexicano del Seguro Social). *See* Mexican Institute of Social Security
India: banks and banking in, 75–85, 89–90, 97, 98n6, 204, 208, 214;

corporations and multinational firms in, 79, 80, 90, 92–93, 95; crises in, 78, 82, 83, 207; economic issues in, 74–82, 84–91, 94–97, 204, 206, 208, 216–17; exchange rates of, 81, 84–85, 90; foreign direct investment in, 86, 87; foreign exchange in, 84–85, 204; global financial crisis of 2008–09 and, 10, 15, 16, 79, 84–86, 89–91, 94, 206; gold imports and investments, 86–87, 94–95, 100n44; growth in, 4, 74, 78, 80, 84–88, 93–95, 97; interest rates in, 78, 79, 80, 82, 86–87, 94–95, 97, 214; mortgage-backed securities in, 16, 83; Mukherjee's term as finance minister, 91–93; national elections in, 16; oil subsidies in, 94; political issues in, 15, 75–76, 88–95, 97, 99n22; reforms in, 15–16, 21, 74–83, 88–93, 95, 204, 214, 227; remittances from abroad to, 207; response to the global financial crisis of 2008–09, 74–88, 95, 97, 206–07, 224; stimulus package in, 16, 75, 77–78, 97, 211; taxation in, 77, 93, 95; trade in, 16, 77, 81, 84–87, 94, 95, 99n31, 207, 219, 223–24; U.S. and, 207. *See also* Asia; Emerging economies; ICICI Bank; Reserve Bank of India

India and the Global Financial Crisis (Reddy), 89

Indonesia: Asian financial crisis of 1997–98 and, 104, 211; banks and banking in, 214; business regulations in, 112; corruption in, 112–13; currency reserves in, 105; economic issues in, 109, 113, 115–16, 117, 209; financial crises in, 4, 17; foreign investment in, 109; infrastructure of, 113; political issues in, 103, 109–10; reforms in, 204; trade in, 219, 223. *See also* Asia; Asia–Southeast; Emerging economies

Industrial Bank of Korea (IBK), 59, 66

Institutional Revolutionary Party (Mexico), 136

International financial institutions (IFIs), 10, 13, 15, 203, 211. *See also individual institutions*

International Monetary Fund (IMF): Argentina and, 152, 155, 157–58, 160, 161, 169; Brazil and, 157, 158; China's stimulus package and, 13; bailouts for Asia and Latin America, 6; global financial crisis of 2008–09, 102; India and, 74, 93; Korea and, 51, 53–54, 58, 204, 214; Mexico and, 189

Japan: foreign exchange reserves of, 218; global financial crisis of 2008–09 and, 13; interest rates in, 225; Korea and, 61–62; regional production networks of, 108; stimulus package of, 13, 17, 211; trade in, 223. *See also* Asia; Asia–East

KAMCO. *See* Korean Asset Management Corporation

Kam Wing Chan, 35

Karp, Philip, 27

Katada, Saori, 1–24, 202–30, 231

KDB. *See* Korea Development Bank

KEXIM. *See* Korea Export-Import Bank

Khosla, Jitesh, 92

Kim Dae-Jung, 53–54, 62

Kirchner, Néstor, 159, 160

Korea: aging of the population in, 67; Asian financial crisis of 1997–98 and, 48–54, 57–62, 66–69, 104, 204, 211, 213; banks and banking in, 49–53, 56–59, 62, 64–69, 204, 213–14, 216; *chaebol* (business conglomerates) in, 52, 54; democratization in, 54; domestic politics in, 15; economic issues in, 15, 48–66, 69, 204, 206, 209, 213, 217; education level of, 49; exchange rates of, 49, 51, 53, 55, 58, 69, 204, 214; financial crises in, 4, 15, 17; global financial crisis of 2008–09 and, 15, 49–52, 58–59, 206; growth in, 4,

66–67; historical background of, 52–54; interest rates and, 61, 64; policy learning by, 15; political issues in, 204; reforms in, 15, 21, 48–49, 52–60, 62, 67–68, 204, 213, 227; rescue package for, 53; response to the global financial crisis of 2008–09, 48, 51, 59, 62–69, 206; small and medium-sized enterprises (SMEs) in, 59, 66; stimulus package of, 15, 48, 49, 62, 64–66, 68; stock market in, 57, 58; swap lines and, 65, 67, 207; taxation in, 64; trade in, 15, 49, 51–52, 54–55, 59–63, 67–69, 162, 207, 223; unification with North Korea, 67; U.S. and, 207. *See also* Asia; Asia–East; Bank of Korea; Emerging economies; Financial Supervisory Commission; Financial Supervisory Service; Industrial Bank of Korea; International Monetary Fund

Korea Development Bank (KDB), 59

Korea Export-Import Bank (KEXIM), 59

Korean Asset Management Corporation (KAMCO), 56

Korean Stock Exchange, 56

Korean War (1950-53), 52

Labor Party (Brazil), 158

LAC countries. *See* Latin American and Caribbean countries

LAC-7 (seven largest economies in Latin America and the Caribbean), 20, 24n39

Laos, 103, 117

Lardy, Nicholas, 36, 37, 40–41

Latin America: Asia and, 131; Asian financial crisis of 1997–98 and, 104; banks and banking in, 124, 213; China and, 129–30, 142, 143, 144, 221, 222; commodities in, 11, 17–18, 21, 142, 144, 183, 205, 221, 223; debt crisis of 1982 and, 6, 124. 205, 213; economic issues in, 123–34, 141, 175, 194–95, 205, 209–10, 217, 225; exchange rates in, 126, 213; foreign exchange reserves in,

205, 217–18; foreign investment in, 129; global financial crisis of 2008–09 and, 4, 8, 11, 17, 123, 132–34; growth in, 124, 125t, 133, 144, 183, 227; policy learning in, 134, 141; political issues in, 123, 134, 141, 142, 144; public debt in, 126; reforms in, 8, 17, 21, 141, 213–16, 227; remittances from migrants in the U.S. and, 127; response to the global financial crisis of 2008–09 and, 124–27, 134, 141–43, 225; stimulus packages in, 212; taxation in, 142–43; trade in, 61, 84, 127–29, 131, 142–43, 183, 205, 220–23; U.S. and, 126–29, 132–33, 142, 144. *See also* Central America; Emerging economies; Pacific Rim; South America; *individual countries*

Latin American and Caribbean (LAC) countries, 20, 24n39, 195

Latin American Integration Association. (ALADI; Asociación Latinoamericana de Integración), 132–33, 162

Latin American 7, 162, 179n29, 216–17, 219–20, 223

Law of Fiscal Responsibility (Brazil; 2000), 158

Lee Myung-Bak, 62, 67

Legislation: American Recovery and Reinvestment Act (U.S.; 2009), 36; Commercial Bank Law (China; 1995), 29; Convertibility Law (Argentina; 1991), 167; Financial Services Modernization Act (U.S.; 1999, 2; Fiscal Responsibility and Budget Management Act (India; 2003), 77; Foreign Exchange Management Act (India; 1977), 81; Foreign Exchange Regulation Act (India; 1974), 81; General Anti-Avoidance Rule (India), 93; Glass-Steagall Act (U.S.; 1933), 2 ; Law of Fiscal Responsibility (Brazil; 2000), 158

Lehman Brothers, 50–51, 64, 78, 80, 82, 85, 168, 188–190

Lins, Maria Antonieta Del Tedesco, 18, 19, 148–80, 231

Local investment platform companies (LIPCs). *See* China

Long-Term Capital Management (LTCM; hedge fund management firm; U.S.), 104

Mahatma Gandhi National Rural Employment Guarantee Scheme (India), 94

Mah, Jai S., 60

Malaysia: Asian financial crisis of 1997–98 and, 104, 111; banks and banking in, 214; business regulations in, 112; corruption in, 112; currency reserves in, 105; economic issues in, 115–16, 117; financial crises in, 4, 17; investor confidence and, 111; political issues in, 103. *See also* Asia; Asia–Southeast; Emerging economies

Market Stabilization Scheme (MSS; India), 85, 90

MDGs. *See* Millennium Development Goals

Mekong River (China), 113

Menem, Carlos, 151

Menem (Carlos) administration (Argentina), 159

Mercosur (Southern Common Market), 128–30, 153, 155, 162, 164

Mexican Central Bank. *See* Bank of Mexico

Mexican Institute of Social Security (IMSS; Instituto Mexicano del Seguro Social), 191–92

Mexico: banks and banking in, 126, 182, 189–90, 192, 198, 208, 216; China and, 130, 184; commodities in, 183, 185, 187–88; crises in, 151, 159, 182, 188, 191, 196, 198, 213; economic issues in, 19–20, 126, 134, 136, 156, 181–88, 191–98, 205–06, 217; employment issues in, 191–93, 196–97; exchange

rates in, 156, 183–85, 188, 189, 197–98; financial crises in, 4, 111; foreign currency swap lines and, 207; foreign exchange reserves, 183, 185, 190, 198, 205, 208; foreign investment in, 169f, 183, 185, 187, 189; global financial crisis of 2008–09 and, 18, 20, 126, 134, 182, 185–88, 193, 196–98, 206–08; gross savings of, 172f; growth of, 20, 126, 151, 181–85, 191–93; interest rates in, 126, 170f, 182, 189–90, 192, 208; oil in, 182, 183, 185, 187–88, 192, 205; political issues in, 142, 184; poverty in, 197; pre-crisis period in, 183–85; recovery of 2010–12 in, 20, 192–99, 207; reforms in, 17, 18, 21, 182, 184, 188, 192, 197–99, 227; remittances received from abroad, 183, 185–86, 205, 207; rescue package for, 53; response to the global financial crisis of 2008–09 and, 136, 138, 142–43, 181, 188–90, 192, 206–08; stimulus package of, 182, 189, 207, 211–12; taxation in, 142–43, 189; tourism in, 186–87; trade in, 18, 20, 130, 142, 162, 182–88, 192–93, 197–98, 205, 207, 219–23, 226; U.S. and, 127, 182–85, 188–89, 192, 196–99, 205, 207, 220–21, 226. *See also* Bank of Mexico; Emerging economies; Latin America

Millennium Development Goals (MDGs), 114

Ministry of Finance (Brazil), 156

Ministry of Finance (India), 75–76, 89, 91

Ministry of Finance (Korea), 55

Ministry of Railways (China), 40

Ministry of Supervision (China), 38

Modi, Narendra, 95, 97

Moody's, 161

Mortgage-backed securities, 16, 83, 168

MSS. *See* Market Stabilization Scheme

Mukherjee, Pranab, 91–93

Mumbai (India), 89

Myanmar. *See* Burma

NAFTA. *See* North American Free Trade Agreement

NAO. *See* National Audit Office

Nassif, André, 173

National Action Party (Mexico), 184

National Audit Office (NAO; China), 37, 39

National Democratic Alliance (NDA; India), 95, 97

National Reform Development Council (China), 36

Naughton, Barry, 36

NDA. *See* National Democratic Alliance

Nicaragua, 131

North America, 13, 14, 102,107, 116, 192, 222. *See also individual countries*

North American Free Trade Agreement (NAFTA), 192

North Korea, 67

OECD. *See* Organization for Economic Cooperation and Development

Oil: Argentina, 162; Asia, 61; Brazil, 162; India, 94; Mexico, 19, 127, 182, 183, 185, 187–88, 192, 205; Venezuela, 137, 223

O'Neill, Paul, 157

OPEC. *See* Organization of the Petroleum Exporting Countries

Organization for Economic Cooperation and Development (OECD), 1, 4, 7, 52, 149, 174

Organization of the Petroleum Exporting Countries (OPEC), 84

Pacific Rim: definition of, 2; economic issues of, 210, 217; financial crises in, 8, 10; global financial crisis of 2008–09, 10; response to the global financial crisis of 2008–09, 202, 210, 222; trade and, 222. *See also* Emerging economies; *individual countries and regions*

Panagariya, Arvind, 78

Panama, 134, 142

Paraguay, 129, 142

Park Chung-Hee, 52, 67

Park Geun-Hye, 67

Paul, Omita, 92

PEMEX (Petróleos Mexicanos), 187–88

Peña Nieto, Enrique, 136

People's Bank of China, 31, 37, 65. *See also* China

People's Republic of China (PRC). *See* China

Peru: Asia and, 131; commodities in, 17–18; economic issues in, 137, 140; exchange rates in, 138; global financial crisis of 2008–09, 18, 137; interest rates in, 140; political issues in, 139, 140–41, 142; reforms in, 17, 18; response to the global financial crisis of 2008–09, 138, 140–41, 141, 222; stimulus package of, 140; trade in, 18, 129, 131, 162, 183, 219, 222; U.S. and, 129. *See also* Emerging economies; Latin America; South America

Petróleos Mexicanos. *See* PEMEX

Petroleum. *See* Oil

Philippines: business regulations in, 112; corruption in, 112; currency reserves in, 105; economic issues in, 110, 115–16, 209; foreign investment in, 111; political issues in, 103; trade in, 219. *See also* Asia; Asia–Southeast; Emerging economies

Piñera, Sebastián, 139

Poland, 194

Policy learning, 2, 10, 11, 20, 227. See also *individual countries and regions*

Political issues, 75, 95, 97. See also *individual countries and regions*

Political parties: Bharatiya Janata Party (India), 95; Chinese Communist Party (CCP), 13, 35–36, 38; Congress Party (India), 91, 93, 97; Institutional Revolutionary Party (Mexico), 136; Labor Party (Brazil), 158; National Action Party (Mexico), 184; National

Democratic Alliance (NDA; India), 95, 97; Trinamool Congress (India), 92–93; United Progressive Alliance (UPA; India), 91, 92, 93, 94; Workers Party (Brazil), 136

PRC (People's Republic of China). *See* China

PROEF. *See* Program to Strengthen Federal Financial Institutions

PROER. *See* Program to Support the Restructuring and Strengthening of the National Financial System

PROES. *See* Program of Incentives for State Participation in Banking Activities

Program of Incentives for State Participation in Banking Activities (PROES; Brazil), 161

Program to Strengthen Federal Financial Institutions (PROEF; Brazil), 161

Program to Support the Restructuring and Strengthening of the National Financial System (PROER; Brazil), 159, 161

Rajan, Raghuram, 89, 93

RBI. *See* Reserve Bank of India

Real Plan (Brazil), 148, 168

Reddy, Y. V., 89

Rendón, Silvio, 140

Reserve Bank of India (RBI), 16, 75–78, 80–85, 89–90, 95, 98n6, 204

Resource curse, 223

Roussef, Dilma, 143, 173

Roussef (Dilma) administration, 178

Russia, 4, 104, 152

SEBI. *See* Securities and Exchange Board of India

Securities and Exchange Board of India (SEBI), 92

September 11, 2001, 148

Singapore: business regulations in, 112; corruption in, 112; economic issues in, 103, 110–11, 112; foreign currency swap lines and, 207; global financial crisis of 2008–09, 111; political issues in, 103. *See also* Asia; Asia–Southeast; Emerging economies

Singh, Manmohan, 93

Sinha, U. K., 92

Sixth Pay Commission (India), 94

Slovak Republic, 194

SMEs (small and medium-sized enterprises). *See* Korea

SOEs (state-owned enterprises). *See* China

South America: capital flows of, 21, 227–28; China and, 129, 143, 205, 222; commodities and, 143, 205, 223; economic issues in, 133, 175; European Union and, 222; global financial crisis of 2008–09 and, 19, 124, 133, 134; Latin American neighbors and, 222; political issues, 205; reduction of external debt in, 126; response to the global financial crisis of 2008–09, 138, 142, 143, 205; stimulus packages in, 136; trade in, 126, 129, 134, 142, 143, 222; U.S. and, 134, 144, 205, 222. *See also* Emerging economies; Latin America; Pacific Rim; *individual countries*

Southern Common Market. *See* Mercosur

Southern Cone (South America), 127

South Korea. *See* Korea

Stallings, Barbara, 15, 42–73, 231

Standard Chartered, 58

State-owned enterprises (SOEs). *See* China

Stiglitz, Joseph, 89

Subbarao, Duvvuri, 89

Thailand: Asian financial crisis of 1997–98 and, 104, 211; business regulations in, 112; corruption in, 112; currency reserves in, 105; economic issues in, 115–16, 117; financial crises in, 4, 17; floods in, 108–09, 113–14;

political issues in, 103; reforms in, 204. *See also* Asia; Asia–Southeast; Emerging economies

Township and village enterprises (TVEs). *See* China

Trade issues: crisis outcomes and, 219–22; free trade, 10; government intervention in, 10; reforms, 10; terms-of-trade shifts in 2000-09, 224t; trade concentrations, 221t; trade liberalization, 220t; Washington Consensus and, 10; world trade, 3. *See also* China-ASEAN Free Trade Area; Dominican Republic-Central America-United States Free Trade Agreement; Emerging economies; North American Free Trade Agreement; Washington Consensus; *individual countries and regions*

Transparency International, 112

Trinamool Congress (political party; India), 92–93

T. Rowe Price, 92

Turkey, 149

TVEs (township and village enterprises). *See* China

United Kingdom. *See* Britain

United Progressive Alliance (UPA; India), 91, 92, 93, 94

United States (U.S.): Argentina and, 162; Asian financial crisis of 1997–98 and, 104; attacks of 9/11, 2; Brazil and, 162; Canada and, 184; China and, 107, 184; dotcom bust in, 2, 148; economic issues in, 109, 111, 118, 143–44, 183, 185, 186, 199, 207; financial market deregulation in, 2, 3; global financial crisis of 2008–09 and, 4, 8, 11, 13, 106, 127, 132–33, 168, 185–86, 188, 199; growth of, 3, 19, 183; hedge funds in, 3; housing market in, 3; interest rates and, 2–3, 11, 126, 173, 189–90, 224–25, 228; Korea and, 53, 60, 61–62, 65; Mexico and, 184, 185; mortgage crisis in, 228n7; political issues in, 107, 144;

private financial institutions in, 90; remittances from migrants in, 127, 185–86; stimulus package of, 13, 211, 225; subprime mortgages in, 2–3; trade in, 17, 20, 184, 185, 207. *See also* Federal Reserve; Lehman Brothers

UPA. *See* United Progressive Alliance

Uruguay, 129, 131, 142

U.S. *See* United States

UTI Mutual Fund (India), 92

Velasco, Andrés, 139

Venezuela: Argentina and, 160; banks and banking in, 218; economic issues in, 134–35, 136–37, 143, 194, 217, 218; foreign exchange reserves of, 218; global financial crisis of 2008–09 and, 4, 18, 218; growth of, 137; interest rates in, 225; policy learning in, 134, 141; political issues in, 141–42, 144; response to the global financial crisis of 2008–09 and, 134, 136–37; trade in, 128, 183, 219, 220, 223; U.S. and, 128. *See also* Emerging economies; Latin America; South America

Vietnam, 103, 104, 112, 115–16, 117. *See also* Asia; Asia–Southeast; Emerging economies

Vodafone, 93

Washington Consensus (WC): Argentina, 18–19, 141, 173; Asia, 8, 214; Brazil, 173; China, 27, 31, 116, 203; Ecuador, 141; Latin America, 8, 134, 177; measures of 6, 10; Mexico, 126; Venezuela, 141

Wen Jiabao, 32, 34

Wise, Carol, 1–24, 148–80, 202–30, 231

Woori Bank, 59

Workers' Party (Brazil), 136

World Bank, 41, 49, 53, 112–13

World Trade Organization (WTO), 12, 27, 60, 162, 173, 184

Yu Yongding, 31